Oxford Studies in Philosophy of Law

Oxford Studies in Philosophy of Law

Volume 5

Edited by

LESLIE GREEN
University of Oxford

BRIAN LEITER
University of Chicago

OXFORD
UNIVERSITY PRESS

OXFORD
UNIVERSITY PRESS

Great Clarendon Street, Oxford, OX2 6DP,
United Kingdom

Oxford University Press is a department of the University of Oxford.
It furthers the University's objective of excellence in research, scholarship,
and education by publishing worldwide. Oxford is a registered trade mark of
Oxford University Press in the UK and in certain other countries

© the several contributors 2024

The moral rights of the authors have been asserted

First Edition published in 2021

Published in the United States of America by Oxford University Press
198 Madison Avenue, New York, NY 10016, United States of America

British Library Cataloguing in Publication Data
Data available

Library of Congress Control Number: 2024937139

ISBN 9780198919629

DOI: 10.1093/9780198919650.001.0001

Printed and bound in the UK by
Clays Ltd, Elcograf S.p.A.

Links to third party websites are provided by Oxford in good faith and
for information only. Oxford disclaims any responsibility for the materials
contained in any third party website referenced in this work.

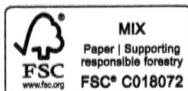

MIX
Paper | Supporting
responsible forestry
FSC
www.fsc.org
FSC® C018072

Contents

List of Contributors

Editors

Leslie Green is Emeritus Professor of the Philosophy of Law, University of Oxford, UK.

Brian Leiter is Karl N. Llewellyn Professor of Jurisprudence and Director of the Center for Law, Philosophy & Human Values, University of Chicago, USA.

Contributors

James Edwards is Associate Professor, Faculty of Law, University of Oxford, UK.

John Horty is Professor, Philosophy Department and Institute for Advanced Computer Studies, University of Maryland, USA.

Ezequiel Monti is Assistant Professor, Universidad Torcuato di Tella, Buenos Aires, Argentina, and María Zambrano Fellow, Universitat Pompeu Fabra, Barcelona, Spain. https://orcid.org/0000-0001-5931-3536.

John Oberdiek is Distinguished Professor of Law, Rutgers University, Camden, NJ, USA.

Nicole Roughan is Associate Professor, Faculty of Law, University of Auckland, New Zealand. https://orcid.org/0000-0003-1486-6393.

Nicolaos Stavropoulos is Professor of Law and Philosophy, University of Oxford, UK. https://orcid.org/0000-0003-4442-1969.

Michel Troper is Professeur émérite, Université de Paris Nanterre (faculté de droit), Paris, France.

A.P. Simester is Amaladass Professor of Criminal Justice, National University of Singapore, Singapore. https://orcid.org/0000-0003-2697-640X.

The Practice Theory

Nicolaos Stavropoulos

1.

On a typical day, before we receive some service, we will stand in line. At the bag drop off, the store checkout, the box office, the ATM, once all available service points are taken, the rest of us will form a line. Sometimes we are nudged by railings or cordons, or explicitly directed to form a line by service agents. But most of us will also start a line spontaneously where no barriers exist and no one is telling us to do so, and new arrivals will join the back of the line unprompted, all patiently waiting to be served in the order in which they each arrived. It is our settled practice to act in this way. We don't reflect, each time the check-out is busy, about whether we should start or join a line. We stand ready to form or join one if and when the circumstances arise. We consider it our duty to do so. Looking at our own practice, we feel that the practice matters in this way and expect everyone else to conform. We would strongly disapprove, at least privately, of anyone cutting or drifting along the line, and would feel shame or guilt if we ourselves did so. We each suppose that others feel the same.

The practice theory, in the form originally developed in the first edition of *The Concept of Law*, says that these behavioural and psychological facts fundamentally explain how it is that we have an obligation to start or join a queue in certain circumstances.[1] Our feeling that our practice

---

[1] Thus, the practice theory is a theory of obligations. Hart's original statement of the practice theory is in *The Concept of Law* as published in 1961. In due course I will consider variants of the theory that may be suggested by Hart's reflections in what became the Postscript that first appeared in the second edition of the book in 1992; Penelope Bulloch and Joseph Raz (eds.) (Oxford: Clarendon Press, 1992). Notice that, while Hart did not use the term 'practice theory' in the original statement of the theory, he came to embrace the term in the Postscript: "The account I have given of

of queuing matters, together with our standing disposition to conform to the practice and to criticize those who don't, transform our practice from a mere pattern of action to a binding, duty-imposing standard. This is not a standard that is given to us, which we endorse and try to follow. It is not a standard which anyone need have announced, directed us to follow, or even formulated or expressed in any form. It is a standard that depends on what we do, not on what anyone says. The standard is *constituted* by our regarding the pattern of our own action as a

these has become known as 'the practice theory' of rules....My practice theory of social rules has been extensively criticized by Dworkin...". See *The Concept of Law* 255. Leslie Green goes so far as to say that the term 'the practice theory of rules' was *coined* by Hart: "...*The Concept of Law* changed the direction of Anglo-American legal theory. For one thing, it introduced and clarified a set of questions that came to dominate the literature...Hart also coined the idiom in which we debate the answers to such questions: 'the practice theory of rules', 'the internal and the external point of view', 'primary and secondary rules', 'the rule of recognition', 'core and penumbra', 'content-independent reasons', 'social and critical morality'. These terms and distinctions are now part of cultural literacy for legal theorists writing in English." Green, 'The Concept of Law Revisited', *Michigan Law Review* 94 (2006), at 1688.

Notice that, although Hart talks of 'the practice theory of rules' or 'the practice theory of social rules', the practice theory remains a theory of obligations, not rules. As I explain in detail in the text, Hart appeals to rules constituted by social practices in order to explain what it is for an obligation to exist. Green makes the same point. "The practice theory thus proposes a general account of legal, moral and conventional obligations: *what it is* for an act to be obligatory is the same in each context, though the criteria that determine which acts are obligatory vary" (emphasis in the original). Green, 'Law and Obligations', in Jules Coleman, Kenneth Himma, and Scott Shapiro (eds.), *The Oxford Handbook of Jurisprudence and Philosophy of Law* (Oxford: Oxford University Press, 2004), ch. 13. Thomas Adams has recently claimed that Hart could not have been committed to the practice theory in the *Concept of Law*, a claim which as Adams admits contradicts Hart himself and most scholarship. (Hart was misled by Dworkin, Adams says.) See Adams, 'Practice and Theory in *The Concept of Law*', in John Gardner, Leslie Green, and Brian Leiter (eds.), *Oxford Studies in the Philosophy of Law*, Volume 4 (2021), 1–31. Adams assumes that the practice theory would have to be an account of the nature of rules and argues that Hart's discussion of rules in the book does not amount to such an account. In fact, as noted, the practice theory is an account of the nature of obligations that appeals to rules constituted by social practices. In a footnote, Adams notices that Hart claims that appeal to such rules is necessary to the explanation of obligations in general but says Hart was wrong to do so (see note 40 in his paper). Hart's claim in question is my main topic. Adams says that, while Hart does not offer an account of the nature of rules, he does offer an account of acceptance of rules. I address this version of the practice theory in Part 4. Adams's second argument for the claim that Hart couldn't have held the practice theory is that he claimed that legal rules can be valid without being practiced. It is uncontroversial that Hart held that view. However, correctly understood, Hart's view reinforces rather than undermines his commitment to the practice theory. Hart's point was that the underlying practice of recognition makes standards that are valid but not practiced possible and remains the foundation of such standards' bindingness. See further discussion of the practice of recognition in Part 4 below and work cited there.

All citations to *The Concept of Law* (hereinafter, CL) are to the third edition; Penelope Bulloch and Joseph Raz (eds.), with an Introduction by Leslie Green (Oxford: Clarendon Press, 2012). Like Hart, I shall use 'duty' and 'obligation' as equivalent.

binding standard.[2] The *content* of the standard is fixed by the pattern of our actions. The *normative status* of the standard—its being a standard—consists in our attitude to the pattern, namely regarding the pattern as a standard. Ultimately, we have a duty to queue in certain situations just because we tend to queue in those situations and we feel a certain way about our own behaviour.

This explanation purports to apply to the phenomenon of queueing a general account of what it is for an agent to have an obligation to take some action in some circumstances. The general account says that there is such an obligation when and because some "existing standard of conduct" requires the action in the circumstances. And for such a standard to exist is for some practice to exist among a group to which the agent in some sense belongs, where most are disposed to take the action in the circumstances and share an attitude of regarding their own practice as a binding standard. When these conditions are met, the practice gives everyone in its purview a reason to conform.[3] For an obligation to

---

[2] Surgeons are taught that, once scrubbed in, you must never let your hands fall below your waist—and if you do, your hands are presumed to be contaminated and you need to go back to the scrub station and start over. Plausibly, surgeons regard that policy as a binding standard and act on it. As a result, a pattern of behaviour emerges—once scrubbed in, surgeons will characteristically stand with hands clasped in front of the body at chest height—and (one hopes) noncompliance would tend to be met with disapproval. But in this case, the pattern of behaviour is a consequence, not the ground of the standard. The pattern of behaviour obtains because agents regard an independently existing standard as binding and try to follow it. They might regard the policy as a binding standard on substantive grounds of antisepsis, or perhaps on the grounds that they have been instructed to treat the policy as a standard by someone who has the authority to bind them in that way. Either way, the obtaining of the standard is analytically prior to and explains the obtaining of the pattern of behaviour. It is the practice theory's key claim that it's the other way around. A standard obtains because agents regard the pattern of their own behaviour as a standard. Thus, the obtaining of the pattern of behaviour is analytically prior to and explains the obtaining of the standard.

The practice theory would treat the phenomenon of someone's binding others by announcing a standard and instructing others to conform to it as a separate, derivative phenomenon which presupposes the existence of an underlying social practice of recognizing the instructor's power to bind others by such acts of communication. The duty to conform to such a standard would therefore ultimately rest on the duty of recognition imposed by the underlying social practice of recognizing others' powers to create duties in that way. I return to this matter below. As we will see, the practice theory has great difficulty accounting for the possibility of binding standards not grounded in a practice of conforming to the standards or of recognizing others' power to impose duties by communicating standards.

[3] The practice theory is unclear on the question of who is bound by a practice that meets these conditions. What makes someone who regularly fails to conform to some practice an insider bound by the standard the practice supposedly sets rather than an outsider not caught by it?

obtain is, in addition, for such a standard to be backed by "demand for conformity" that is particularly intense and "social pressure…upon those who deviate" that exceeds some threshold of seriousness. The obligation is specifically moral in character where pressure to conform is meant to induce shame, remorse, and guilt.[4] And it is proto-legal if physical sanctions are the "prominent or usual" form of pressure.[5]

In this taxonomy, at formal dinner you have reason to start with the flatware furthest from the plate, a reason that ultimately obtains just in virtue of people's regarding their practice of doing so as binding. In case you don't do as they do, people may be taken aback but are unlikely to insist that you conform, so in this case the reason does not rise to an obligation. But in the case of queueing, people are likely to care about conformity and might try to shame you into moving to the back of the queue if they notice you trying to slip to the front. The difference in the likely reactions of those who practice queuing explains why, in this case, an obligation—a moral one—obtains. And if you face physical sanctions in the name of the community for hurting somebody, you have a proto-legal duty not to do so. The practice theory holds these claims to be conceptual—to be accounts of what it means to say that some agent has an obligation to take some action—and, because conceptual, to amount to an explanation of what obligations *are*.[6]

The practice theory says that, in all these cases, the relevant practice is normatively significant. But it's not claiming that some nonsocial, inherently normative factors give the practice such significance and thus

---

[4] CL 86. These are sometimes described as obligations of positive morality. Later I shall discuss the relevance of so-called critical morality to the practice theory of obligation.

[5] CL 86.

[6] "'He ought to' and 'He has an obligation to' are not always interchangeable expressions but are alike in carrying an implicit reference to existing standards of conduct […]. Rules of etiquette or correct speech are certainly rules: they are more than convergent habits or regularities of behaviour; they are taught and efforts are made to maintain them; they are used in criticizing your own and other people's behaviour in the characteristic normative vocabulary." CL 86; "[T]he existence of [social] rules…is the normal, though unstated, background or proper context for [the] statement [that a person has an obligation]; and…the distinctive function of such statement is to apply such a general rule to a particular person…" CL 85. In the Preface to CL, Hart claims that the nature of certain phenomena is revealed by examination of the "standard uses of the relevant expressions and of the way in which these depend on a social context, often unstated". It is remarkable that the claim on p. 85 employs the exact notion of unstated context that is said in the Preface to reveal the nature of the phenomenon to which the relevant expression refers.

make it the case that there is a reason to conform. If that were the claim, the explanation of how it is that we have a duty to conform to some practice would have to start outside the practice, at the prior, inherently normative considerations that give the practice that role, and there is no reason to expect that all practices would qualify. In fact, we should expect that many would not. Rather, the claim is that each practice gives *itself* normative significance. To regard our own practice as a reason or binding standard is what it is for the practice to *be* a reason or binding standard. The actions favoured by the reason or mandated by the standard are all and only those that make up the pattern of actions that is the object of our attitude. Of necessity, the reasons or duties perfectly map onto the pattern. All settled practices give rise to reasons or duties to conform. Mafia practices give rise to metaphysically impeccable mafia duties. And no duty to take some action can exist in the absence of a practice of taking the action.[7]

These claims come with a certain ambition. They purport to articulate an alternative to "metaphysical conceptions of obligation or duty".[8] Metaphysical conceptions understand obligation or duty "as invisible objects mysteriously existing 'above' or 'behind' the world of ordinary observable facts."[9] The practice theory rejects such "obscure metaphysics".[10] In providing an account of obligation or duty that makes no appeal to entities 'behind' ordinary observable facts, it aims to demystify obligation, albeit without losing sight of what the metaphysicians aimed to capture by appeal to such nonnatural entities: the normative character of obligation.

---

[7] For the reasons canvassed in Kripke, *Wittgenstein on Rules and Private Language: An Elementary Exposition* (Cambridge, MA: Harvard University Press, 1982), it's doubtful that the social facts of social practice, on which the practice theory exclusively relies, can by themselves uniquely determine any standard. Plausibly, an indefinite number of standards would be consistent with these facts, and the theory has no resources to discriminate among such standards. I am setting aside this profound problem, focusing instead on a more narrow commitment of the theory: that, necessarily, the standard determined by the social facts of the practice requires all and only what agents do in their settled practice. Suppose it didn't. Suppose that the standard so determined required that agents do something that is not in fact their practice to do; or that they not do something that it is in fact their practice to do. For that to be the case, the standard would have to reflect, and therefore to be partly determined by, some factor external to the practice, by reference to which these parts of established practice would turn out to be violations. But that would directly contradict the thesis that the standard is determined by the facts of the practice alone.

[8] *CL* 84.   [9] *CL* 84.   [10] *CL* 84.

Hart famously argued that a previous attempt to provide an account that avoids 'obscure metaphysics' failed to combine these commitments. The earlier attempt tried to account for an obligation to take some action in terms of the likelihood of suffering some setback in the event of failing to take the action. Hart's best-known point in this connection is that a violation of some duty is not merely a ground for predicting that some hostile reactions will follow but also a reason for such reactions.[11] The predictive theory therefore leaves the normativity of obligation out of the picture.

What went wrong with the predictive theory? Hart offers an intriguing and less well understood diagnosis. The predictive theorists must have noticed, he conjectures, that whether someone has an obligation to do something does not depend on *that person's* psychology—how he feels about doing that thing, whether he believes or fears he might get in trouble for not doing it, or more generally on that person's beliefs and motives. You may be motivated to do something that is demanded or expected of you, perhaps because you believe you will be in trouble if you don't, without being obligated to do it. Or you may lack all motivation to do that thing, perhaps because you believe you can get away with not doing it, but you may still be under an obligation to do it. Hart suggests that this may have led the theorists to despair of keeping psychology in the picture, proposing instead to drop it altogether and, as Hart puts it, to treat claims of obligation not as psychological claims but as claims about what is likely to happen to those who fail to conform.[12]

The misstep that Hart attributes to the prediction theorists is not of course that they considered psychological candidates for a role in their account. By Hart's lights, psychology *must* remain in the picture if an account of obligation is to capture its normative character. Hart's suggestion is rather that their mistake lies in the fact that they restricted

[11] CL 84. Hart offers a further well-known objection. A person can be under an obligation to do something, even if there is no chance that he would suffer for not doing that thing. Even though, in general, obligations are associated with a system of sanctions for breach, in individual cases, the claim that a person has an obligation to do something and a claim that *that person* is likely to suffer for not doing it may diverge. See CL 84–5. As I explain in the text, Hart thought that the predictive theory's focus on the individual was the source of the theory's failure.
[12] CL 83.

their focus to the psychology of the *individual* and, when this didn't pay off, supposed that they had to drop psychology altogether. The consequence was that they lost sight of the normativity of obligation.

How can the practice theory do better? The key is its suggestion that we widen our perspective to take into view the psychology of those around an agent under a putative obligation: to see how *the group* feels about conformity and nonconformity. The social perspective shows how it is possible for an agent to be under an obligation to do something irrespective of the agent's own attitudes. The attitudes that matter are those of the group. As we saw, for the agent to be so obligated is for the group to regard its own practice of doing that thing as a standard that binds everyone in the group. If the group feels that way, everyone *is* bound.

The practice theory thus purports to represent an alternative the predictive theorists missed. It keeps psychology in the picture and claims to be able to account for the fact that the existence of an obligation is not merely an occasion but a reason for disapproval: it says that it's a reason that consists in the fact that the group regards its own behaviour as binding. Thus, the practice theory purports to represent a viable, better alternative to obscure metaphysics, since it appeals to no more than ordinary behavioural facts and manifest attitudes towards such facts, yet claims to remain true to the normative nature of duty.

Plainly, these claims are about so-called 'normative reasons' for action. A normative reason for action is a consideration that favours some action by some agent in certain circumstances. By contrast, a motivating reason for action is a consideration that an agent *regards* as a normative reason for some action in some circumstances and on which the agent acts. The practice theory purports to account for *normative* reasons in terms of considerations that agents regard as normative reasons and on which they act—that is, in terms of motivating reasons. (Recall that it says that for me to have a reason to queue is for us to share an attitude of regarding our practice of queueing as a reason to conform.) If the practice theory purported to account for *motivating* reasons in terms of considerations which agents regard as normative reasons and on which they act, it would be true but trivial. Moreover, it couldn't hold that, by explaining claims of obligation or duty as claims about agents' psychology (in the sense of claims about the agents' regarding some factors as normative reasons[13]), it was presenting an alternative to "obscure metaphysics". It's trivially true, not a competitor to metaphysical conceptions that appeal to "invisible objects mysteriously existing 'behind' the world of ordinary, observable facts", that explanations of motivating reasons are psychological in that sense.[14]

I shall refer to the practice theory so understood as the *pure practice theory*. Later I shall consider some alternatives. I think it's plain that the pure practice theory is Hart's theory—Hart's writings hardly leave any doubt. He explicitly makes the claims that I just reviewed, which add up to the pure practice theory. Moreover, much else that he says makes more sense if we attribute to him the pure theory than it otherwise would. I will therefore continue to attribute the pure practice theory to him and in the next section I will explore some further claims that he makes on its behalf. However, my main purpose here is not historical. The pure practice theory is important in its own right. A more important question therefore is whether the pure practice theory is sound and, if not, whether it can be amended to survive objections.

The practice theory feels archaic but remains important. Although no doubt it has its followers as a general explanation of obligation, the best-known application of the theory is to the case of legal obligation, and the theory's largest follower base can be found in the legal academic world. Hart thinks that a legal obligation obtains just when and because

---

[13] Recall that, by the practice theory, a duty is a reason backed by intense demand for conformity and serious pressure on deviants.

[14] CL 83–4. Notice that an explanation is psychological in the relevant sense if it appeals to the agent's regarding some factors as reasons for some action. It doesn't follow that the factors the agent so regards are themselves some mental states of the agent such as the agent's beliefs. More precisely, the factors may be the content of the agent's beliefs, not the fact that the agent has them. If you say that the fact that I was running late to our appointment was my motivating reason for texting you "running late", you have said something about my psychology, namely that I regarded my being late as a reason to alert you. The fact that I was running late, if it's a fact, is not the fact that I had this attitude. Rather, it's a fact about the time and place of our appointment, the time at which I sent the text, my location when I did so, and so on. It is the fact that forms the content of my attitude, or, differently, the fact at which my attitude is directed. Derek Parfit, *What Matters*, Volume 1 (New York: Oxford University Press, 2011), 538–9, says that, in the case of false beliefs, the psychological alternative may make more sense: in such a case we might say that the fact that I falsely believed that I was late was why I sent the text. However, that is not the same as saying that the reason that I thought I had and on which I acted was the fact that I had that belief.

it follows from a general standard communicated or implicitly endorsed by an agent or institution who is regarded, in the settled practice of judges and other officials, as having the power to place people under obligations by conveying or endorsing standards. The key social practice is therefore a practice of recognition of others' powers to create duties in this way, and Hart calls the rule that he thinks that practice constitutes the rule of recognition.[15]

Hart's account is widely considered successful. Many legal philosophers today make claims about "the rule of recognition" of this or that country, debate whether "the rule" can tolerate disagreement about its content and, if so, how much, and otherwise speak as if it were beyond dispute that legal obligations ultimately existed in virtue of such a rule.[16] And in the UK, where Hart's influence is outsize, senior judges will sometimes make explicit reference to "the UK rule of recognition" and debate the conditions under which it may change.[17]

I have discussed elsewhere the mechanics of Hart's appeal to the practice theory to explain the nature of legal obligation.[18] Here I examine the practice theory in its general form, as a basic account of the nature of reasons and obligations. I shall discuss some of the theory's implications about the nature of legal obligations only to illustrate or clarify the claims of the general, basic account.

Now obviously, if the general account proves to be untenable, a conception of law based on it must fail. But a conception of law that purports to be based on the theory may also be threatened in another way. Some of the claims it makes about law may not only fail to be supported by the practice theory but in fact be incompatible with it. To give one

---

[15] "We may suppose that our social group has not only rules which, like that concerning baring the head in church, makes [sic] a specific kind of behaviour standard, but a rule which provides for the identification of standards of behaviour in a less direct fashion, by reference to the words, spoken or written, of a given person." *CL* 57. Cf. *CL* 124.

[16] A small sample: Matthew Adler and Kenneth Himma (eds.), *The Rule of Recognition and the U.S. Constitution* (New York: Oxford University Press, 2009); Julie Dickson, 'Is the Rule of Recognition Really a Conventional Rule?' (2007), 27 *Oxford Journal of Legal Studies* 373–402; Brain Leiter, 'Explaining Theoretical Disagreement' (2009), 76 *University of Chicago Law Review* 1215–50.

[17] A recent example is *R. (Miller) v Secretary of State for Exiting the European Union*, [2017] UKSC 5, passim.

[18] 'Words and Obligations' in Andrea Dolcetti, Luís Duarte d'Almeida, and James Edwards (eds.), *Reading H. L. A. Hart's 'The Concept of Law'* (Oxford: Hart Publishing, 2013).

example, a familiar claim in legal philosophy is that it doesn't follow from the fact that some agent has a legal obligation to take some action in some circumstances, that the agent has any reason to take the action in the circumstances. The claim is strictly incompatible with the pure practice theory. For the theory, to have an obligation to do something *is* to have a reason to do it, indeed a reason backed by serious social pressure. If one did have an obligation to do something, it couldn't be a further question whether one had a reason to do that thing.

It follows that, by the lights of the practice theory, legal obligations, being ultimately grounded in the social practice of officials, are not a pale or provisional or diminished form of obligation. There is no further ingredient that genuine obligations have but legal obligations so understood lack. Their social credentials are exactly the right ones. As obligations go, legal obligations are as good as it gets.

To think otherwise might be motivated by the common thought that nonmoral obligations are merely provisional, whose status as obligations outright is subject to moral validation. A familiar example is the view that a legal obligation to take some action is in the first instance an obligation only in some diminished sense. If there is a moral obligation to obey the law, the legal obligation achieves full-blooded status indirectly.[19]

But that thought has no place in the pure practice theory. To the contrary, the theory holds moral obligation to be just another species of socially constituted obligation—the only kind there is. The theory can of course accept that nonmoral and moral obligations may differ yet overlap in content. It can hold moral obligations to be distinctive in various ways. Hart said that moral obligations are typically considered important; are not subject to deliberate modification; can be violated only voluntarily; and are enforced through tools meant to induce shame.[20]

---

[19] On this view, there needn't be any direct moral support for the action in itself. A moral obligation to obey could still provide indirect moral support for the action via support of the capacity of some nonmoral factor—that some legal institution issued a command, for example—to constitute a reason for the action. When that factor obtains—e.g. when a command is issued—it comes to *be* a reason for the action. See Section 4 below for further discussion of the possibility of indirect moral validation.

[20] CL 86; 168–70.

But there is no sense in which they are ontologically superior or more robust than any other.[21]

The theory further implies that domains of obligation are separate and self-contained. This is not a substantive claim of the theory, based on some deep difference it has identified in the nature of each, but a trivial implication of the claim that obligations consist in a certain shared attitude to some social pattern of action. It follows that we can distinguish between resulting domains of obligation to the precise extent that we can distinguish between social patterns of action at which the special attitude is directed. It's an obvious further implication that each domain so identified is self-contained. By hypothesis, the factors that matter to the constitution of obligation are internal to each practice; what happens elsewhere is not germane. The 'separation of law and morals' is not an upshot of some fundamental difference in the nature or normative standing of legal and moral obligations. It's simply a particularly well-known implication of the claim that obligations are individuated by underlying patterns of action and attitude. Legal and moral obligations must be distinct just because and to the extent that their social bases are distinct, in precisely the same way that legal obligations and mafia obligations, or obligations to join a queue and promissory obligations, are distinct.[22]

---

[21] Hart said that a mark of obligation is that it restricts one's freedom to do as one wishes and binds one to act in ways that may go against one's self-interest. On this score, there is no sense in which legal and other nonmoral obligations are weaker than moral ones. If anything, to the extent that legal obligations are backed by credible threats of sanction (as Hart thinks they are), they work to change the calculation of self-interest in a way that ensures the agent honours them: though the obligation may be against the agent's ex ante interest, factoring in a well-designed sanction would ensure that the agent's self-interest will now lie in performance. A legal obligation may then come out in one way stronger than a moral one with the same content. By getting the shameless to conform, legal obligations may succeed where morality would fail.

[22] Differences in the social bases of legal and moral obligations may include the manner in which disapproval to nonconformity tends to manifest in each case.

We must be careful not to conflate two very different ways of defending a practice-based conception of obligation in some domain. One, obligation is constituted by social practice therefore is specific to the domain defined by each practice. Two, obligation is not fundamentally social. Domain-specific obligations are the genuine, outright obligations that exist from the point of view of the practice that constitutes each domain. On the first alternative, legal obligations would be constituted by some pattern of action and shared attitudes to the pattern within the legal domain (e.g. by the settled practice of judges and their shared attitude of regarding the practice as binding) because that's what it is for obligations to exist. On the second, legal obligations would be constituted by such a pattern of action and shared attitudes to

The pure practice theory seems therefore incompatible with a number of typical claims made by conceptions of obligation that appear to be based on it. We might weaken the practice theory in various ways to eliminate the incompatibility. But I think that weakening the theory in those ways would create serious problems for the theory and thereby destabilize any conception of law based on it. Setting law aside, the question whether the practice theory's least plausible claims can be stripped out without affecting the coherence or plausibility of the rest is interesting in its own right. In what follows, I shall consider a number of problems with the pure practice theory and explore whether they can be fixed by restricting its ambition.

2.

I have said that the pure practice theory claims that obligations are in their nature social such that all obligations, whatever their specific character, are grounded in some social practice. It may seem that, in characterizing the theory in this way and attributing it to Hart, I overlooked what Hart calls critical morality. Perhaps, correctly understood, the theory claims that obligations *other than* those grounded in critical morality—the only or most robust, full blooded kind of obligation—are grounded in social practice.

But this thought misunderstands the theory. By the lights of the theory, obligations of critical morality could not exist. If critical morality could give rise to obligations, there would have to be some more basic account that explained what obligation is and thus how it is that some obligations are socially constituted and other obligations are not. But then the practice theory wouldn't be basic. It would no longer be a theory of what it is to have a reason or duty. It would have to be derivative from the more basic theory and apply that theory to the particulars of social practices. But as we saw, the practice theory aims to be, itself, basic.[23]

---

it because these factors determine the outright, therefore not fundamentally social, obligations that are deemed to exist from the point of view of the practice that constitutes the legal domain. Hart insisted to the end that his view was the former and saw no reason to abandon it in favour of the latter. See 'Commands and Authoritative Legal Reasons', in *Essays on Bentham* (Oxford: Clarendon Press, 1982), the very last piece of work that Hart published.

[23] To be clear, this is a claim about the logic of the theory, not a historical claim about what Hart thought. Since it purports to be an account of what it is for an obligation to exist, the practice theory allows for no further, more basic account of obligation.

For the practice theory, as Hart explains, critical morality is the domain of ideals that one can use as guides for one's personal choices and on the basis of which one can criticize some social practice and call for its reform. In fact for Hart, the critical role of such ideals is severely restricted. The ideals cannot break completely free from actual moral practices. They remain connected to recognized values and duties and their power is restricted to commending, though not mandating, actions that go above and beyond, or to encouraging practices of accepted morality to move further along in the direction of rationality and generality. Thus Hart makes no more than a limited concession to—as he puts it—the moralists, who insist on the critical role of morality as a source of *nonsocial* standards against which to evaluate individual conduct and social practices. Hart rejects such a role for morality, emphasizing instead certain social functions as critical morality's distinguishing mark.[24]

It's essential to ideals so understood that they cannot rise to obligations, unless and until the ideals are endorsed in actual practice—until reform of the practice has taken place. And if that happens, the ideals will have been transformed into the only kind of obligation there is: the social kind. Once reform is complete—once people settle into a practice of taking the actions recommended by the ideals and come to regard their practice as a binding standard—the ideals play no role in explaining how it is that people now have a duty to take the actions. As always, the explanation is that they now have the duty in virtue of the fact that they regard their practice of taking the actions as a binding standard.[25]

That is how Hart understands the matter. In fact, it may be optimistic to suppose that critical morality as Hart understands it can even serve in

[24] *CL* 181–3. Notice that Hart uses 'essence', 'nature', and 'definition' as roughly equivalent; see *CL* 156. But he only considers the possibility that the moralists propose to bring the key critical role into the definition of morality by *stipulation*. He does not consider the possibility that the question about the critical role of morality is a matter for theory not stipulation. The moralists might hold that, on the best account of its nature, morality is such that it plays the key critical role.

[25] Joseph Raz, 'H. L. A. Hart (1907–1992)' (1993), 5 *Utilitas* 148: "One may express views belonging to one's 'critical morality' as Hart calls it, i.e. views about what moral practices the society should have but does not and how people ought to behave according to them. It would be a misuse of language to talk of rights and duties in such a context. One has a duty to be a vegetarian only if the community has a moral practice requiring this."

the limited critical role that Hart assigns to it: as grounds on which one may criticize actual practices and campaign for their reform.

Suppose that in our practice of queueing we treat only one factor as relevant to the order in which we are to be served: the order in which we arrived. A critic urges us to change our practice. The critic thinks that the practice as it stands is unfair, because it's disproportionately onerous on the old. As the practice stands, how long a person standing in a queue will have to wait to be served is determined strictly by how many are ahead and how long it will take to serve them. But for any place in the queue, it's harder to wait, and therefore the burden associated with that place is larger, the older one is. The critic says that to correct the unfairness we should change the practice to let senior citizens overtake, perhaps up to a certain point, anyone manifestly younger waiting ahead of them.

In the real world, the critic's appeal would be not only coherent but plausible. Queueing is but one way to manage congestion and allocate its costs. Though common, queuing is not truly universal even in societies that take pride in their queuing discipline. Those who patiently waited in line to get into the venue will swarm the bar once inside. And those who waited to drop off their bags upon entering the terminal will accept assignments of priority based on status at the boarding gate—or will swarm the gate if the airline does not enforce a priority scheme.[26] In some cases the pattern is mixed. Where lanes merge, many hesitate, even where there are signs directing them to "use both lanes". Some move over to the nonmerging lane a mile ahead of the choke point, clearing the way for others to overtake hundreds of those already waiting. But it's plausible to suppose that, where a practice of queueing *is* settled, it would be unfair on others who have been standing in line, and it would therefore justifiably infuriate them, if you were to cut to the front.[27]

---

[26] Swarming does not entail conflict or inefficiency. When a flight is called and passengers swarm the gate, as long as they remain calm and mindful of the crowd around them, spontaneously yielding to each other at the choke point at just the right time, the flow will be smooth and fast—not unlike people spontaneously finding their way around each other as they walk in different directions on a crowded sidewalk. The airport gate scene near the end of *Bullitt* is a great illustration of perfectly civilized swarming.

[27] Perhaps fairness in the allocation of costs is a constraint on the efficient management of congestion. Expectations sustained by a practice of management by queue are probably also

If fairness plays this role in the explanation of the normative significance of the practice—if it is among the background factors that give the
practice its normative role—then an appeal to fairness in support of a
change in the settled aspects of a (hypothetical) practice would make
sense. One could coherently criticize us on the grounds that the burdens
of congestion are a function of both the time it takes to be served and
the strains of waiting, such that a scheme that orders people by time of
arrival will succeed in allocating the burdens fairly only if it gives seniors
some priority. If so, considerations of fairness would speak to the question of whether we should persist with our practice as it stands or should
instead adjust it to let seniors go to the front of the line. Crucially, the
fact that such considerations are relevant would not be a psychological
fact about us—that we regard them as relevant—but a normative fact
not reducible to our psychology which would justify certain actions as
well as attitudes and would obtain regardless.

In this approach, it is not the case that our disposition to queue and to
feel that our practice is binding explains our duty to join the queue.
Rather, the duty to join the queue, which obtains on other grounds, justifies and thereby makes it intelligible that we should be disposed to
queue and feel bound to do so. And, if the duty explains why a practice
should reform, as opposed to being explained by the practice ex post
reform, then, even where reform is not in issue, the duty would explain
the practice, rather than the practice explaining the duty.

In the Hartian world, we can't argue like that. The theory says that
reasons consist in a shared attitude directed at a pattern of action. To be
fair to Hart, this claim need not imply that we each have reason to do all
and only what we each already do. If enough of us settle into a practice
and regard it as binding, by the lights of the theory it *is* binding even on

---

relevant. Where the practice is unsettled but circumstances are otherwise similar—there is
congestion which entails costs that ought to be allocated—it's harder to say what action would
constitute conformity to the background reasons. Much depends on the content and distribu-
tion of expectations. Arguably, we ought to use both lanes up to the point they merge, and it's
permissible to swarm the unmanaged boarding gate unless people start to form a line. Notice
that we don't need to suppose that a reason not to take the benefits without sharing in the
burdens generally explains how it is that you have a duty to conform to a practice that
entails both.

member of the group that doesn't feel that way.[28] But we are here dealing with a different problem. What we are trying to understand is not
individual deviation from collective recognition of some duty. It is,
rather, deviation that *lies in* collective recognition of some duty. But the
practice theory lacks the resources to explain how we together could get
it wrong.

By hypothesis, it's not the case that we are currently disposed to participate in and regard as a binding standard a practice that orders by
arrival but gives priority to the elderly. To the contrary, the hypothesis is
that there is no such practice and, instead, we currently regard our
standing practice, which is sensitive to order of arrival alone, as such a
standard. To make things easier on the Hartian critic, suppose that we
already do *other* things in the name of fairness. Still, by hypothesis, it's
not the case that we accept that we should dilute our practice of ordering by arrival and let the elderly through on grounds of fairness (or on
any other grounds). It follows that, by the lights of the theory, we do *not*
have reason to dilute our existing standard. In fact, it would be a violation of the duty the standard imposes on us to let the seniors through.[29]
How can the Hartian critic *criticize* us for doing what, by his lights, it is
our *duty* to do? How can it be that we *ought* to start acting differently?

By the practice theory, if we *did* come round to making it our practice
to let senior citizens through and to feel that our newly adjusted practice
bound us, we'd thereby come to have a reason to let the seniors through.
But the critic can't appeal to that fact in a campaign for reform. He can't
appeal to a reason that by hypothesis would obtain only if our actions
and attitudes were other than as they are, as justification *for* changing
our actions and attitudes in the relevant way.

The Hartian seems to be facing a dilemma. Either there is a reason for
reform, in which case it's not true that to have a reason to do something
is for most everyone to do it and to feel a certain way about doing it. Or
there is none, in which case it's a mystery why what the putative critic is
saying would count as criticism, and why we should care.

---

[28] As we saw, the practice theory maintains that the psychological foundation of obligation
is social, not individual.

[29] Recall that the duty under our hypothetical practice is the duty of new arrivals to join the
back of the queue and wait until everyone who arrived before is served.

orm

The lesson is that to preserve the possibility that a practice should be other than it is, we need to appeal to normative factors external to the practice that play this critical role. Since any practice is vulnerable to such criticism, we must appeal to some nonsocial, irreducibly normative factors—just as Hart's metaphysicians supposed.[30] By restricting itself to social factors, the practice theory loses sight of the critical role of the normative—just like the predictive account did. Adding psychology, whether individual or social, to the mix doesn't deliver normativity. Even if we add facts about how a group of people would feel about certain actions, we can't convert facts about how people would act into facts about how people should act.

Hart speaks in a certain tone of the moralists who demand that morality retain its critical bite beyond, and even cut against, what we already do. He purports to concede some scope for criticism and advocacy for reform of standing practices on grounds of critical morality. But he is in no position to make the concession—unless he gives up his claims about how duty works.

The inability of the practice theory to explain how it's possible for our standing practices to be flawed and for us to have reasons to reform or abandon them cuts deep. It seems perfectly intelligible that we might have a reason or even a duty to do other than as we do. It seems not merely coherent but plausible that duty can exist absent or in the face of a social practice of recognition. One can sensibly claim that, as things stand, we all have a duty to ride a bicycle to work, even if few do. Some people campaigned for the education of girls before it was customary to provide it, indeed against a firmly settled practice of not providing any.[31]

---

[30] Contrary to what Hart supposed, such normative factors need not be understood as mysterious entities standing 'behind' or 'above' the world of natural facts. The normative domain may include as its basic element a relation, namely the relation of some natural or normative fact's being a reason for some agent to hold some attitude or take some action in certain circumstances. Thomas Scanlon develops that position in *Being Realistic about Reasons* (Oxford: Oxford University Press, 2014), esp. Lecture 2. See also Scanlon, 'Reasons: A Puzzling Duality', in R. Jay Wallace, Philip Pettit, Samuel Scheffler, and Michael Smith (eds.), *Reason and Value: Themes from the Moral Philosophy of Joseph Raz* (Oxford: Oxford University Press, 2004), 237–40.

[31] There's still a lot of work to do. "According to UNESCO estimates, 130 million girls between the age of 6 and 17 are out of school and 15 million girls of primary-school age—half of them in sub-Saharan Africa—will never enter a classroom." World Bank, https://www.worldbank.org/en/topic/girlseducation (archived on 1 September 2020).

These people were not plausibly suggesting that, if customs were modified, it would *then* wrong girls not to educate them. They were claiming that it was wronging girls already, and that the customs ought to be modified to make things right. They appealed to the fact that people were wronging girls *in* excluding them from schooling as a reason *why* people ought to extend girls the benefit of education. Claims of obligation are most forcefully advanced in support of reform, not conformity. And many unpracticed duties plausibly exist.

It would be remarkable if such claims turned out to be deeply confused. Of course the claims, while intelligible, might still be fundamentally misguided. Perhaps, though reasons as we understand them transcend and are not ultimately explained by our actions and attitudes, in fact no such reasons exist. One might try to defend the practice theory on such terms, but it would be an uphill struggle. Moreover, the practice theory was not historically advanced as a kind of deep scepticism about the surface of normative thought or as an error theory. True, Hart did think that reasons were a kind of motivation, and this led him to the implausibilities we have been discussing. But the theory was supposed to reflect the way we ordinarily think and talk about the normative and to be true to the psychology of acting for a reason, not show us to be deeply confused or mistaken.

Instead of considering attempts to defend the practice theory on the basis of scepticism about ordinary practical thought, I shall turn to the more modest strategy of abandoning the practice theory's original ambition to explain what it is to have a reason or obligation yet retain the rest of its claims. Before I do so, I need to say more about how best to understand the idea that social practices can be normatively significant.

3.

Like all contingencies, social practices can matter. As prominent signs at the far end of the Channel Tunnel indicate, people drive on the other side of the road over there. That people drive on the other side matters. Because they do, you have a reason to drive on the other side too. And, on the way back, as equally prominent signs on the home end indicate, people drive on the side of the road you started out on, so you ought to switch back to driving on that side. Moving back and forth, the normative valence of driving on a given side of the road flips from obligatory at one end to madness at the other. Our duties to drive on one or the other side of the road vary with and supervene upon local driving practices. What explains these relations?

In this case the obvious answer is that you have a moral duty not to expose others to risk of harm, which implies, with some further premises about roads and the vehicles that use them, that you ought to drive on the same side as everyone else. This fact makes local driving practices a part of your circumstances that is relevant to your antecedent moral duties related to harm. *Should you be in a place where people are driving on a given side, you ought to drive on that side.* The fact that people in France tend to drive on the right implies that, if you keep to the right you will be on the same side as everyone else, which is what you have ex ante reason to do, whereas if you keep to the left you will be going against the traffic, which is what you have ex ante reason not to do. That fact then gives you reason to drive on the right in France. (For the same reasons, now combined with different local facts, the opposite is true for Britain.) The normative significance of French driving practices is therefore indirect and derivative, assigned to the practices by substantive nonsocial normative facts such as the fact expressed in the normative conditional just mentioned and more fundamentally the fact, on which the conditional is based, that people have a general duty not to harm others.[32]

The case of driving emphasizes the normative significance of what people do in their social practice—the pattern of their action. Other cases highlight what people expect others to do, or how they understand linguistic and other signals or roles. Practices of polite behaviour vary wildly across cultures and traditions. To be polite is among other things to signal that you hold others in high regard and enjoy interacting with them, to protect them from losing face, to play your part in mutual non-acknowledgement of material better kept out of sight, and otherwise to

---

[32] This is not to deny that, at a more fundamental level, the duty not to harm others may itself be explained by a further, more basic normative fact, though it may be more controversial what that fact might be. It seems reasonable to suppose that the claim that a duty not to harm others explains the duty to drive on the same side as everybody else must be consistent with a wide range of views about what explains, at a more fundamental level, the duty not to harm, as well as with the view that that duty is a moral primitive.

participate in the delicate dance that sustains smooth interaction.[33] To do all that effectively, you need information about what is expected and what is considered respectful or would cause disruption or offence. You need to know how effectively to signal that you hold others in high regard, or what material others would expect you to leave unacknowledged or wouldn't know how to respond to, and how to tell that apart from material that people would expect you to acknowledge overtly and would take offence if you didn't. So, if you have a reason to protect people's expectations and avoid offending them, you need to tune in with and learn from local practices. And plausibly you do have such a reason. If so, existing practices of polite behaviour, including the expectations and other attitudes they create and sustain, and the meaning participants normally attach to certain expressions or other signals, bear on your action. As before, they do so because we have antecedent reason to pursue and protect smooth interaction with others such that, if doing or saying something, or refraining from doing or saying it, would serve this purpose, then you have reason to do or say that thing or to refrain from doing or saying it.

It may be tempting to present the explanation of the normative significance of practices such as these in the following way. The social facts of the practice—that people in France drive on the right, that in polite society people don't talk and expect others not to talk about one's achievements[34]—determine the *content* of the relevant reason or duty given by the practice; while the relevant background normative fact gives the reasons or duties so determined their normative *force*. Differently, we might say that the practice determines *what* action you would have reason to take, *if* you had reason to conform to the practice, and the background nonsocial normative facts determine whether or not you *do* have reason to conform to it.

But putting the matter this way would be a distortion, for two closely related reasons. First, if background normative factors give some practice normative relevance, they do so *transparently*, by giving normative

---

[33] I am drawing on Thomas Nagel's famous 'Concealment and Exposure' (1998), 27 *Philosophy & Public Affairs* 3–30.
[34] The second example is Nagel's.

roles to what we do or say or think within the practice. They are not factors that give normative roles to (socially determined) standards that require that we do or say or think these things; nor are they reasons why social practices should be capable of determining by themselves such standards or duties.[35]

This remains true, even as the practices may focus, clarify, refine, or reduce uncertainty over preexisting responsibilities, or provide tools for incurring them or "new ways of breaching old duties".[36] If some language is conventionally associated with insult, then one should refrain from using the language because of the normatively important consequences of doing so: the risk, if not the certainty, that one's audience will take offence. It's not the convention that makes use of the language impermissible. Rather, it's the normative conditional just mentioned, which, given the social fact that the relevant language *is* conventionally associated with insult, makes the fact that using the language will cause offence a reason not to use it. Though the reason might not exist if the convention were different—say, if the language were conventionally associated with affection rather than insult—it's not a reason to respect the convention but a reason to respect the people you are talking to in circumstances where the convention obtains. Thus, the duty is not based on the recognition of the validity of some social norm but on the evaluation of the consequences of alternative courses of action in the relevant social circumstances.[37]

Second, it follows from the fact that what gives the social facts of the practice normative relevance is certain substantive nonsocial normative facts—therefore by hypothesis factors external to the practice—that it remains possible that what we should be doing given the practice is other than what we are already doing. Since the practice can go beyond

---

[35] In the next section I shall consider a version of the practice theory on which background normative factors give social practices normative relevance nontransparently, by giving force to socially defined standards or duties or conferring on social practices the power to set such standards or duties.

[36] The quote comes from Ronald Dworkin, *Justice for Hedgehogs* (Cambridge, MA: Belknap Press, 2011), 310. As Dworkin goes on to notice, "convention cannot achieve what the rationale of underlying moral facts would not sanction".

[37] In Owens's terminology, the duty is socially conditioned but not conventional. See Owens, 'Wrong by Convention', *Ethics* (2017), 1–23. See also his discussion of practice dependence and convention in Ch. 3, *Bound by Convention: Obligation and Social Rules* (Oxford: Oxford University Press, 2022).

or fall short of what the background reasons support, the duties that may obtain need not *map* onto the standing practice.

It is in principle possible that the precise normative significance of some social practice is such that we have reason to do exactly what is done already. Any appearance that it *must* be so may be the product of the inevitably artificial, stylized character of the examples. True, when in France, you should do as others do in France, namely drive on the right. The fact that gives you the reason to do so is that the others are on that side.[38] But it's not always so simple. In real life, the way in which the normative gives the social normative roles can be fine grained rather than binary. There is no deep reason why duty should map onto the pattern of action that forms the settled part of a social practice.[39] As we saw in the discussion of our toy example of a queueing practice that responds only to order of arrival, I may have reason, the same reason, to join the queue but also to let the old man through.

The normative transparency of social practices implies that a rule that required the actions that make up the relevant practice could only serve as a summary of the normative situation and would have no force itself.[40] To the extent that people talk or think about a rule requiring the actions, they needn't all have in mind the same rule. Moreover, even if they did, such a 'rule of the practice' would be redundant in explanation. The same considerations that would explain the duty to take the actions would also explain the rule that by hypothesis required them. Whatever explains why I owe it to others to stand in line also explains the 'queuing rule'. And the factors that explain why players should draw near the batsman when a slow bowler is bowling—and make it intelligible for players to think that anyone in their circumstances ought to draw near the batsman—would also explain a 'slow-bowler rule' that required that they do.

---

[38] "[A] good underwriter needs an independent mindset akin to that of the senior citizen who received a call from his wife while driving home. 'Albert, be careful,' she warned, 'I just heard on the radio that there's a car going the wrong way down the Interstate.' 'Mabel, they don't know the half of it,' replied Albert, 'It's not just one car, there are hundreds of them.'" Warren Buffett, letter to shareholders 2011, https://www.berkshirehathaway.com/letters/2011ltr.pdf, 9 (accessed on 5 March 2024). Going against the flow may be a good idea sometimes in finance but never on the road.

[39] Recall, once again, that the role of the normative factors is not to validate or reject a socially given standard or to give reasons why practices should be able to set, by themselves, such standards.

[40] Cf. John Rawls's discussion of the summary conception of rules, 'Two Concepts of Rules' (1955), 64 *Philosophical Review* 3, 19. See also my 'Words and Obligations', note [18], 131–2, 143, on the summary conception of rules.

If so, a practice may fail to give any reason or obligation to conform, or may give reason to do more or less than what's done. Social recognition is neither necessary nor sufficient for obligation.

Notice that there is no implication that reasons or duties given by social practices can only be generic. The distinctive character and scope of practice-dependent obligations can be accounted for substantively. That some obligations are distinctive in kind (e.g. are promissory or legal obligations or obligations of some role) may be a consequence of the fact that they are incurred through procedures that enable or facilitate a certain kind of interaction and at the same time afford protections against some characteristic, morally significant vulnerability that is entailed by the relevant kind of interaction.[41] And that some obligations bind members of a certain group may be an implication of the fact that they obtain in virtue of some custom or circumstance specific to the group.

4.

A restricted form of the practice theory might concede that at least some reasons or obligations—for example reasons and obligations of critical morality—that are *not* ultimately social are possible. The concession is not available at the basic level. If obligations come in two flavours and the theory only explains one, the theory can't be basic but must be part of a broader theory that is based on an account of obligation simpliciter. The theory of obligation simpliciter would then explain how it is that some obligations come in one flavour and others in the other.[42]

One possibility is that the basic account is disjunctive such that the practice theory is one of two entirely independent explanations of reasons and obligations. There are two parallel separate normative worlds, one containing social, the other nonsocial (for example moral) reasons. The possibility sounds extravagant.[43]

---

[41] I explore this hypothesis in connection with legal and other political obligations in 'The Force Hypothesis', in Nicolaos Stavropoulos (ed.), *Interpretivism and its Critics: New Work in Legal Philosophy* (Oxford: Hart Publishing, forthcoming).

[42] See note 23 and discussion above.

[43] Hart makes a closely related point in 'Commands and Authoritative Legal Reasons', note 18, at 267.

A more plausible and familiar idea is that there is only one kind of reason or obligation, and the practice theory offers a partial account of the single kind.

One such possibility is that the practice theory is an account of what it is for an agent *to accept* a reason or an obligation. Once again, of necessity, such an account would be parasitic on a more basic account of what reasons or obligations *are*. We'd need to appeal to the basic account to explain *what* people are accepting when they accept a reason or duty. The theory might be understood to model *guidance*. A variant says that social practices give rise to standards that *guide* an agent's behaviour, in the sense that the agent regards their existence as reasons for the actions that the agent understands the standards to mandate and acts on them. The theory leaves open the conditions under which the standards *govern* behaviour, in the sense of their existence *being* reasons for the actions.[44] While the theory itself would be in terms of social and psychological facts and would speak to *motivation*, it would rely on the basic account to explain what it is for some standard to give *reasons*.[45] For if the theory claimed that for behaviour to be governed by some standard just is for behaviour to be guided by the standard, it would turn into the original, pure practice theory. Notice, moreover, that a theory of guidance by recognition of social standards may accept that reasons and obligations can obtain in virtue of standards other than those that are recognized in some social practice (e.g. standards that obtain because of some practice but are not recognized in the practice), or on grounds that are not social at all.

Another variant says that social practices determine only what *counts* as your duty within some practice, or, differently, what duties you have in the eyes of the practice. That too presupposes the existence of a further basic account, which by hypothesis must appeal to factors other than social practices, of what it is to have a duty *outright*. (If the theory said that that is *also* explained by facts about social practices, then it would, once again, become the pure practice theory.)

---

[44] I think that's what Scott Shapiro has in mind in distinguishing between norm-guided and norm-governed behaviour in 'On Hart's Way Out', 4 *Legal Theory* (1998), 469–507.

[45] So this modified version of the practice theory no longer tries to explain reasons in terms of motivations.

Following Parfit, one might put these points by saying that the practice theory purports to explain the normativity of social practices in the rule-implying sense, while it relies on a different theory, which appeals at the fundamental level to nonsocial, inherently normative factors, to explain the normativity of social practices in the reason-implying sense.[46]

If we restrict the ambition of the practice theory in one of these ways, we are led to the *mixed practice theory*. This version is mixed because it concedes the existence of a basic nonsocial account of reasons and duties. The question arises how the two parts combine.

The mixed practice theory addresses, in the first instance, the question of when and how a social practice may give rise to a social rule. Another question is how that information bears on the question whether the practice in question gives rise to reasons or obligations. One possibility is that the two questions are unrelated. Perhaps an account of the normativity of the practice in the reason-involving sense is independent of the account of its normativity in the rule-implying sense. But if this is the case, we can safely ignore the answer to the question about social rules when we turn to the question about reasons or obligations.

To ensure that the rule-implying account remains a distinctive, non-redundant element in the overall explanation of how it is that a social practice may give rise to duties, the mixed theory must replicate the *two-factor*[47] model of the pure practice theory. Like its pure cousin, the mixed theory so understood assumes that one factor, the pattern of action that makes up some practice, determines the content of the

---

[46] Parfit, *On What Matters*, note 14, 935; 976–83.

[47] I shall use 'two-factor' as shorthand for a model of explanation of obligation which splits the explanatory tasks between nonnormative and normative factors in the following way. What people do in their social practice—the pattern of their action—fixes the content of the standard or obligation that the practice constitutes. Some ontologically distinct factor that the model perceives as normative gives the socially defined standard or obligation binding force. On the pure practice theory, the second, supposedly normative factor is a shared attitude of regarding the pattern as a binding standard; the attitude is what it is for the pattern to *be* such a standard. In what follows, I consider mixed theories. These suppose that the second factor is not psychological but is instead some nonsocial, inherently normative fact that plays the same role. I sketched an alternative model in Section 3. On that competing model, nonsocial inherently normative facts give normative roles, not to predefined standards or duties, but to what people do and think within social practices, taking into account linguistic facts, social meanings, normatively significant consequences, and all other relevant circumstances.

obligations that may obtain because of the practice. It differs from its pure cousin in respect of the second factor.

For the pure theory, the second factor, the one that confers normative significance and therefore turns a bare pattern of action into a binding standard that imposes those obligations, is social recognition in the form of a shared attitude of regarding the pattern as a binding standard. In place of psychological endorsement, the mixed theory says that socially recognized standards and duties are subject to validation by some factor that is normative in the reason-implying sense (and is not fundamentally psychological or social). The idea is that the recognized standards and duties under them truly bind only in case they are also independently underwritten by reason. The matter of validation is therefore the business of the basic account of reasons and duties rather than the practice theory. The task of explaining the normativity of social practices is therefore split, and the rule-involving part is supposed to *constrain* the reason-involving one. The task of the latter is to offer an up or down judgment on whether the putative standards and duties identified in the former are indeed binding.[48]

Now, the question arises what the required mode of validation is, if it is to preserve the nonredundancy of the social part of the overall account.

We already noticed that validation operates on a predetermined package of duties. One constraint therefore is that the duties that are subject to validation must be identical with the duties endorsed in social attitudes, such that they perfectly map onto the pattern of action that is so endorsed. But why?

If we suppose, as the pure practice theory does, that having some attitude to a pattern of action is just what it is for a social practice to give rise—indeed to constitute—a binding standard or an obligation to conform, it stands to reason that the content of the obligation or standard should be determined by the pattern of action.[49] It is after all that

---

[48] If the theory conceded that the normative part was not limited to such an up or down judgment but could instead offer a transparent and granular assessment of the normative effect of the social facts, it would be a version of the practice theory in name only.

[49] As we saw, an implication is that the standard or duty would be coextensive with the pattern of action: we would get to do all and only what we do already. This made it impossible to claim that our practice contains mistakes and should be reformed to put it right.

pattern that the attitude, which turns the pattern into a binding standard, takes as its object. The normative ontology of the pure practice
theory therefore directly motivates and supports the two-factor account
of obligation.

But in the mixed theory we are not supposing that having some attitude to a pattern of action is what it is for a social practice to give rise to
a binding standard or a duty to conform. The mixed theory admits that
the explanation of how a social practice may give rise to such a standard
or duty can only be explained by appeal to some nonsocial normative
facts, not attitudes. So one question is why the purview of such normative facts should be restricted to the factors that are the stipulated object
of an attitude of endorsement—the pattern of action. That the pattern is
the object of such an attitude (on the assumption that it is) is just one
among many potentially relevant aspects of the practice. Further potentially relevant aspects include other attitudes including expectations
about each other's behaviour which are caused by the existence of the
practice, the social meaning attached to actions in the practice, the consequences of conformity and deviation and the burdens and benefits
entailed by each, and other ways in which the existence of some practice
may affect agents' relevant circumstances.

These and any other relevant considerations would normally all be
factored into the explanation of how some social practice may affect our
obligations, constitute standards, or otherwise matter. Recall that such
an explanation would appeal to some background normative considerations which would assign to some aspect or consequence of the practice a normative role. For example, it would appeal to principles related
to background duties not to expose others to certain risks of harm,
which would give the fact that all the other drivers are on the right side
the status of a reason for me to drive on that side; or principles related to
background duties to respect the dignity of others, which would give the
fact that using some word would insult the audience the status of a reason for me not to use it; or principles of fairness in the allocation of
burdens and benefits, which would give the fact that others have been
standing in line at the checkout the status of a reason for me to join the
back of the line (and perhaps also to let an old lady who arrives after me
go first).

In the model we are examining, we can't proceed like that. The normative factors to which our explanation may appeal cannot be factors that assign normative roles to some aspect or consequence of the practice and thereby determine its normative effects. It is already given what these effects are (they are duties that perfectly track the pattern of action that constitutes the practice) as is the normative role of the social facts of the practice (it is to determine these effects). So the background normative considerations to which the explanation appeals must be factors that assign to the social facts of the practice, not normative roles, but the capacity themselves to assign such roles and thereby to determine the normative effects of the practice. Such background factors are therefore not reasons why the social facts of the practice should be reasons, but reasons why the social facts should determine reasons.

A model of explanation that meets the constraints suggests itself. The kind of two-factor explanation we've been looking for is associated with the notion of *normative powers*. Normative powers go beyond agents' ability deliberately to change their own or others' normative situation by changing normatively relevant circumstances. Rather, if agents have such powers, they get to change the normative situation directly by choosing to do so.[50] That is, their choice does not bring about the normative change by causally affecting normatively relevant circumstances. Rather, the choice directly effects the normative change.[51] For example, agents get to place themselves under obligations or to give themselves reasons they didn't have before, simply by forming or conveying an intention to do so. In this model, if an agent has the relevant power, the content of the agent's intention determines the content of the reason or obligation that obtains because of the formation or communication of the intention. The normative considerations that confer upon the agent

---

[50]   Thus, an agent who exercises a normative power attaches a normative property or consequence to an act or object by fiat. See Jed Lewinsohn, 'The "Natural Unintelligibility" of Normative Powers', forthcoming, *Jurisprudence*, special issue on 'Reasons and Normativity: Themes from the Philosophy of Joseph Raz'.

[51]   As Raz puts it, an act is an exercise of a normative power "only if it affects a norm normatively and not causally. [...] An act affects a norm causally if its consequences regulate the application of a norm. It affects a norm normatively if the act itself or its result affects the existence or application of the norm." See Raz, 'Voluntary Obligations and Normative Powers' (1972), 46 *Aristotelian Society Supplementary Volume* 79–102, at 94.

the power to change the agent's normative situation by forming or conveying an intention to do so by forming or conveying the intention—the reasons why the agent should have the power—assign normative force to the given contents. In the standard example, to promise is to convey an intention to place oneself under a duty by the very act of conveying the intention. The intention fixes the content of one's duty: it's the duty one conveyed an intention to be placed under. The reasons why one should be able to place oneself under duties just by conveying an intention to do so give the duty so determined normative force.[52] Can we appeal to normative powers so understood to defend the two-factor model of explanation of the normative significance of social practices? I am interested in the character of such a defence, not the details, which may vary.

Normative powers are postulated devices for manufacturing reasons, and the existence of such powers is normally defended by appeal to their capacity to overcome some perceived practical disadvantage that makes it desirable for agents to possess them or, differently, that constitutes the point of possessing the powers.[53] The argument in favour of postulating such powers might go as follows. You need to be able to get others to trust that you will do something in the future but you can only accomplish that if there is some guarantee that when the time comes you will have reason to do it. You cannot reliably procure such a reason by suitably arranging your relevant circumstances. The power to bind yourself by conveying an intention to do so allows you, simply by conveying the intention, to place yourself under a duty to do that thing, a duty that is

[52] Similarly, it can be claimed that to command others to perform some act is to convey an intention to place those to whom the command is addressed under a duty to perform the act, by the very act of conveying the intention. Your command fixes the content of the duty—it's the duty you conveyed an intention that they be placed under. On this view, it's plausible to suppose that not everyone has the power to bind others by commanding them, but if you are one of those who do, the power gives the duty so determined normative force.

[53] The existence of normative powers may be defended other than by appeal to the point of having them. For example, the powers may be claimed to be inherent in rational agency, or ultimately to derive from some social practice of recognition (where the force of such recognition is not itself grounded in any nonsocial normative considerations). I am setting aside these alternatives as they could not provide a basis for the two-factor model of explanation of the normative significance of social practices. Recall that that model supposes that the social facts of some practice set the content of the duties that obtain because of the practice, while some nonsocial normative considerations explain (are the reason) why the content of the duties should be set in that way.

resistant to being outbalanced so can persist in the face of changing circumstances. The powers thereby enable you to enter into valuable transactions or to form valuable relationships that would otherwise be out of reach. The point of having the powers—the fact that possessing the powers opens up these possibilities or, differently, meets the need to have access to these possibilities or your interest in having such access—justifies having the powers and thereby explains how it is that you do have them.[54]

Setting aside the question whether it's necessary to postulate such powers in order adequately to explain phenomena such as promising, the idea of normative powers suggests a strategy for defending the two-factor model of explanation proposed by the mixed practice theory. One might claim that people are endowed with a *social normative power* which allows them together to perform acts and adopt attitudes that constitute a social practice and thereby to incur obligations the content of which is determined purely by these actions and attitudes. Certain nonsocial normative considerations justify this social normative power and thereby give force to the obligations so determined.

In fact, the idea of normative powers cannot support the social normative powers hypothesis and, by extension, the two-factor model of explanation of the normative effect of social practices. To see this, some clarifications are in order.

First, as the examples illustrate, the existence of some normative power is normally defended on the grounds that the power would make it possible to access some normative possibilities which, absent the

---

[54] The most influential account of normative powers is Joseph Raz's. See Joseph Raz, 'Voluntary Obligations and Normative Powers' (1972), 46 *Aristotelian Society Supplementary Volume* 79–102; 'Promises and Obligations', in P. M. S. Hacker and Joseph Raz (eds.), *Law, Morality and Society: Essays in Honor of H. L. A. Hart* (Oxford: Clarendon Press, 1977); Joseph Raz, 'Normative Powers', in *The Roots of Normativity* (Oxford: Oxford University Press, 2022). Some variants are defended in David Owens, *Shaping the Normative Landscape* (Oxford: Oxford University Press, 2012); Seana Shiffrin, 'Promising, Intimate Relationships and Conventionalism' (2008), 177 *Philosophical Review* 481–524; Gary Watson, 'Promises, Reasons, and Normative Powers', in David Sobel and Steven Wall (eds.), *Reasons for Action* (Cambridge: Cambridge University Press, 2009).

Notice that we may be able to explain the phenomena without accepting any of these claims. Thomas Scanlon, 'Reasons: A Puzzling Duality?', in Jay Wallace, Philip Pettit, et al. (eds.), *Reason and Value* (Oxford: Clarendon Press, 2004), and *What We Owe to Each Other* (Cambridge, MA: Belknap Press, 1998), 295–327, offers a competing account. See also Dworkin's account of obligation in *Hedgehogs*, note 36.

power, would be out of reach (and the point of the power lies in securing that very access). We each have the normative power to bind ourselves by our say so, the defence goes, because having it makes it possible for us to arrange things today in such a way that tomorrow we will have a duty to do something. Absent the power, the possibility of fixing today our duties tomorrow would be inaccessible.[55]

What is the equivalent access claim, if we are to appeal to normative powers to explain how some social practice can change our obligations? It's not enough for the social powers hypothesis to identify some normative possibility that would be out of reach absent the *practice*. Any social practice that makes a normative difference thereby opens up the normative possibilities defined by the difference that it makes—whatever the explanation of how it makes that difference. We saw earlier that, on the competing account, the practice of driving on the right makes such a difference by changing relevant circumstances in such a way that it's now mandatory to drive on the right. The emergence of the practice thereby makes it possible to come under a duty to drive on the right (and thereby to share the road with others safely), a possibility which did not exist before. The relevant question for the purpose of testing the social powers hypothesis is different. It is whether social practices could make the normative difference they do make only in virtue of being an exercise of a social power to create duties that are determined by the social facts of the practice alone. The claim therefore must be that the competing, circumstances-based account misidentifies or otherwise misrepresents the normative effects of practices.

Second, the claim we are discussing is not that a social practice of recognition may confer on people a normative power to modify duties by performing certain acts or forming certain attitudes. It's a familiar claim that one's ability to bind oneself by one's say so derives from a social practice of recognizing that one's using the formula 'I hereby

---

[55] For example, it could be claimed that you cannot reliably procure a reason let alone a duty to do as promised, say by encouraging an expectation on the part of the promisee that you will do what you promised to do, an expectation that it would then be wrong to betray and therefore one that you will then have reason to meet. You may fail to elicit such an expectation, and besides the promisee will have reason to form the expectation only if there is reason why you should perform. The reason to perform cannot therefore be grounded in the expectation it would support. To be clear, I don't mean to endorse these claims.

promise to φ' (or equivalent) places one under a duty to φ.[56] And Hart claimed that a general ability to adjust others' duties at will derives from a social practice of recognition of certain acts ("the words of a given person"[57]) as creating binding standards that place others under duties. He thought that that special ability is the key innovation introduced to the basic technology of social duty that makes law possible.[58] (Obviously, in the Hartian scheme, the basic technology, on which the special ability is founded, is not *itself* an exercise of such an ability.) In both cases, the claim is that social practices make it possible for agents to change duties by so choosing precisely by recognizing agents' power to do so.[59]

---

[56] See D. Neil MacCormick, 'Voluntary Obligations and Normative Powers' (1972), 46 *Aristotelian Society Supplementary Volume* 59–78. Owens, *Shaping the Normative Landscape* (note 54), 123–63, argues that the ability to bind oneself by one's say so is intelligible only if it exists in virtue of a social practice of recognition of the binding force of one's say so. MacCormick and Owens are part of a tradition that I discuss further in note 59, below.

[57] See note 15 above.

[58] *CL* 91–9. Such legal standards can therefore be valid even when not practiced. The foundation of their bindingness is the social practice of recognition of the acts that produce them as sources of binding standards. I discuss these points further in Nicolaos Stavropoulos, "Words and Obligations", note 18, 133–5.

[59] Hart is a prominent representative of a distinguished tradition. Hume argued that a promise would be unintelligible or normatively ineffective absent a convention that attached to it a duty to perform. See David Hume, *A Treatise of Human Nature*, in David Fate Norton and Mary J. Norton (eds.) (Oxford: Clarendon Press, 2007), 3.2.5.1. Lewinsohn, note 50, develops one strand of Hume's argument. John Rawls argued that "[i]n the case of actions specified by practices it is logically impossible to perform them outside the stage-setting provided by those practices, for unless there is the practice, and unless the requisite proprieties are fulfilled, whatever one does, whatever movements one makes, will fail to count as a form of action which the practice specifies". See Rawls, note 40, above, 25. Hart argued that "[t]o promise is to say something which creates an obligation for the promisor: in order that words should have this kind of effect, rules must exist providing that if words are used by appropriate persons on appropriate occasions (i.e. by sane persons understanding their position and free from various sorts of pressure) those who use these words shall be bound to do the things designated by them" (*CL* 43). He also argued that "in order that words, spoken or written, should in certain circumstances function as a promise, agreement, or treaty, and so give rise to obligations and confer rights which others may claim, rules must already exist providing that a state is bound to do whatever it undertakes by appropriate words to do. Such rules presupposed in the very notion of a self-imposed obligation obviously cannot derive their obligatory status from a self-imposed obligation to obey them" (*CL* 225).

The Humean point is fundamental to Hart's account of secondary rules, including the rule of recognition, and thus to his account of law. "[W]e shall make the general claim that in the combination of [primary rules that impose duties and secondary rules that provide for operations which lead to the creation or variation of duties] there lies what Austin wrongly claimed to have found in the notion of coercive orders, namely, 'the key to the science of jurisprudence'. [...] What we shall attempt to show, in this and the succeeding chapters, is that most of the features of law which have proved most perplexing and have both provoked and eluded the search for definition can best be rendered clear, if these two types of rule and the interplay

THE PRACTICE THEORY 33

The relevant claim here, however, is not that social practices may be the *source* of some normative power such as the power to bind oneself or others. Rather, it is that social practices are *exercises* of a normative power: the power to create or modify duties by performing certain acts or forming certain attitudes, a power whose source lies in nonsocial, substantive normative considerations—and that this explains why the content of the resulting duties is fixed by the social facts of the relevant practice alone.[60] Those who participate in a social practice get thereby to place themselves under duties, and, just like a promisor whose duty is fixed by the content of an expressed attitude (the act the promisor conveyed an intention to be placed under a duty to perform), the duty of participants is fixed by the content of participants' attitudes, that is, by their regarding the pattern of their own behaviour as binding. The relevant claim is not therefore that practices make normative powers possible, as many think is true of the power to bind oneself through promising or as Hart thought is true of the power to legislate. The claim we are examining is almost the opposite. It's the claim that powers make social practices possible or, more precisely, they make it possible for social practices to affect duties, by conferring on people the ability to adjust their duties by adjusting their attitudes to patterns of their behaviour.

The claim that social practices are sources of normative powers is therefore very different from the claim that practices are exercises of such powers. To argue for the role of practices as sources of powers one needn't even argue directly for the existence of the powers. One could argue that a putative power, if it existed, could only secure some stipulated normative outcome only if the power were generally recognized. We might accept this claim consistent with rejecting the existence of the powers on other grounds. Moreover, it's not implausible to claim that one can successfully bind oneself by explicit undertaking only if such

---

between them are understood. We accord this union of elements a central place because of their explanatory power in elucidating the concepts that constitute the framework of legal thought." *CL* 81. See, further, discussion in the text, p. 34 and note 61 below.

[60] In his recent 'Normative Powers' (note 54 above), 164, Raz suggests that the customs of a large group are clearly *not* exercises of normative powers, whereas those of a small group like a family might be a borderline case.

undertakings are generally recognized as binding, or to claim that legislation can succeed in modifying people's duties only if it is generally
understood to have such effects. Even those who hold that we do not
need to appeal to normative powers to explain the normative effects of
undertakings or legislation and reject the practice theory as an explanation of how social practices matter, could accept that social traction is
necessary for these individual acts reliably and systematically to produce normative effects (though they would of course reject the claim that
such traction need take the form of a shared recognition of the power of
promisors or legislators to create duties by their say so).

By contrast, the claim that social practices are exercises of certain
normative powers entails commitment to the existence of the relevant
powers. It must be supported by arguments that show that some normative advantage could not be secured, some disadvantage overcome, or
some normative possibility accessed, except by supposing that social
practices make a normative difference in virtue of being the exercise of
such powers.

Third, the claim that social practices are exercises of normative
powers implies that practices are relevantly similar to promises and
legislation, both of which are paradigms of acts that an individual may
deliberately perform. In these two cases, the relevant powers would give
one voluntary control over the precise normative effects of those acts,
an almost magical ability to contrive, not just any obligation but an obligation of one's choosing, simply by adjusting or expressing an attitude.
The point of the powers, which is supposed to ground their existence,
very much depends on the fact that they come with voluntary control
and can be exercised as one pleases.

With these clarifications in place, it's worth looking more closely into
how the social powers hypothesis might work. I shall argue that the
hypothesis faces a number of fatal difficulties.

It would help to recall at this point why Hart thought that the introduction of a practice of recognition of someone's power to create duties
by their word was such a breakthrough in the manufacturing of duty.
Hart taught us that social practice is an unwieldy mode of production of
duty. In a simple society where a duty can obtain only when and because
it is practiced, duties would be uncertain, their enforcement inefficient,

and, above all, there would be no way deliberately to modify existing ones. In fact, Hart said, it would not even be possible to release those bound by duty from performance or to transfer to others the benefit of performance, operations which constitute deliberate modifications of individual duties.[61] It is precisely this multilayered unwieldiness that creates the opening for recognizing in some person or institution outside the relevant social practice normative powers over the domain of duty, including the power to identify, enforce, or modify individual or general duties by deliberate action (primarily, by saying so). The very point of existence of such powers, and the reason why they are truly an innovation in the domain of obligation, is that they make it possible to decouple the existence and content of a duty from a practice of conforming to it and instead make duty subject to voluntary control.

Against this background, consider again the present hypothesis, which is precisely that the very mode of production of duty that Hart thought to be unwieldy because beyond deliberate control is itself an exercise of a power to create and fix the content of duties.

What would such a power be like? By hypothesis, no one considered alone could deliberately, just by so choosing, set up a social practice and thereby make duties of the relevant kind obtain. By hypothesis, no one has authority or control over the action and the psychology of others. At best, we'd need to postulate a distributed normative power and suppose that such power allowed people, by somehow aligning their actions and attitudes, by falling into step with each other in action and in spirit, together to change their normative situation by placing themselves under the duty to do as they do. In this case, the hypothesis is that, once a pattern of action settles and people take a certain attitude to it, obligations that exactly match the pattern will thereby obtain.

---

[61] Hart says that "the possibility of [deliberately changing primary rules of obligation] presupposes the existence of rules of a different type from the primary rules of obligation" (CL 93). He further argues that "if there are only primary rules of obligation [people] would have no power to release those bound from performance or to transfer to others the benefits which would accrue from performance. For such operations of release or transfer create changes in the initial positions of individuals under the primary rules of obligation, and for these operations to be possible there must be rules of a sort different from the primary rules" (CL 93). See also note 59 above.

But what would it be for us to be exercising *a power* in aligning our actions and attitudes in the required way? How could we together choose to do something and to regard it as our duty to do it? One possibility is to suppose that we (who?) are a kind of corporate agent who can form intentions and perform acts and can therefore form an intention that we do something and have a duty that we do that thing. If so, it might be in the corporate agent's gift to commit us to its choices. But it's hard to see how such an agent's intentions can fail to be a function of and therefore a construct of the individual intentions of those who make up the group. An ontologically more modest approach might then be to understand the relevant power in terms of individual intentions the object of which is that we together do things, and perhaps also the relations in which these intentions stand.

We might characterize such an intention in terms of the collective act and the resulting duties that give the intention content. Suppose I am looking to arrange things so that we together φ and consider it our duty to φ. The problem is that I can't control what others will do and therefore what pattern of action might emerge, nor can I control how others will feel about any such pattern. This means I have no control over the content of any resulting obligations. I cannot therefore effectively intend that we φ and thereby acquire a duty that we φ. The problem of control therefore implies a problem of content. Aiming for a duty to drive on the right, I might end up with a duty to drive on the left.[62]

Alternatively, we might characterize the intention conditionally. On this approach, suppose that for a group of people that includes me, I intend that we φ and that we thereby acquire a duty to φ conditional on others' intending the same. Now suppose further that the same is true of every other member of the group. If so, it might be coherent to think of us as trying voluntarily to set up a practice of taking the relevant action and to submit to a duty, if a practice obtains, to conform.

---

[62]   Could a more sophisticated conception of shared intention overcome this difficulty? It's hard to see how. Recall that we are looking for a model of shared intention that would secure deliberate control over our actions and duties and thus explain how it's possible, not simply for us to do things together, but for us together to invent standards and duties at will. We are looking, in other words, for an account of group powers, not group action.

But this proposal faces another difficulty: redundancy. Where the condition that is part of my intention is satisfied—where others share the intention and act on it—a practice will emerge. And if a practice emerges, I may come to have a duty to conform. But in those cases where I do have a duty to conform to an existing practice, the duty obtains whether or not I intend to submit to it. In certain cases it may not even matter how others feel—I should conform because many others conform. And where intention to submit to the duty matters, for each one of us it is enough if others intended to submit to it. For it's already the case, regardless of my attitudes, that, when certain further conditions are met, the fact that some people do something and feel they ought to do it makes it the case that I have a duty to do that thing. Differently, I should submit my action to the practice in those conditions, whether or not I am inclined to submit to it. If I form the intention, on the condition that others sign up, that we develop a practice of polite interaction that includes treating certain words as insults and others as signals of respect, and the condition is satisfied, I will acquire a duty to conform to the practice because of the consequences of the fact that the practice now exists, never mind my intention that it exist. And if I am equally lucky in my intention that we start a local chapter of the 'Ndrangheta, I will incur no duties to conform to our newly established practices of loan sharking and extracting protection payments, no matter how enthusiastically we all do conform and how we feel about our conforming. And this applies to everyone else too. In either case, the intention that is meant to give content to our supposed power to incur duties does no work.

None of this is to deny that we can jointly commit to a given project by sharing an intention to pursue it together, that is, by each forming an intention to play their part in its pursuit and to submit to the responsibilities that the project imposes on each, conditional on others forming the same intentions. We can each sign up to playing our part in the performance of the symphony, thereby making it possible for us together to perform it. Arguably, the interdependent intentions play a constitutive role in explaining what it is for us to perform the symphony. Here, the project to which we jointly commit—performance of the symphony— is prior to and independent of our committing to it, and the responsibilities we each incur are the consequence not the creature of our commitment. By contrast, the social powers hypothesis needs more: it needs the possibility of willing our joint project and the responsibilities that attach to its joint pursuit into existence and giving both content, as opposed to simply endorsing a project the content of which is given otherwise and undertaking to do one's part in its pursuit.

The social powers hypothesis seems therefore caught between impotence and redundancy. Why should we be tempted to postulate such powers? It's plausible to suppose that reasons not grounded in exercises of normative powers (whether individual or social) suffice to settle salient practical questions that normally arise in the domain of social practices. If so, such reasons would deprive putative normative powers of operational space and purpose. It's therefore hard to see how reason could validate such powers and thus, indirectly, the effects of their exercise: it's hard to see what point would be served by social practices having the capacity to define duty in the social domain.

Such a device, if it existed, would be disabling, not enabling in social practical life. It would box us in by making duty conditional on general conformity and removing the possibility that duty might outstrip, fall short, or cut against established practice. Such a device would shrink our normative world. If we abandoned it, we would lose nothing.

It's not true that, to be able to do things together, we must in each case submit our action to a standard defined by established social practice. Maybe the right thing to do is that which we all do. But it wouldn't follow that it's right because we all do it. Perhaps we do it because it's right. As Dworkin pointed out many years ago, we'd do just fine if we acted on a standard that the practice 'justified'—a standard that reflected the direct, unmediated normative significance of the practice, therefore one that could go beyond or fall short of the settled practice. We'd do just fine *even if we disagreed, as is likely, about what that standard was.*[63]

Nor is it true that working under standards of that kind would not be true to the ordinary psychology of engaging with social practices or the

---

[63] Ronald Dworkin, 'Social Rules and Legal Theory' (1971), 81 *Yale Law Journal* 855–90, at 867. Cf. discussion in Section 3, above.

ordinary way of thinking about them. People can act unreflectively, 'without deliberation', in doing as others do. But if circumstances demand it, they will happily turn reflective and argumentative about what their practice truly requires.

It's easy to concoct perfectly coherent hypotheticals of people with these traits. Consider the Sophisticates: they deliberately set out to develop a practice that responds well to the problem of efficient management of congestion under the constraint of fair allocation of its costs (just like a nonprofit airline might). They hold themselves to the standard, whichever it is, that their practice would 'justify', and would adjust their practice to meet the standard if it turned out that the standard required other than what they currently do. If they did all that, they would probably do exactly as *we* do already. Nothing would change if we turned into the Sophisticates. We wouldn't be missing out *practically* if queuing operated on such a basis. Such a practice would be exactly as *stable* and *predictable* as current queueing practice is. We probably already *have* turned into the Sophisticates. (Just spend a few minutes watching the line at a bus stop in central London.)

It is easy to devise such examples to test the hypothesis that the two-factor model is the correct one because people's attitudes have a certain character. On this hypothesis, people aim to place themselves under duties by choosing together to do so; they 'claim' the normative powers the model assigns them. We can then stipulate that the key attitude does not obtain and see what happens. There is an asymmetry. We couldn't devise similar tests for the competing model of ordinary normative explanation by stipulating that some key attitude does not obtain. There is no key attitude in the relevant sense. The ordinary model simply calculates the normative effect of attitudes together with all other relevant factors, whatever these are.

This fact about ordinary normative explanation has some further consequences. Remember that, as the mixed practice view accepts, substantive normative facts are not attitudes, nor are social obligations the only kind. So reasons, values, moral concerns, unpracticed moral obligations, and the like, remain in the ontology of the social normative powers theorist. These continue to do their work, whether or not the powers exist.

Even someone who holds that social practices are exercises of a normative power would not therefore deny (how could he?) that your action within some social practice is subject to ordinary including moral standards or duties. He would not deny that, because others are already queuing, I may have reasons of fairness to join the back of the queue. But he would say that responding to these reasons would not count as compliance with the queueing rule. The social power theorist would not deny that, in France, given that others are driving on the right, to keep us all safe I should also drive on the right. But he would say that in doing so I am not complying with the rule of the road in France.

So the social powers theorist could accept that duties to conform to social practices can obtain through the usual mechanisms. But he might say that the *distinctive* duties, those that count as the characteristic duties incurred because of the practice, can only obtain through a special mechanism: through the exercise of the power of groups to place themselves and others under duties just by settling into a pattern of action and taking a certain attitude to the pattern.

As we saw, while the ordinary mechanism is fine grained, tracking normatively relevant distinctions given the circumstances, the special mechanism is binary. Either the power obtains, or it does not. If it does, all and only that which is done in some settled practice is validated, or nothing is. (Since the bar is so high, we should expect many failures.) This point is not affected by the fact that the social powers theorist may also make fine grained calls as to what agents have reason to do, taking into view all circumstances. The mechanism is binary, but not because it asks whether there is a duty to do something in some circumstances, factoring in the existence of a practice of doing it. For this would, of course, be the question asked by the competing, ordinary model of explanation. Rather, it is binary because it asks whether there is a reason why people should have the power to *make* it their duty to do that thing by settling into a pattern of doing it and holding themselves to the pattern.

In sum, the insistence, on the part of the powers version of the mixed practice theory, on preserving the pure practice theory's doctrine of determination, even as it rejects the pure theory's normative ontology—the pure theory's very motivation for the doctrine—seems ad hoc. Its remaining complaint, that reasons and duties otherwise constituted wouldn't count as reasons or duties imposed by the relevant practice, looks rather feeble. The practice theory hoped to contribute to the understanding of an interesting normative phenomenon, not to teach us how to use words. The simple alternative seems to be able smoothly to account for the phenomena. Pending further argument, we have no reason to turn to the practice theory in order to understand how social practices can make a normative difference.

5.

I have argued that, in its original, pure form, the practice theory is an account of what it is to have an obligation. It purports to offer an alternative to 'metaphysical' theories on which we must appeal to nonnatural factors in order to capture the normative character of obligation. The practice theory holds instead that obligations are ultimately a social construct, made of shared attitudes to patterns of action. I have argued that, by restricting itself to social factors, the theory loses sight of the critical role of the normative. The metaphysicians were right. We need to appeal to nonsocial normative facts to explain how social practices may give rise to duties, constitute standards, or otherwise matter.

It may seem that we can have it both ways. Perhaps we can mix normative realism with the practice theory's doctrine of determination. We could hold that, when nonsocial normative factors give some social practice normative significance, they do so en bloc, by assigning normative force to the standards or duties determined by the social facts of the practice alone.

I have argued that in fact normative realism and the social determination doctrine don't mix. If nonsocial normative factors explain why social practices matter, they do so by explaining how exactly they matter, taking into account all relevant considerations. This implies that socially dependent duties might outstrip, fall short, or cut against established practice. The normative powers model, applied to the case of collective action, is a poor fit. There is no good reason why the capacity of social practices to change the normative situation should be limited to what is endorsed in practice. The social determination doctrine is a leftover from the pure practice theory—from thinking reason is a construct all the way down—and can't stand once we give up on that radical constructivism.[64]

Nicolaos Stavropoulos, *The Practice Theory* In: *Oxford Studies in Philosophy of Law, Volume 5*. Edited by: Leslie Green and Brian Leiter, Oxford University Press. © Nicolaos Stavropoulos 2024. DOI: 10.1093/9780198919650.003.0001

[64] I presented a draft of this article at the UCLA Legal Theory Workshop. I am grateful to participants for discussion and to Mark Greenberg for written comments. I am grateful to Thomas Adams and Hasan Dindjer for written comments on an earlier draft and to George Letsas and Jed Lewinsohn for discussion. I am grateful to Angelo Ryu for detailed written comments and suggestions and for discussion of a recent draft.

Precedent and Open Texture

John Horty

1. Introduction

Suppose that two parents have established a household rule according to which their children are allowed to go out and play Saturday mornings only if their rooms are clean. What does it mean, in this setting, for a child's room to be "clean"—how can it be determined whether this predicate applies to a child's room? The parents might attempt a definitional account, perhaps stipulating that a child's room is clean just in case the floor is vacuumed and the bed is made up with fresh sheets. But what if the shelves have not been dusted and are covered with clutter? On the other hand, what if the bed is not made up with fresh sheets, but the reason is that no fresh sheets are available and the washing machine is in use? The parents might refine their initial definition, perhaps leading to: a child's room is clean just in case the floor is vacuumed, shelves are dusted, and the bed is made up with fresh sheets unless no fresh sheets are available and the laundry room is busy. But what if the trash has not been emptied? What if clothes are not folded and put away? Given the unbounded collection of possible complicating considerations, it is hard to imagine how any definitional account of what it means for a child's room to be clean could be successful.[1]

The phenomenon at work in this example is what H. L. A. Hart describes as *open texture*, a feature of ordinary predicates that he illustrates with his famous example of vehicles in the park:

---

[1] Recent discussions of the problems confronting definitional accounts of predicate meaning can be found in Chapter 1 of Elbourne (2011) and throughout Ludlow (2014); a classic account, focusing on theories of sentence comprehension and concept learning, is provided by Fodor et al. (1980).

A legal rule forbids you to take a vehicle into the public park. Plainly this forbids an automobile, but what about bicycles, roller skates, toy automobiles? What about airplanes? Are these, as we say, to be called "vehicles" for the purpose of the rule or not?

And just as famous as Hart's example is his semantic proposal—involving a "core" and a "penumbra"—for understanding the meaning of open-textured predicates:

> If we are to communicate with each other at all, and if, as in the most elementary form of law, we are to express our intentions that a certain type of behavior be regulated by rules, then the general words we use—like "vehicle" in the case I consider—must have some standard instance in which no doubts are felt about its application. There must be a core of settled meaning, but there will be, as well, a penumbra of debatable cases in which words are neither obviously applicable nor obviously ruled out. These cases will each have some features in common with the standard case; they will lack others or be accompanied by features not present in the standard case.[2]

According to Hart's proposal, then, an open-textured predicate—such as "clean," applied to a child's room—is associated with a core of settled meaning, which determines a set of cases to which the predicate clearly applies, as well as a set of cases to which it clearly fails to apply. The predicate would clearly apply, for example, to a glittering room: bed crisply made, fresh sheets, floor perfectly vacuumed, clothes neatly folded and put away, shelves dusted, trash properly disposed of. The predicate would clearly fail to apply to a filthy and chaotic room: bed unmade, dirty sheets, clothes and trash scattered around an unvacuumed floor, cluttered, dust-covered shelves. In addition to these clear cases, however, Hart's view allows for a range of penumbral cases to which the predicate neither clearly applies nor clearly fails to apply. It is not hard to

---

[2] The passages quoted in this paragraph are from Section 3 of Hart (1958), where he first discusses the concept of an open-textured predicate, although in this paper he describes these predicates using the phrase "open character" instead. This discussion is then elaborated upon and extended in Chapter 7 of Hart (1961), where the concept of open character is now described as "open texture," a phrase that Hart adopted from Waismann (1945).

imagine that the room of a typical child would fall within this penumbra: bed sloppily made though perhaps with fresh sheets, floor vacuumed toward the center but debris visible around the edges, trash disposed of, shelves still cluttered but haphazardly dusted.

Although Hart illustrates his concept of open texture with the hypothetical example of vehicles in a park, the problems of determining applicability of particular open-textured predicates in various penumbral situations are common in the law. Sometimes these problems can seem to be comical, even ludicrous, until the stakes are appreciated. For example, the British court system once considered the question whether Pringles could properly be classified as "potato chips." The reason this question found its way into the courts is that, in the United Kingdom, food is generally exempt from the value-added tax, with only a few exceptions—including potato chips. In an effort to avoid this tax, amounting to roughly $160 million, the manufactures of Pringles were therefore intent on establishing that Pringles should be classified not as potato chips but rather as "savory snacks," on the grounds that they contain corn, rice, and wheat, in addition to potato flour.³ At other times, the importance of the problems involved in determining the applicability of open-textured predicates is almost self-evident. These include the various cases in employment law testing the distinction between "employees" and "contractors," as well as the range of cases exploring applicability conditions for socially fraught predicates such as "marriage" or "rape" or "person."⁴

Because of the intrinsic interest and practical importance of the issues surrounding open-textured predicates, a substantial literature on the topic has evolved within legal theory.⁵ For the most part, however, this literature focuses on what might be thought of as broader issues related to open texture—the role of defeasible legal rules, policy arguments concerning the application of these rules, the impact of open-textured

---

³ After multiple levels of appeal, this effort failed, with the result that Pringles were officially classified as "potato chips" and the manufactures were forced to pay a value-added tax; see Cohen (2009).

⁴ A useful discussion of the changing conditions for applicability of the predicates "rape" and "person" can be found in Schiappa (2003).

⁵ Some highlights include Baker (1977), Bix (1991), MacCormick (1991), Lyons (1999), Tur (2001), Schauer (2008), and Schauer (2013).

predicates on theories of legal interpretation. The legal literature on the topic does not provide anything like a semantic account of open-textured predicates, or at least, not in the sense that a contemporary semanticist would recognize.

The goal of the present paper is to offer such an account, particularly of open-textured predicates in the law, but an account that may be applicable to uses of these predicates in language more broadly.[6] The central idea is that judgments involving open-textured predicates—whether Pringles are potato chips, whether a child's room is clean—are evaluated against a background set of previous authoritative decisions involving these predicates, and that these previous decisions then constrain later applications of the same predicates in exactly the way that precedent cases constrain later decisions in the common law.

Because this account draws on the mechanism of precedential constraint to help explain the use of open-textured predicates, it falls within a strong tradition of research connecting work in the philosophy of language with issues in legal theory.[7] Much of this work concentrates on the illumination, or lack thereof, to be derived from an application within legal theory of ideas originally developed in logic or the philosophy of language—such as formal treatments of vagueness, for example.[8] The present paper moves in the opposite direction, applying ideas first developed in the study of legal reasoning to illuminate an issue within the philosophy of language itself, the phenomenon of open texture. What makes this shift in explanatory direction possible is a growing body of research in the field of artificial intelligence and law that has brought a new precision to the study of legal reasoning, and led to the development of ideas and tools that can then be applied elsewhere.

In particular, the account of open texture presented here is based on a treatment of precedential constraint—characterized as the *reason model*

---

[6] The idea that an account along these lines can be applied in language more broadly, not just legal language, arose in discussion with Cumming and is currently under development in joint work; see Cumming (2023) for an initial proposal. A difference between Cumming's work and the current account is that Cumming formulates his proposal using a full default logic—much richer and more expressive than the special-purpose formalism employed here, which corresponds only to a fragment of default logic.

[7] See Endicott (2022) for an overview.

[8] A study of vagueness in the law from a perspective that combines legal, linguistic, and logical considerations is presented in Endicott (2000); a later collection on the same topic is found in Keil and Poscher (2016).

of constraint—that is derived directly from recent research in artificial intelligence and law, as well as from an earlier proposal due to Grant Lamond.[9] According to the reason model, what matters about a precedent case is the court's assessment of importance among the competing reasons presented by that case, which is represented as a priority ordering among these reasons. Later courts are then constrained not necessarily to follow the rules set out in precedent cases, or even to modify those rules only in certain ways, but simply to reach decisions that are consistent with the priority ordering that has been established earlier. The development of the common law is pictured, not as the elaboration of an increasingly complex system of rules, but instead as the gradual construction of an increasingly rich priority ordering among reasons.

Because the goal of this paper is to show how the reason model of precedential constraint can be adapted to provide a semantic account of open-textured predicates, we begin with a brief but precise formulation of the reason model itself. This is accomplished in the next two sections, with Section 2 presenting the formal framework within which this model is developed, and then Section 3 moving through the series of definitions that constitute the model. Section 4 then shows how the ideas from the reason model can be generalized to a semantic treatment of open-textured predicates, by providing an account of the constraints governing their applicability. Section 5 concludes with a discussion of some open issues and directions for future work.

2. Basic concepts

2.1 Factors and fact situations

We suppose that a situation presented to a court for decision can be represented as a set of *factors*, where a factor is a legally significant fact

---

[9] See Lamond (2005) for his initial proposal. The first version of the account presented here is found in Horty (2011), later developed in Horty (2015); a book-length exposition is presented in Horty (2024). This account has been related to other approaches from artificial intelligence and law in Horty and Bench-Capon (2012), compared to analogical approaches in Rigoni (2014), limited in scope in Broughton (2019), and explored from a formal perspective in Prakken (2021). More recently, a different interpretation of Lamond's original proposal, and one that connects it more closely with traditional ideas from legal theory, has been presented in Mullins (2020).

or pattern of facts bearing on that decision. This style of representation has been used to analyze case-based reasoning in a number of complex legal domains within artificial intelligence and law, where it originated in the work of Edwina Rissland and Kevin Ashley.[10] Cases in different areas of the law will be characterized by different sets of factors, of course. In the domain of trade-secrets law, for example, where the factor-based analysis has been explored most extensively, a case typically concerns the issue of whether the defendant has gained an unfair competitive advantage over the plaintiff through the misappropriation of a trade secret; and here the factors involved might turn on, say, questions concerning whether the plaintiff took measures to protect the trade secret, whether a confidential relationship existed between the plaintiff and the defendant, whether the information acquired was reverse-engineerable or in some other way publicly available, and the extent to which this information did, in fact, lead to a real competitive advantage for the defendant.[11]

Many factors can naturally be taken to have polarities, favoring one side or another. In the domain of trade-secrets law, the presence of security measures favors the plaintiff, since it strengthens the claim that the information secured was a valuable trade secret; reverse-engineerability favors the defendant, since it suggests that the product information might have been acquired through legitimate means. As a simplification, we will assume, not just that many, or even most, factors have polarities, but that all factors are like this, favoring one particular side. In addition, we rely on the further simplifying assumption that the reasoning under consideration involves only a single step, proceeding at once from the factors present in a situation to a decision—directly in favor of the plaintiff or the defendant—rather than moving through a series of intermediate legal concepts.

---

[10] See Rissland and Ashley (1987) and Ashley (1989) for their initial proposals, Rissland (1990) for an overview of research in artificial intelligence and law that places this work in a broader perspective, Ashley (1990) for a canonical presentation, and then Rissland and Ashley (2002) for later reflections on the factor-based representation of legal information.

[11] The most detailed analysis in this domain is presented by Aleven (1997), who analyzed 147 cases from trade-secrets law in terms of a factor hierarchy that includes five high-level issues, eleven intermediate-level concerns, and twenty-six base-level factors. The resulting knowledge base is used in an intelligent tutoring system for teaching elementary skills in legal argumentation, which has achieved results comparable to traditional methods of instruction in controlled studies; see Aleven and Ashley (1997).

Formally, then, we start by postulating a set of legal factors bearing on some particular issue. We will let $F^\pi = \left\{ f_1^\pi,...,f_n^\pi \right\}$ represent the set of factors favoring the plaintiff and $F^\delta = \left\{ f_1^\delta,...,f_n^\delta \right\}$ the set of factors favoring the defendant. Given our assumption that each factor favors one side or the other, the entire set $F^{\pi/\delta}$ of legal factors will be exhausted by those favoring the plaintiff together with those favoring the defendant: $F^{\pi/\delta} = F^\pi \cup F^\delta$. As this notation suggests, we take π and δ to represent the two sides in a dispute, plaintiff and defendant, and where s is one of these sides, we let $\bar{s}$ represent the other: $\bar{\pi} = \delta$ and $\bar{\delta} = \pi$.

Based on this set $F^{\pi/\delta}$ of factors, we define a *fact situation X* of the sort presented to the court for judgment simply as some particular subset of the factor set: $X \subseteq F^{\pi/\delta}$. And where X is a fact situation of this kind, we let X^s represent the factors from X that support the side s, so that: $X^\pi = X \cap F^\pi$ and $X^\delta = X \cap F^\delta$. Of course, any interesting situation will contain factors favoring both sides of a given dispute. For example, the situation $X_1 = \left\{ f_1^\pi, f_2^\pi, f_1^\delta, f_2^\delta \right\}$ contains two factors each favoring the plaintiff and the defendant, with those factors favoring the plaintiff contained in $X_1^\pi = \left\{ f_1^\pi, f_2^\pi \right\}$ and those favoring the defendant contained in $X_1^\delta = \left\{ f_1^\delta, f_2^\delta \right\}$.

2.2 Reasons, rules, cases, case bases

When presented with a fact situation, a court's primary task is to reach a decision, or determine an outcome. Given our assumption that reasoning proceeds in a single step, we can suppose that the *outcome* of a case is a decision either in favor of the plaintiff or in favor of the defendant, with these two outcomes represented as π or δ respectively.

In addition to reaching a decision for one side or the other, we generally expect the court to supply a rule, or principle, to serve as justification for its decision.[12] Rules of this kind will be characterized in terms of reasons, where a *reason for a side* is some set of factors uniformly

---

[12] Although I will refer to case rules as "rules," I take no stand on the question whether they should actually be classified as rules or as principles; I think of these case rules as relatively specific, a property associated with rules, as opposed to principles, by Raz (1972), but also as defeasible, a property associated with principles, as opposed to rules, by Dworkin (1967).

favoring that side; a *reason* can then be defined as a set of factors uniformly favoring one side or another. To illustrate: $\left\{f_1^\pi, f_2^\pi\right\}$ is a reason favoring the plaintiff, and so a reason.

Since reasons, like fact situations, are sets of factors, we can stipulate that a reason U *holds* in a situation X just in case each factor from U belongs to X, so that U is a subset of X, or $U \subseteq X$. And we can also define a relation of strength among reasons for a side according to which, where U and V are reasons for the same side, then V *is at least as strong a reason as U for that side* just in case U is a subset of V, or $U \subseteq V$. To illustrate: The reason $\left\{f_1^\pi\right\}$ holds in the fact situation $X_1 = \left\{f_1^\pi, f_2^\pi, f_1^\delta, f_2^\delta\right\}$, since $\left\{f_1^\pi\right\} \subseteq X_1$, and of the two reasons $\left\{f_1^\pi\right\}$ and $\left\{f_1^\pi, f_2^\pi\right\}$, the second favors the plaintiff at least as strongly as the first, since $\left\{f_1^\pi\right\} \subseteq \left\{f_1^\pi, f_2^\pi\right\}$.

Given this notion of a reason, a *rule* can now be defined as a statement of the form $U \to s$, where U is a reason supporting the side s. For convenience, we introduce two auxiliary functions— *Premise* and *Conclusion* —picking out the premise and conclusion of a rule, so that, if r stands for the rule just mentioned, we would have $Premise(r) = U$ and $Conclusion(r) = s$. And we will say that a rule is *applicable* in a situation whenever the reason that forms its premise holds in that situation. To illustrate: The statement $\left\{f_1^\pi\right\} \to \pi$ is a rule, since $\left\{f_1^\pi\right\}$ is a reason supporting the plaintiff. If we take r_1 to stand for this rule, we would have $Premise(r_1) = \left\{f_1^\pi\right\}$ and $Conclusion(r_1) = \pi$. And r_1 is applicable in the situation X_1 above, since $Premise(r_1) = \left\{f_1^\pi\right\}$ holds in this situation.

The rules defined here are to be interpreted as defeasible, telling us that their premises entail their conclusions, not as a matter of necessity, but only by default. Continuing with our illustration, what the rule $r_1 = \left\{f_1^\pi\right\} \to \pi$ means, very roughly, is that, whenever the premise $\left\{f_1^\pi\right\}$ of the rule holds in some situation, then, as a default, the court ought to decide that situation for the conclusion π of the rule—or perhaps more simply, that the premise of the rule provides the court with a pro tanto reason for deciding in favor of its conclusion.[13]

---

[13] The connections among default rules, reasons, and oughts sketched in this paragraph are developed in detail in Horty (2012).

On the basis of the concepts introduced so far—fact situations, rules, outcomes—a *case* can be defined as a situation together with an outcome and a rule through which that outcome is justified: such a case can be specified as a triple of the form $c = \langle X, r, s \rangle$, where X is a situation containing the factors presented to the court, r is a rule, and s is an outcome.[14] For illustration, consider the case $c_1 = \langle X_1, r_1, s_1 \rangle$, where the fact situation of this case is the familiar $X_1 = \left\{ f_1^\pi, f_2^\pi, f_1^\delta, f_2^\delta \right\}$, where the case rule is the familiar $r_1 = \left\{ f_1^\pi \right\} \rightarrow \pi$, and where the outcome of the case is $s_1 = \pi$, a decision for the plaintiff. This particular case, then, represents a situation in which the court, when confronted with the fact situation X_1, decided for the plaintiff by applying or introducing the rule r_1, according to which the presence of the factor f_1^π—that is, the reason $\left\{ f_1^\pi \right\}$—leads, by default, to a decision for the plaintiff.

Finally, with this notion of a case in hand, we can now define a *case base* as a set Γ of precedent cases. It is a case base of this sort—a set of precedent cases—that will be taken to represent the common law in some area, and to constrain the decisions of future courts.

3. Constraint by reasons

According to the reason model, we recall, what matters about a precedent case is the precedent court's assessment of the relative importance of the reasons presented by that case for each of the opposing sides. This assessment can be represented as a priority ordering on reasons, with later courts then required to reach decisions that are consistent with the priority ordering derived from the decisions of earlier courts.

In order to develop this idea, we need to explain how a priority ordering on reasons can be derived from the decisions of earlier courts, and then what it means for the decision of a later court to be consistent with that ordering.

---

[14] Our representation of cases embodies the simplifying assumption that the particular rule underlying a court's decision is plain, ignoring the extensive literature on methods for determining the *ratio decidendi* of a case; and we suppose, as a further simplification, that a case always contains a single rule, ignoring situations in which a court might offer several rules for a decision, or in which a court reaches a decision by majority, with different members of the court offering different rules, or in which a court might simply render a decision in a case without setting out any general rule at all.

3.1 A priority ordering on reasons

To begin with, then, let us return to the case $c_1 = \langle X_1, r_1, s_1 \rangle$—where $X_1 = \{f_1^\pi, f_2^\pi, f_1^\delta, f_2^\delta\}$, where $r_1 = \{f_1^\pi\} \to \pi$, and where $s_1 = \pi$—and ask what information is carried by this case; what is the court telling us with its decision? Well, two things. First of all, with its decision for the plaintiff on the basis of the rule r_1, the court is registering its judgment that $Premise(r_1) = \{f_1^\pi\}$, the reason for its decision, is more important—or has higher *priority*—than any reason for the defendant that holds in X_1, the fact situation of the case.[15] How do we know this? Because if the court had viewed some reason for the defendant that held in the situation X_1 as more important, or higher in priority, than $Premise(r_1)$, the court would have found for the defendant on the basis of that reason, rather than for the plaintiff on the basis of $Premise(r_1)$. And second, if the court is telling us explicitly that the reason $Premise(r_1)$ itself has higher priority than any reason for the defendant that holds in X_1, then the court must also be telling us, at least implicitly, that any other reason for the plaintiff that is at least as strong as $Premise(r_1)$ must likewise have a higher priority than any reason for the defendant that holds in this situation.

We can recall that a reason U for the defendant holds in the situation X_1 just in case $U \subseteq X_1$, and that a reason V for the plaintiff is at least as strong for the plaintiff as the reason $Premise(r_1)$ just in case $Premise(r_1) \subseteq V$. If we let the relation $<_{c_1}$ represent the priority ordering on reasons derived from the particular case c_1, then, the force of the court's decision in this case is simply that: where U is a reason favoring the defendant and V is a reason favoring the plaintiff, we have $U <_{c_1} V$ just in case $U \subseteq X_1$ and $Premise(r_1) \subseteq V$. To illustrate: Consider the reason $\{f_1^\delta\}$ for the defendant and the reason $\{f_1^\pi, f_2^\pi, f_3^\pi\}$ for the plaintiff. Here, we have $\{f_1^\delta\} \subseteq X_1$ as well as $Premise(r_1) \subseteq \{f_1^\pi, f_2^\pi, f_3^\pi\}$. It therefore follows that $\{f_1^\delta\} <_{c_1} \{f_1^\pi, f_2^\pi, f_3^\pi\}$—the court's decision in the case c_1 entails that the reason $\{f_1^\pi, f_2^\pi, f_3^\pi\}$ favoring the plaintiff is to be assigned a higher priority than the reason $\{f_1^\delta\}$ favoring the defendant.

---

[15] When comparing the relative importance of reasons, it is more common to say that one carries greater weight than the other, or that one is weightier than the other. I prefer to speak in terms of priority, rather than weight, for two reasons: first, the priority ordering on reasons to be defined here is nonlinear, while the concept of weight tends to suggest linearity; second, the ordering to be defined here allows only ordinal comparisons among reasons, while the concept of weight suggests that cardinal comparisons must be available as well.

Generalizing from this example, we reach the following definition of the priority ordering among reasons derived from a single case:

Definition 1 (Priority ordering derived from a case) Where $c = \langle X, r, s \rangle$ is a case and U and V are reasons favoring the sides $\overline{s}$ and s respectively, the relation $<_c$ representing the priority ordering on reasons derived from the case c is defined by stipulating that $U <_c V$ if and only if $U \subseteq X$ and $Premise(r) \subseteq V$.

This priority ordering on reasons derived from a single case can be lifted to an ordering derived from an entire case base in the natural way, through the stipulation that one reason has a higher priority than another according to the case base whenever that priority is supported by some case from the case base:

Definition 2 (Priority ordering derived from a case base) Where Γ is a case base and U and V are reasons, the relation $<_\Gamma$ representing the priority ordering on reasons derived from the case base Γ is defined by stipulating that $U <_\Gamma V$ if and only if $U <_c V$ for some case c from Γ.

And using this concept of a priority ordering derived from a case base, we can now define a case base itself as inconsistent if the ordering it supports yields conflicting information about the priority among reasons—telling us, for some pair of reasons, that each has a higher priority than the other—and consistent otherwise:

Definition 3 (Inconsistent and consistent case bases) Where Γ is a case base with $<_\Gamma$ its derived priority ordering, Γ is inconsistent if and only if there are reasons U and V such that $U <_\Gamma V$ and $V <_\Gamma U$, and consistent otherwise.

3.2 Constraint

We now present the reason model of constraint itself, building on the concept of case base consistency. The guiding idea, once again, is that, in deciding a case, a constrained court is required to preserve the consistency of the background case base. Suppose, more exactly, that a court constrained by a consistent background case base is confronted with a new fact situation. Then what the reason model tells us, in the first instance, is that the court is permitted to base its decision on a particular rule only if augmenting the background case base with a decision based on that rule maintains consistency:

Definition 4 (Reason model constraint on rule selection) Against the background of a consistent case base Γ, the reason model permits a court to base its decision in some situation X on the rule r, applicable in X and supporting the side s, if and only if the augmented case base $\Gamma \cup \{\langle X, r, s \rangle\}$ is consistent.

This definition can be illustrated by imagining that the background case base is $\Gamma_1 = \{c_1\}$ containing as its single member the familiar case $c_1 = \langle X_1, r_1, s_1 \rangle$—where, again, $X_1 = \{f_1^\pi, f_2^\pi, f_1^\delta, f_2^\delta\}$, where $r_1 = \{f_1^\pi\} \to \pi$, and where $s_1 = \pi$. Suppose that, against this background, the court confronts the fresh situation $X_2 = \{f_1^\pi, f_2^\pi, f_1^\delta, f_2^\delta, f_3^\delta\}$ and considers finding for the defendant in this situation on the basis of the reason $\{f_1^\delta, f_2^\delta\}$, leading to the decision $c_2 = \langle X_2, r_2, s_2 \rangle$, where X_2 is as above, where $r_2 = \{f_1^\delta, f_2^\delta\} \to \delta$, and where $s_2 = \delta$. Is the court permitted to carry through with this plan, according to the reason model?

Well, as we can see, $Premise(r_1) = \{f_1^\pi\}$, the reason for the decision in the initial case, holds in the new situation X_2 as well, since $\{f_1^\pi\} \subseteq X_2$. And of course, the new reason $Premise(r_2) = \{f_1^\delta, f_2^\delta\}$ favors the defendant at least as strongly as itself—that is, $Premise(r_2) \subseteq Premise(r_2)$, or $Premise(r_2) \subseteq \{f_1^\delta, f_2^\delta\}$. It therefore follows from Definition 1 that c_2, the court's envisaged decision, would assign the reason $\{f_1^\delta, f_2^\delta\}$ for the defendant a higher priority than the reason $\{f_1^\pi\}$ for the plaintiff—that is, $\{f_1^\pi\} <_{c_2} \{f_1^\delta, f_2^\delta\}$. But Γ_1 already contains the case c_1, from which, in a similar fashion, we can derive the priority relation $\{f_1^\delta, f_2^\delta\} <_{c_1} \{f_1^\pi\}$, telling us exactly the opposite. Since the augmented case base

$$\Gamma_2 = \Gamma_1 \cup \{c_2\}$$
$$= \{c_1, c_2\}$$

resulting from the court's envisaged decision contains both these cases, we would then have both $\left\{f_1^\delta, f_2^\delta\right\} <_{\Gamma_2} \left\{f_1^\pi\right\}$ and $\left\{f_1^\pi\right\} <_{\Gamma_2} \left\{f_1^\delta, f_2^\delta\right\}$ by Definition 2, so that, by Definition 3, this augmented case base would be inconsistent. By Definition 4, then, we can conclude that the court is not permitted to decide for the defendant in the situation X_2 on the basis of the rule r_2, since c_2, the resulting decision, would introduce an inconsistency into the background case base.

Of course, it does not follow from the fact that the court is not permitted to decide the situation X_2 for the defendant on the basis of the particular rule r_2 that it is not permitted to decide this situation for the defendant at all—in this situation, there are other rules on the basis of which the court is permitted to reach a decision for the defendant. Suppose, for example, that the court considers finding for the defendant on the basis of the reason $\left\{f_1^\delta, f_3^\delta\right\}$, leading to the decision $c_3 = \langle X_3, r_3, s_3 \rangle$, where $X_3 = X_2$, where $r_3 = \left\{f_1^\delta, f_3^\delta\right\} \to \delta$, and where $s_3 = \delta$. The augmented case base

$$\Gamma_3 = \Gamma_1 \cup \left\{c_3\right\}$$
$$\left\{c_1, c_3\right\}$$

resulting from this decision would then be consistent. As before, the previous case c_1 supports the priority $\left\{f_1^\delta, f_2^\delta\right\} <_{c_1} \left\{f_1^\pi\right\}$, and the new decision c_3 would now support the priority $\left\{f_1^\pi\right\} <_{c_2} \left\{f_1^\delta, f_3^\delta\right\}$, so that we would then have both the case base priorities $\left\{f_1^\delta, f_2^\delta\right\} <_{\Gamma_3} \left\{f_1^\pi\right\}$, and $\left\{f_1^\pi\right\} <_{\Gamma_3} \left\{f_1^\delta, f_3^\delta\right\}$. But there is nothing inconsistent about this pair of priorities.

Now imagine that the court does, in fact, decide the situation X_2 in this way, augmenting the background case Γ_1 with the new decision c_3, leading to the augmented case base $\Gamma_3 = \Gamma_1 \cup \left\{c_3\right\}$. According to the reason model, this decision would then represent a step in the normal development of a legal system, which proceeds more generally as follows: A court confronts a new situation X against the background of a consistent case base Γ, with an associated ordering $<_\Gamma$ on reasons. The court is permitted to base its decision only on a rule r supporting an outcome s such that the case base $\Gamma' = \Gamma \cup \left\{c\right\}$ is consistent, with the result that the background case base is augmented with this new decision.

The next court confronting the next new situation Y must then work against the background of the augmented case base Γ', which gives rise to the strengthened ordering $<_{\Gamma'}$ on reasons. This new court is likewise permitted to base its decision only on a rule r' supporting an outcome s' such that the case base $\Gamma'' = \Gamma' \cup \{\langle Y, r', s' \rangle\}$ is consistent, thus further augmenting the case base, further strengthening the underlying priority ordering on reasons, and the process continues.

The hypothesis of the reason model is that this is how the common law develops in the normal, incremental case—by building up a stronger and stronger priority ordering on reasons through a series of decisions that are, at each stage, consistent with the existing case base.

3.3 Requirements and permissions

Definition 4 characterizes only the rules on the basis of which a court is permitted to justify its decisions. But of course, once this idea is in place, it can be used to define the conditions under which a court is permitted, or required, to reach a decision for one side or another—through the natural stipulation that a court is permitted to reach a decision for a side if some rule on the basis of which it is permitted to justify its decision supports that side, and required to reach a decision for a side if every rule on the basis of which it is permitted to justify its decision supports that side:

Definition 5 (Reason model constraint on decision) Against the background of a consistent case base Γ, the reason model permits a court to decide the situation X for the side s if and only if some rule on the basis of which the court is permitted to decide that situation supports s. Likewise, the reason model requires the court to decide X for the side s if and only if every rule on the basis of which the court is permitted to decide that situation supports s.

For illustration: We have seen that, against the background of Γ_1, the court is permitted to decide the fact situation X_2 on the basis of the rule r_3 supporting δ, the defendant. And it is easy to see that the court is likewise permitted to decide this situation on the basis of r_1, supporting π, the plaintiff. It follows from Definition 5, therefore, that the court is permitted to decide this situation for each side, but not required to decide for either. By contrast, suppose that, against the background of the same case base, the court is now faced with the situation $X_4 = \left\{ f_1^\pi, f_1^\delta \right\}$. It then follows that the only rule on the basis of which the court is permitted to justify its decision is r_1, so that the court is required to decide this new situation for π, the plaintiff.

It is just worth noting that the notions of requirement and permission introduced in Definition 5 conform to the rules of standard deontic logic. We can see, for example, that a court is required to decide a situation for the side s just in case it is not permitted to decide that situation for $\overline{s}$, the opposite side. And as long as it is working against the background of a consistent case base, the court will never be required to decide the same situation for one side and also for the other; it will always be required to reach a decision only for one side, or required to reach a decision only for the other, or permitted to reach a decision for either side.

4. Open texture

4.1 A semantic account

We now turn, at last, to the central task of this paper: showing how the treatment of precedential constraint sketched so far can be adapted to supply a semantic account of open-textured predicates. The first step is to interpret π and δ—previously regarded simply as grammatically indeterminate symbols indicating a decision for the plaintiff or the defendant—explicitly as predicates, so that, where X is a fact situation, the application of π to X means that the situation is decided for the plaintiff, while the application of δ to X means that the situation is decided for the defendant. If π and δ are predicates, it seems clear that they must be open-textured predicates, since a judgment about their applicability in some situation is determined not by appeal to definition but by assessing the various competing considerations that might favor a decision for the plaintiff or the defendant. And it is clear also that the predicates π and δ are contraries, in the traditional sense that they cannot both apply in a particular situation, but that, at any given point, it may not yet be determined which applies.

Once we have agreed to regard π and δ as open-textured predicates, the next step is simply to generalize the analysis already set out for the particular predicates π and δ to open-textured predicates more broadly. We begin by stipulating that, just as π and δ can be thought of as contraries, each open-textured predicate p is associated with some contrary p'. To illustrate: If p represents the predicate "clean," applied to a child's room, then p' represents the predicate "not clean." If p represents the predicate "potato chips," applied to a manufactured comestible, such as Pringles, then p' represents the predicate "not potato chips." If p represents the predicate "employee," applied to an individual performing a service for pay, such as an Uber driver, then p' represents the predicate "contractor." A pair consisting of an open-textured predicate p and its contrary p' represents the two sides of a *dispute*. As before, we will let s range over these two sides, and where s is one of the sides, $\overline{S}$ is the other: $\overline{p} = p'$ and $\overline{p'} = p$.

For each dispute between a pair of open-textured predicates p and p', we postulate a set $F^p = \left\{ f_1^p, \ldots, f_n^p \right\}$ of factors favoring the decision that the predicate p should be applied to some object or situation under consideration, and a set $F^{p'} = \left\{ f_1^{p'}, \ldots, f_n^{p'} \right\}$ of factors favoring the decision that, instead, the predicate p' should be applied. If we take p and p' to represent "clean" and "not-clean," for example, then F^p might include the factors that, in a particular child's room, the bed is crisply made, or the floor carefully vacuumed, while $F^{p'}$ might include the factors that unfolded clothes are strewn about, or that trash has not been emptied. If we take p and p' to represent the predicates "potato chips" and "not potato chips," then F^p might include the factor that a particular manufactured comestible contains at least 40% potato flour, while $F^{p'}$ might include the factor that it contains other ingredients as well, such as corn, rice, or wheat flour. If we take p and p' to represent the predicates "employee" and "contractor," then F^p might include the factors that, for a particular individual, the company directs "when, where, and how" that individual's work is done or that the individual is required to "undergo company-provided training," while $F^{p'}$ might include the factors that there is no need for the individual in question to perform "on-site services" or that the individual performs the required services using "independently-obtained supplies or tools."[16]

Following our earlier pattern, we let $F^{p/p'} = F^p \cup F^{p'}$ represent the entire set of factors bearing on the dispute between p and p'. And we define a fact situation X that gives rise to this dispute as some subset of $F^{p/p'}$—that is, $X \subseteq F^{p/p'}$—divided into those factors $X^p = X \cap F^p$ favoring application of the predicate p and those factors $X^{p'} = X \cap F^{p'}$ favoring application of the predicate p'. Again, the most interesting situations are those containing factors favoring opposite sides of some dispute, such as the situation presented by a typical child's room, as described earlier, the situation presented by Pringles, which contain 42% potato flour but substantial amounts of corn, wheat, and rice flour, and the situation presented by Uber drivers, who undergo company-provided training but perform services off site using their independently provided vehicles.

From this point forward, the account set out already, centered around the dispute between application of the particular open-textured predicates π and δ, generalizes in a straightforward way to any dispute between application of the open-textured predicates p or p' more broadly. A reason U for a side s of the dispute between p and p' is defined as a set of factors uniformly favoring that side—that is, $U \subseteq F^s$—and a reason bearing on this dispute is defined as a reason for one side of the dispute or the other. As before, the reason U is said to hold in a fact situation X just in case each factor from U belongs to X, or $U \subseteq X$. A rule for the sides of the dispute between p and p' has the form $U \rightarrow s$, where U is a reason for s, and such a rule is applicable in some situation X just in case the reason U that form its premise holds in that situation. A case *bearing on* the dispute between p and p' is a structure of the form $c = \langle X, r, s \rangle$, where X is a fact situation giving rise to this dispute and r is a rule applicable in that fact situation and

---

[16] These particular factors are extracted from the United States Internal Revenue Service 20-factor test for differentiating employees from contractors.

supporting the side s. And a case base Γ bearing on this dispute is a set of cases bearing on the dispute.

Exactly as before, a priority ordering among reasons supporting opposite sides of the dispute between P and P', and derived from a particular case bearing on this dispute, can be set out as in Definition 1, and then extended to a priority ordering derived from a case base as in Definition 2. The notion of a consistent case base can be set out as in Definition 3. Finally, against the background of a case base Γ bearing on the dispute between P and P', the rules on the basis of which the court is permitted to arrive at a decision in a particular situation X giving rise to this dispute can be specified as in Definition 4, and the decisions that the court is required or permitted to reach specified as in Definition 5.

4.2 The Super Scoop

We now shift from Max's room, Pringles, and Uber drivers to another example, based on a series of United States federal court cases involving the question whether the Super Scoop—a dredge, at the time the largest in the world—could properly be classified as a "vessel." This question was brought before the courts by Willard Stewart, a marine engineer working on the Super Scoop, who was injured on the job through, as he claimed, the company's negligence and sought compensation for damages. Stewart had two routes to recovery. He could file a claim through the Longshoreman and Harbor Workers' Compensation Act, a federal statute that would provide the equivalent of workers' compensation, but would exclude negligence. Or he could file under the Jones Act, another federal statute specifically enacted to protect seamen, due to the extraordinary perils of work at sea, containing the language

> Any seaman who shall suffer personal injury in the course of his employment may, at his election, maintain an action for damages at law, with the right of trial by jury...

and so allowing recovery for negligence.[17]

---

[17] 46 U.S.C. App. §688(a). The Act has since been further amended and recodified at 46 USC 30104.

Because Stewart hoped to claim negligence under the Jones Act, it was necessary for him to establish that he had been employed by Dutra as a "seaman" at the time of his injury. Although this term is not defined in the Jones Act itself, a gloss on the statute specifies that whether or not an individual is a seaman depends on that individual's connection with a vessel. The nature of Stewart's connection with the Super Scoop was never an issue, since all parties acknowledged that he had been employed as a member of its crew. The question remained, however, whether the Super Scoop could legitimately be classified as a "vessel"—or more exactly, a "vessel in navigation"—as this predicate was understood in the Jones Act, and on that issue, there were considerations naturally favoring different sides. On one hand, the Super Scoop shared a number of characteristics with more typical vessels. It had a captain and crew, as well as various marine appurtenances, such as ballast tanks and navigation lights; and, importantly, it was registered with and subject to regulations of the United States Coast Guard. On the other hand, the Super Scoop was incapable of self-propulsion, but had to be towed from one location to another, and its primary purpose was construction, rather than navigation.

Stewart's suit against Dutra began in the District Court of Massachusetts, which found that the Super Scoop was not a vessel, so that Stuart could not proceed under the Jones Act, a decision that was upheld by the First Circuit Court of Appeals in *Stewart v. Dutra Construction Co., Inc.*[18] The decision was then appealed again to the United States Supreme court, which reversed the Appeals Court judgment, ruling instead that the Super Scoop was a vessel, and allowing Stewart to proceed with his Jones Act suit.[19]

We will not consider here the reasoning either of the District Court or of the Supreme Court, but focus only on the decision of the First Circuit Court of Appeals, which was explicitly based on the precedent established in *Di Giovanni v. Traylor Bros, Inc.*, an earlier case before the same court, and dealing with the same issue.[20] This case concerned, not a dredge, but a barge, the Betty F, bearing a crane used for bridge construction. The Betty F was similar, in many ways, to the Super Scoop, with a captain and crew, requiring Coast Guard registration, but

---

[18]   230 F.3d 461 (1st Cir. 2000).   [19]   543 U.S. 481 (2005).
[20]   959 F.2d 1119 (1st Cir. 1992).

without the capacity for self-propulsion, and with construction rather than navigation as its primary business; in addition, at the time of the incident in question, the Betty F had been largely stationary for over a month. This incident occurred when Rocco Di Giovanni, a workman on the Betty F, slipped and fell, due to the negligence of Traylor in failing to address a hydraulic fluid leak. Like Stewart, Di Giovanni hoped to bring suit as a seaman under the Jones Act. Again, the sole point of contention was whether or not the Betty F could be classified as a vessel, a question that had been presented to the First Circuit Court of Appeals, which decided that the Betty F could not be so classified, on the grounds that "if a barge, or other float's 'purpose or primary business is not navigation or commerce,' then workers assigned thereto...are to be considered seamen only when it is in actual navigation or transit."[21] Confronted with an analogous issue in *Stewart*, the court felt that it was bound by its own precedent, and so concluded that the Super Scoop could not be classified as a vessel either.

To model, or at least approximate, the situation confronting the First Circuit Court in *Stewart* within the current framework, we let the open-textured predicates v and v' represent the judgments that some marine platform is or is not a vessel. Among the factors favoring v, that the object is a vessel, we let f_1^v indicate that it has a captain and crew and f_1^v that it is subject to Coast Guard regulations. Among the factors favoring v', that the object is not a vessel, we let $f_1^{v'}$ indicate that it is not capable of self-propulsion, $f_2^{v'}$ that its primary business is not navigation, and $f_3^{v'}$ that it has been largely stationary for at least a month.

Using this notation, the situation presented by the Betty F to the *Di Giovanni* court can be represented as $X_5 = \left\{ f_1^v, f_2^v, f_1^{v'}, f_2^{v'}, f_3^{v'} \right\}$—and we simplify by imagining that the court was considering this situation against the background of an empty case base $\Gamma_4 = \varnothing$ containing no decisions at all concerning applicability of the predicate "vessel."[22] Given this information, and reasoning, as we imagine, against this

---

[21] 959 F.2d at 1123 (1st Cir. 1992).

[22] This is a significant simplification, since, by the time of *Di Giovanni*, there was already a substantial case base concerning applicability of the predicate "vessel." It is also worth noting that any decision is permitted against the background of an empty case base, so that the court is free to rely on its own judgment to decide whether an open-textured predicate is applicable;

background case base, the court then concluded that the Betty F should not be classified as a vessel on the grounds that its primary business was not navigation—that is, on the basis of the rule $r_5 = \left\{ f_2^{v'} \right\} \rightarrow v'$—leading to the decision $c_5 = \langle X_5, r_5, s_5 \rangle$, where X_5 and r_5 are as above and where $s_5 = v'$. The augmented case base resulting from this earlier decision, and constraining the reasoning of the later *Stewart* court, is therefore

$$\Gamma_5 = \Gamma_4 \cup \left\{ c_5 \right\}$$
$$\left\{ c_5 \right\},$$

with the situation presented by the Super Scoop to the *Stewart* court itself represented as $X_6 = \left\{ f_1^v, f_2^v, f_1^{v'}, f_2^{v'} \right\}$, differing from that presented by the Betty F situation only in omitting $f_3^{v'}$, and so forming a slightly stronger case for the conclusion v. Nevertheless, as the reader can verify, the reason model of constraint requires a finding for v' in the situation X_6 considered against the background of Γ_5—that is, a decision that the Super Scoop is not a vessel, just as the *Stewart* court itself concluded. In fact, the court justified its decision through a further application of the *Di Giovanni* rule, leading to $c_6 = \langle X_6, r_6, s_6 \rangle$ as the decision in *Stewart*, where X_6 is as above, where $r_6 = r_5$, and where $s_6 = v'$.

4.3 A comparison to Hart

With this semantic account of open-textured predicates before us, we can now draw a comparison with Hart's own proposal, presented in the canonical passage quoted in the Introduction of this chapter. In this passage, we recall, Hart argues that an open-textured predicate has a "core of settled meaning," which determines a range of cases in which "no doubts are felt about its application," but that such a predicate may also allow for a range of penumbral cases in which the predicate is neither "obviously applicable nor obviously ruled out." The current account, however, does not postulate a separate core of settled meaning

---

once this decision is incorporated into the case base, the court's judgment then gains legal authority, constraining later decisions.

to determine situations in which no doubts are felt about the applicability of an open-textured predicate. Instead, it relies only on a background set of precedent cases that requires the application of that predicate in certain situations, and requires the application of its contrary in others. In the same way, the present account does not postulate a set of penumbral situations in which an open-textured predicate is neither obviously applicable nor obviously ruled out, but supposes only that there may be a range of situations in which the background set of precedent cases requires application neither of the predicate nor of its contrary, but permits the decision to go either way.

I think of the current account of open texture as providing a sympathetic reconstruction of Hart, capturing in a formal semantic theory much of what is most important in his proposal. At the same time, I also want to argue that an explicit reliance on a background set of precedent decisions, as in the current account, has advantages over any appeal to a separate core of settled meaning. I will try to establish this point by, first, deflecting Hart's own argument, if it is interpreted as favoring a separate core of settled meaning, and then highlighting one benefit of relying, instead, on a background set of precedents.

We begin, then, with Hart's argument for a core of settled meaning. The argument is brief, and contained in the canonical passage already cited. Here, Hart takes as his premise the claim: "If we are to communicate with each other at all…then the general words we use—like 'vehicle' in the case I consider—must have some standard instances in which no doubts are felt about its application." And from this he moves directly to his conclusion: "There must be a core of settled meaning…." But this argument fails if it is interpreted as favoring a separate core of settled meaning, apart from the background set of precedent cases. After all, in the example we have just considered, once the court had decided that the Betty F cannot be classified as a vessel, it follows at once that it is no longer permissible to apply the predicate "vessel" to the Super Scoop either—there is, in Hart's language, no longer any doubt about application of this predicate to the Super Scoop. Yet this judgment does not depend on any separate core meaning of the predicate "vessel," but only on the relation between the situation at hand and the background set of precedents.

Turning now to our positive argument: the current account, with its explicit reliance on a background set of precedent decision, seems to allow a better explanation than an account based on a core of settled meaning for the linkage, or coordination, between judgments concerning application of open-textured predicates to different items that were originally in the penumbra. Imagine, for example, the state of affairs as it existed before applicability of the predicate "vessel" had been investigated for either of the two marine platforms under consideration, the Betty F and the Super Scoop—imagine, once again, that the background set of decisions on the issue was simply $\Gamma_4 = \varnothing$. At that point, it is natural to suppose that either decision concerning applicability of the open-textured predicate to each of these items would have been permissible, or in Hart's terminology, that both would have fallen within the predicate's penumbra. Once it was decided in *Di Giovanni* that the Betty F should not be classified as a vessel, however—that is, once the background case base had shifted from Γ_4 to $\Gamma_5 = \{c_5\}$—the later *Stewart* court was required to reach the same decision concerning the Super Scoop, since the *Di Giovanni* rule applied to the Super Scoop as well, and the Super Scoop displayed no features on the basis of which it could be distinguished.

What can explain the Super Scoop's change of status—from an item lying within the penumbra of the open-textured predicate "vessel," for which either decision concerning applicability would have been permitted, to an item whose exclusion from the category of vessels is now required? The current account offers an explanation, since the required classifications depend on the background set of precedent cases, and this set has changed, from Γ_4 to Γ_5—it now contains *Di Giovanni*, which, in accord with the reason model, requires the judgment that the Super Scoop is not a vessel. It is more difficult to find an explanation for this change of classification on any view according to which the classification of an item—as a vessel, not a vessel, or lying in the penumbra—is supposed to depend on a separate core of settled meaning for the open-textured predicate.

One way to understand the difficulty is to ask: if there is a separate core of settled meaning for the predicate "vessel," did this core of settled meaning change with the *Di Giovanni* decision? And here we face a dilemma. If the core of settled meaning did not change, and the core of settled meaning is what determines the classification of an item, then, since the Super Scoop lay within the penumbra prior to the *Di Giovanni* decision, it should remain in the penumbra afterward. On the other hand, if the core of settled meaning for the predicate "vessel" did change with the *Di Giovanni* decision, then that could explain the change of classification, of course. But in that case, if the core of settled meaning of an open-textured predicate can vary with the set of precedent decisions concerning applicability of that predicate, and variation in this set of precedent decisions can account for changes of classification all on its own, as in the reason model, then it is reasonable to wonder what additional work the separate core of settled meaning is supposed to be doing.

5. Discussion

The goal of this paper has been to suggest that the reason model of precedential constraint can be generalized to provide a semantic account of open-textured predicates, primarily in a legal setting, but applicable to other uses of open-textured predicates as well. This suggestion could be developed in a number of ways. As a first example, our treatment of open texture could be adapted to provide an account of the closely related phenomenon of vagueness. Here, the idea would be that vague predicates form a special class of open-textured predicates whose applicability is determined by factors keyed to values along dimensions with a particular, often numerical structure—for the vague predicate "tall," say, the relevant dimension would be that of height, and the set of relevant factors might include being at least 6′2″ in height, for instance, or no more than 5′11″ in height.[23]

As a second example, the current treatment of open texture relies on a set of factors whose own applicability, or not, is assumed to be clear.

---

[23] See Horty (2019) for an investigation of the reason model of constraint based on dimensional factors of this kind, and then Cumming (2023) for a treatment of vagueness based on these dimensional factors.

And often, this assumption is appropriate—it is at least relatively clear, for instance, whether a particular marine platform has a captain, or ballast tanks. In other cases, however, the factors in terms of which open-textured predicates are analyzed may themselves be open-textured. The question whether a marine platform should be classified as a vessel also depends, for instance, on whether it is largely stationary, or whether it has navigation as its primary purpose. But "largely stationary" and "has as its primary purpose" are straightforward examples of monadic and dyadic open-textured predicates. In order to apply to examples like this—with open-textured predicates analyzed in terms of other open-textured predicates—the current account would have to be extended to apply, not simply to a single open-textured predicate analyzed in terms of a set of concrete underlying factors, but to hierarchies of interlocking open-textured predicates.[24]

Rather than exploring directions for further technical development, however, I want to close by addressing two more philosophical concerns.

First, I claim to have provided a semantic account of open-textured predicates—but can the account provided here really be characterized as semantic? The dominant approach to semantics in contemporary philosophy is truth-conditional, with the goal of specifying, in a systematic way, the conditions under which sentences are true—so, for example, the conditions under which a sentence like "The Super Scoop is a vessel" is true. The goal of the present account, by contrast, is not to specify the conditions under which sentences are true, but instead, the conditions under which the court is required or permitted to affirm certain statements, as well as the reasons on the basis of which it is permitted to justify its decisions—it tells us whether, for example, against the background of a set of previous decision, the court is required to affirm that the Super Scoop is a vessel, required to affirm that it is not a vessel, or both permitted to affirm that it is a vessel and also permitted to affirm that it is not a vessel. The present account is thus developed at an entirely different level from the standard truth-conditional approach to semantics—it is normative, working at the level of requirements and permissions, rather than factual.

---

[24] See Canavotto and Horty (2023) for a proposal.

My response to this first concern is that, while truth-conditional semantics may be the dominant semantic approach, there are any number of other approaches—such as proof-theoretic, or verificationist, semantics, conceptual-role semantics, dynamic semantics, or inquisitive semantics, just to mention a few. Stepping back from this tangle of terminology, and the associated tangle of competing semantic theories, I adopt here a perspective most closely associated with the work of Michael Dummett, according to which a theory of meaning is, at bottom, a theory of understanding—the function of a semantic theory is to provide an account of what it is that a speaker knows by virtue of under-standing a language.[25] From this perspective, the current account can be seen as offering the—arguably reasonable—suggestion that what a speaker knows who understands the meaning of an open-textured predicate is not some set of necessary and sufficient conditions under which that predicate is applicable, but instead: taking into account the existing authoritative uses of that predicate, what reasons are permitted to justify further applications of the predicate or its contrary, and when the application of that predicate or its contrary is itself either permitted or required.

The second concern involves the generality of the proposed account. The example of the Super Scoop illustrates how, in the legal setting, constraints derived from previous decisions force coordination in the application of open-textured predicates. But I have also suggested that applications of open-textured predicates in natural language are con-strained in a similar way: Over the course of a conversation, which can last for seconds or for centuries, a stock of prior applications of an open-textured predicates is established. Individuals who wish to participate in this conversation, rather than starting a new one, are then required to use these predicates in a way that respects the constraints established in their previous applications.

Can the account of open texture presented here really be generalized in this way, from legal predicates to open-textured predicates more generally? I think this is a hypothesis worth considering, but of course,

---

[25] This perspective can be found throughout Dummett's work, receiving its earliest exten-sive discussion in Dummett (1975).

even as a hypothesis, it would have to be explored in much more detail—there are many ways in which the use of open-textured predicates in natural language differs from their use in the law. In the legal setting, for example, the set of precedent cases bearing on the further application of an open-textured predicate is carefully documented and curated; if questions arise, there are recognized methods of argument for determining whether or not some previous decision functions as an authoritative precedent in a new situation. In the more fluid setting of a natural language, by contrast, we could expect the set of precedent cases constraining the use of open-textured predicates to be indefinite, local, and changing; speakers might well exercise creativity by flouting norms, ignoring previous cases that should count as precedents, or granting authority to previous cases that should not. Another difference between open-textured predicates in legal language compared to natural language more generally is that, while the authority of past decisions over present cases in the law is carefully documented, the nature of the authority on the basis of which previous uses of open-textured predicates might constrain current uses in natural language more generally is much less clear. My suspicion is that these constraints result from an unnoticed, or at least underexplored, principle of conversational coordination in natural languages, which leads to coordination in the use of open-textured predicates.[26] If this suspicion, or something like it, is correct, then the legal doctrine of precedent, like so much else in the law, can be seen as a more stylized, self-conscious, and rigorous development of a mechanism that is already at work in our everyday interactions.[27]

---

[26] For a central account of meaning coordination in natural language, see, of course, Lewis (1969), who himself appeals to precedent but only as a mechanism for aligning mutual expectations. Empirical research along these lines can be found in Clark and Marshall (1981) and Clark and Wilkes-Gibbs (1986), and then in Garrod and Anderson (1987), who introduce the term "entrainment" for the kind of meaning coordination under consideration; this term was later adopted in Clark (1991) and Ludlow (2014). The current suggestion is that a precedent is more than just a kind of signpost for use by speakers to coordinate expectations, but that, instead, precedential constraint has a normative force, explicated here by the reason model, in bringing about what Garrod, Anderson, Clark, and Ludlow refer to as meaning entrainment.

[27] I am very grateful for help from Ilaria Canavotto, Sam Cumming, and an anonymous reviewer for this volume.

References

Aleven, Vincent (1997). *Teaching Case-Based Argumentation through a Model and Examples*. PhD thesis, Intelligent Systems Program, University of Pittsburgh.

Aleven, Vincent and Ashley, Kevin (1997). "Evaluating a learning environment for case-based argumentation skills." In *Proceedings of the Sixth International Conference on Artificial Intelligence and Law* (ICAIL-97), pages 170–179. The Association for Computing Machinery Press.

Ashley, Kevin (1989). "Toward a computational theory of arguing with precedents: accommodating multiple interpretations of cases." In *Proceedings of the Second International Conference on Artificial Intelligence and Law* (ICAIL-89), pages 93–110. The Association for Computing Machinery Press.

Ashley, Kevin (1990). *Modeling Legal Argument: Reasoning with Cases and Hypotheticals*. MIT Press.

Baker, Gordon (1977). "Defeasibility and meaning." In Hacker, Peter and Raz, Joseph, editors, *Law, Morality, and Society: Essays in Honour of H. L. A Hart*, pages 26–57. Oxford University Press.

Bix, Brian (1991). "H. L. A Hart and the open texture of language." *Law and Philosophy*, 10:51–72.

Broughton, Gabriel (2019). "Vertical precedents in formal models of precedential constraint." *Artificial Intelligence and Law*, 27:253–307.

Canavotto, Ilaria and Horty, John (2023). "Reasoning with hierarchies of open-textured predicates." In *Proceedings of the Nineteenth International Conference on AI and Law* (ICAIL-23), pages 52–61. The Association for Computing Machinery Press.

Clark, Herbert (1991). "Words, the world, and their possibilities." In Pomerantz, James and Lockhead, Gregory, editors, *The Perception of Structure*, pages 263–277. American Psychological Association.

Clark, Herbert and Marshall, Catherine (1981). "Definite reference and mutual knowledge." In Joshi, Aravind, Sag, Ivan, and Webber, Bonnie, editors, *Elements of Discourse Understanding*. Cambridge University Press.

Clark, Herbert and Wilkes-Gibbs, Deanna (1986). "Referring as a collaborative process." *Cognition*, 22:1–39.

Cohen, Adam (2009). "The Lord Justice hath ruled: Pringles are potato chips." *New York Times*, May 31, 2009.

Cumming, Samuel (2023). "Semantic reasons." *Nous*, 57:641–666.

Dummett, Michael (1975). "What is a theory of meaning?" In Guttenplan, Samuel, editor, *Mind and Language: Wolfson College Lectures* 1974, pages 97–138. Oxford University Press.

Dworkin, Ronald (1967). "The model of rules." *University of Chicago Law Review*, 35:14–46. Reprinted in Dworkin (1977), pp. 14–45.

Dworkin, Ronald (1977). *Taking Rights Seriously*. Harvard University Press.

Elbourne, Paul (2011). *Meaning: A Slim Guide to Semantics*. Oxford University Press.

Endicott, Timothy (2000). *Vagueness in Law*. Oxford University Press.

Endicott, Timothy (2022). "Law and language." In Zalta, Edward, editor, *The Stanford Encyclopedia of Philosophy* (Spring 2022 Edition). Stanford University. Available at http://plato.stanford.edu/archives/spr2022/entries/law-language/.

Fodor, Jerry, Garrett, Merrill, Walker, Edward, and Parkes, Cornelia (1980). "Against definitions." *Cognition*, 8:263–367.

Garrod, Simon and Anderson, Anthony (1987). "Saying what you mean in dialogue: a study in conceptual and semantic co-ordination." *Cognition*, 27:181–218.

Hart, H. L. A. (1958). "Positivism and the separation of law and morals." *Harvard Law Review*, 71:593–629.

Hart, H. L. A. (1961). *The Concept of Law*. Oxford University Press. Second edition published in 1994; pagination refers to the second edition.

Horty, John (2011). "Rules and reasons in the theory of precedent." *Legal Theory*, 17:1–33.

Horty, John (2012). *Reasons as Defaults*. Oxford University Press.

Horty, John (2015). "Constraint and freedom in the common law." *Philosophers' Imprint*, 15(25):1–27.

Horty, John (2019). "Reasoning with dimensions and magnitudes." *Artificial Intelligence and Law*, 27:307–345.

Horty, John (2024). *The Logic of Precedent: Constraint, Freedom, and Common Law Reasoning*. Forthcoming with Cambridge University Press.

Horty, John and Bench-Capon, Trevor (2012). "A factor-based definition of precedential constraint." *Artificial Intelligence and Law*, 20:181–214.

Keil, Geert and Poscher, Ralf (2016). *Vagueness and Law: Philosophical and Legal Perspectives*. Oxford University Press.

Lamond, Grant (2005). "Do precedents create rules?" *Legal Theory*, 11:1–26.

Lewis, David (1969). *Convention: A Philosophical Study*. Harvard University Press.

Ludlow, Peter (2014). *Living Words: Meaning Underdetermination and the Dynamic Lexicon*. Oxford University Press.

Lyons, David (1999). "Open texture and the possibility of legal interpretation." *Law and Philosophy*, 18:297–309.

MacCormick, Neil (1991). "On open texture in law." In Amslek, Paul and MacCormick, Neil, editors, *Controversies about Law's Ontology*, pages 72–83. Edinburgh University Press.

Mullins, Robert (2020). "Protected reasons and precedential constraint." *Legal Theory*, 26:40–61.

Prakken, Henry (2021). "A formal analysis of some factor- and precedent-based accounts of precedential constraint." *Artificial Intelligence and Law*, 29:559–581.

Raz, Joseph (1972). "Legal principles and the limits of law." *Yale Law Journal*, 81:823–854.

Rigoni, Adam (2014). "Common-law judicial reasoning and analogy." *Legal Theory*, 20:133–156.

Rissland, Edwina (1990). "Artificial intelligence and law: stepping stones to a model of legal reasoning." *Yale Law Journal*, 99:1957–1981.

Rissland, Edwina and Ashley, Kevin (1987). "A case-based system for trade secrets law." In *Proceedings of the First International Conference on Artificial Intelligence and Law* (ICAIL-87), pages 60–66. The Association for Computing Machinery Press.

Rissland, Edwina and Ashley, Kevin (2002). "A note on dimensions and factors." *Artificial Intelligence and Law*, 10:65–77.

Schauer, Frederick (2008). "A critical guide to vehicles in the park." *New York University Law Review*, 83:1109–1134.

Schauer, Frederick (2013). "On the open texture of law." *Grazer Philosophische Studien*, 87:197–215.

Schiappa, Edward (2003). *Defining Reality: Definitions and the Politics of Meaning.* Southern Illinois University Press.

Tur, Richard (2001). "Defeasibilism." *Oxford Journal of Legal Studies*, 21:355–368.

Waismann, Frederich (1945). "Verifiability." In *Proceedings of the Aristotelian Society, Supplementary Volume 19*, pages 119–150. Harrison and Son. Reprinted in Anthony Flew, editor, *Logic and Language*, pages 117–144, Blackwell Publishing Company, 1951; pagination refers to this version.

John Horty, *Precedent and Open Texture* In: *Oxford Studies in Philosophy of Law, Volume 5*. Edited by: Leslie Green and Brian Leiter, Oxford University Press. © John Horty 2024. DOI: 10.1093/9780198919650.003.0002

Officials, Subjects, and the Recognition Challenge for (International) Legality

Nicole Roughan

> A legal system...is a social order characterized by a significant division of labor in sustaining the practice of holding accountable that constitutes a given society's law. Put another way, what makes law (that is, what accounts for its existence) in a society that possesses a legal system is the practice of secondary rules of change, adjudication, and enforcement by one set of actors (officials) who rule over another set of actors (subjects).
>
> David Lefkowitz[1]

Introduction

It has become seriously unfashionable to ask, let alone to worry, whether international law's lack of a rule-based systemic structure upsets its status as law, or undermines its claim to legality.[2] Not only do theorists of international law mount plausible defences of its systematicity,[3] but

---

[1] David Lefkowitz, 'What Makes a Social Order Primitive? In Defense of Hart's Take on International Law" (2017), 23 *Legal Theory* 258, 273. See also Lefkowitz, *Philosophy and International Law: A Critical Introduction* (Cambridge University Press 2020), 36.

[2] Leaving open, for now, whether the concept of law and the ideal of legality are understood to be integrated or separate. My longer work on officials argues that some distinction and relation between law's agents and subjects is central to both an austere concept of law and a robust condition of legality. Space precludes defending that full account here. The present terminology refers to legality to capture both the status of law and the ideal of law, but will specify when it makes a difference, for the present argument, to talk about satisfying only the more austere concept.

[3] These include efforts to find foundational or unifying rules, including a rule of recognition. See e.g. Mehrdad Payandeh, 'The Concept of International Law in the Jurisprudence of H. L. A. Hart' (2010), 21 *European Journal of International Law* 967, 989–93; and Jean

for philosophers of law the question itself seems a bit pointless given the availability of sophisticated accounts of legal ordering that do not explain law in rule-based systemic terms.[4] If jurists can make do with variants of legal ordering that do not turn on rule-based systematicity, and philosophers of law can ground legal (as well as systematic) credentials in places other than rules of recognition and the union of primary and secondary rules, what would be the point of returning to Hartian theory to worry about international law's status as law?

This chapter argues that international law faces a recognition challenge more serious than many contemporary philosophers of international law acknowledge in their responses to Hart. While Hart thought international law lacked a foundational *rule* of recognition,[5] more basic challenges surround collective recognition of the role of the legal official or 'official of law',[6] its distinction from the role of law's subject, and recognition within the official-subject relation. These issues affect not only law's systematicity, but also law's claim to authority and its differentiation from mere force. The 'blurring' of official and subject roles does not simply support a conclusion that international law is an "anomalous system[7]", or is 'not a system, but an order',[8] but upsets an official-subject distinction and relation that is central to legality itself.

This challenge is not specific to international law, but the international legal context highlights how disruptions to the recognition of official-subject relations pose a challenge for legality. Just as the lack of centralized coercive mechanisms makes international law a prime candidate to

---

D'Aspremont, *Formalism and the Sources of international Law: A Theory of the Ascertainment of Legal Rules* (Oxford University Press 2011); other accounts find systematicity in principles (e.g. Campbell McLachlan, 'The Principle of Systemic Integration and Article 31(3)(c) of the Vienna Convention' (2005), 54 *The International and Comparative Law Quarterly* 279) or in practices of interpretive communities creating relations between norms (e.g. Mario Prost, *Concept of Unity in Public International Law* (Hart Publishing 2012).

[4] On the distinction between legal system and legal order, see Keith Culver and Michael Giudice, *Legality's Borders: An Essay in General Jurisprudence* (Oxford University Press 2010).

[5] H. L. A. Hart, *The Concept of Law*, 2nd edn (Clarendon Press 1994), 236.

[6] This term is used, in preference to 'legal official', to avoid the account of an official as simply holding a legal office. See John Gardner, 'Twilight of Legality' (2018), 43 *Journal of Legal Philosophy* 1; and Nicole Roughan, 'Office-Holding to Officiality' (2020), 70 *University of Toronto Law Journal* 231.

[7] Gardner, 'Some Types of Law', in Douglas Edlin (ed.), *Common Law Theory* (Cambridge University Press 2007).

[8] Culver and Giudice (n. 4).

shed light on the role of coercion in a theory of law,[9] attention to what Richard Collins has termed the 'problematic'[10] or potentially 'redundant'[11] notion of the official in international law provokes general jurisprudential insights surrounding the role of the official and officials' relations to subjects.

The present work responds to two major trends in international legal theory that seek to work around (rather than with) ideas of the official. One trend explains and/or justifies diffuse publicness in international law; the other explains and/or justifies interactional and transactional international law. Against both approaches, the present work argues that both publicness and interactionism in international law will be upset by blurry recognition of the roles and relations of officials and subjects. It then situates a concern for officiality within foundational theories of international legality that insist upon the value of rule of law-type protections for individuals as 'ultimate' and/or direct subjects of international law.[12] International legality, I argue, depends upon the recognition of officiality.

Those claims are defended in three parts. Following this introduction, Part 1 looks beyond familiar concerns about who counts as an international legal official, to examine the blurring of both a role of official and official-subject relations. That argument requires attention to what it is to be an official, which is examined in Part 2's analysis of key general jurisprudential devices that centre upon the recognition of official/subject distinctions, roles, and relations.[13] Part 3 returns to the specific international context to examine possibilities for either rescuing or rejecting the requisite recognition of international

---

[9] Liam Murphy, 'The Normative Force of Law: Individuals and States' (2018), 3 *Oxford Studies in Philosophy of Law* 87. See also Murphy, 'Law beyond the State: Some Philosophical Questions' (2019), 28 *European Journal of International Law* 203. And see Murphy, 'The Normative Force of Law', in *What Makes Law: An Introduction to the Philosophy of Law* (Cambridge University Press 2014).

[10] Richard Collins, 'The problematic concept of the international legal official' (2016), 6 *Transnational Legal Theory* 608.

[11] Ibid. 611.

[12] Samantha Besson, 'The Authority of International Law—Lifting the State Veil' (2009), 31 *Sydney Law Review* 343; Jeremy Waldron, 'Are Sovereigns Entitled to the Benefit of the International Rule of Law?' (2011), 22 *European Journal of International Law* 315.

[13] This selection omits leading accounts in jurisprudence that do not turn on this distinction, including those of Dworkin and Kelsen. This selection is explained at n. 59.

officiality and subjection, and responds to scepticism about the importance of officiality.

A final preliminary point limits this chapter's ambition. Both the existence and normative significance of the *role* of the official depend not upon the mere establishment of institutional offices replete with formal competencies and functions, but upon normative social practices of recognition. Examining those practices would require extensive descriptive, interpretative, and evaluative analyses that may offer different and shifting answers within different international regimes.[14] Given its methods, the present work does not conclude upon the substantive issue of whether the blurring of international officiality and subjection is sufficient to undermine international legality. The chapter therefore does not claim that the recognition challenge facing international legality denies international law the status of law (and/or the attainment of an ideal of legality, if that is understood separately). It aims to show how and why it could do so.

1. 'Problematic' or 'Redundant' Officials of International Law

The clearly stratified structure of state legal systems entices much statist philosophy of law to skip quickly over a distinction and division between law's subjects and officials. That luxury cannot be afforded in international law, where recognitive practices surrounding officiality and subjection are muddied by the formally flattened and fragmented structure of the international legal order. International law's decentralized character, and the structure in which states both participate in law-making and are simultaneously the primary subjects of international legal ordering, have led some theorists of international law to confront the idea of the official with more urgency than statist jurisprudence typically displays.

Earlier interventions include the influential work of Keith Culver and Michael Giudice, who argue that the idea of the international legal official is beset by problems of circularity and indeterminacy that are more

---

[14] Such fragmentation has implications for officiality, discussed in part three.

acute for international than for state legal orders.[15] Collins has argued that the very idea of the official (which he characterizes as a bootstrapping device used by analytical jursiprudes to avoid justifying the hierarchies inherent in state legal ordering) is inapt for the more heterarchical and transactional international legal order.[16] In contrast, sophisticated accounts of publicness in international law,[17] or analyses of public administration and public authority,[18] seem to rest on implicit but often loose notions of the official agent. Put together, these approaches suggest both indeterminacy in 'who counts as' an official of international law, and indeterminacy over the existence and normative significance of such a role.

a. Indeterminacy in 'who counts as' an international official

Culver and Giudice explain that to be an official is to 'occupy a special position within the legal system by virtue of the rules of office'.[19] Lefkowitz is more specific, describing officials as 'actors occupying offices constituted by rules that empower them to make, apply, and enforce the law'.[20] If 'legal officials' are understood as those who occupy formally institutionalized offices that confer normative power to make, apply, and/or enforce legal rules, then various international legal regimes are replete with such agents. The proliferation of international courts, tribunals, and administrative bodies has expanded what was once a fairly small number of such 'office-holders' into a much larger, albeit 'fragmented' set.[21]

---

[15] Culver and Giudice (n. 4).   [16] Collins (n. 10) 611.

[17] Benedict Kingsbury, 'International Law as Inter-Public Law' (2009), 49 *Nomos* 167; Armin Von Bogdandy, Philipp Dann, and Matthias Goldmann, 'Developing the Publicness of Public International Law: Towards a Legal Framework for Global Governance Activities' (2008), 9 *German Law Journal* 1375.

[18] Armin von Bogdandy, Matthias Goldmann, and Ingo Venzke, 'From Public International to International Public Law: Translating World Public Opinion into International Public Authority' (2017), 28 *European Journal of International Law* 115.

[19] Culver and Giudice (n. 4) 10.

[20] Lefkowitz, 'What Makes a Social Order Primitive?' (n. 2) 274. See also Lefkowitz, *Philosophy and International Law* (n. 2) 37.

[21] Martti Koskenniemi, *Fragmentation of International Law: Difficulties Arising from the Diversification and Expansion of International Law* (International Law Commission 2006).

Even a bare view of the official as an office-holder, however, is not as clear-cut as it sounds. As Culver and Giudice argue, this view harbours considerable indeterminacy about who counts as an international official. How high-ranking must an office-holder be before they are an official and not a mere bureaucrat, if there is such a distinction?[22] If the category includes not only office-holders in international regimes, but also judges of international courts and tribunals, as well as state agents or even states themselves, the category loses purchase and has porous boundaries. Building on those concerns, Collins suggests that, while municipal legal orders can resolve doubts about who counts as an official through recourse to clear-cut officials further up a systemic institutional hierarchy, indeterminacy surrounding international officials cannot be resolved by going one step higher up a chain.[23]

Scholarship invoking the international official often fleshes out its content by relying on ellipses that assume the audience knows who the officials are.[24] Some scholars expressly defend a labelling or 'folk' explanation, in which legal officials are simply those who are identified as such by the relevant community of actors (including other 'officials'),[25] Others favour a pragmatic understanding of the international official, reversing the flow of the standard Hartian circularity (in which the practices of a more or less stable category of 'officials' generates a rule of recognition) so that all those whose practices contribute

---

[22] On bureaucratic logics of international officiality, see Alexander Somek, 'A Bureaucratic Turn?' (2011), 2 *European Journal of International Law* 345. Cf. Ingo Venzke, 'International Bureaucracies from a Political Science Perspective: Agency, Authority and International Institutional Law' (2008), 9 *German Law Journal* 1401.

[23] Collins (n. 10) 617–18; Culver and Giudice (n. 4) 16.

[24] Alex Green, in an astute paper, , refers to "state representatives, international courts and tribunals, and so on". See Alex Green, 'The Precarious Rationality of International Law: Critiquing the International Rule of Recognition' (2022), 22 *German Law Journal* 1613, at 1618. See also Murphy, 'Law beyond the State' (n. 9) 210: 'what matters for customary international law is the practice and opinions of state officials, not the beliefs and attitudes of international legal officials generally, including, for example, international judges and officials of international legal organizations'. These works are referenced not to criticise the authors' arguments, rather as instances of a widespread scholarly reliance on an assumed category of officiality.

[25] See e.g. Brian Tamanaha, *A General Jurisprudence of Law and Society* (Oxford University Press 2001), 142: 'A "legal" official is whomever, as a matter of social practice, members of the group (including legal officials themselves) identify as "legal" officials'. This position is relied upon in Green (n. 23).

to generating a relatively stable rule of recognition should (therefore) be regarded as officials.[26]

Such expansiveness introduces additional candidates who might 'count as' officials, beyond formal international office-holders. Some are individuals, such as those 'most highly-qualified publicists' whose teachings the ICJ Statute empowers its judges to rely upon as sources of law.[27] Others include non-state actors as observers or delegates to deliberative, negotiating, or law-making conferences;[28] a cadre of international arbitrators whose practices contribute towards 'judicialization' of that field; and foreign office lawyers.[29] Are these all officials of international law? Are judges of national courts, when they apply international law through monistic or dualistic structures?

Indeterminacy over who counts as an official does not preclude making distinctions. As Liam Murphy points out, international lawyers and theorists analysing customary international law readily differentiate between state officials and international legal officials.[30] International legal doctrines also offer classifications and determinations of 'official' statuses for particular agents of both states and international organizations, entitling them to various immunities, due process protections, or imposing obligations. The impact of indeterminacy may not upset the mere identification of officials. However, a more troubling indeterminacy has more far-reaching implications. This involves doubts not over

---

[26] E.g. Jean D'Aspremont, 'Herbert Hart in Today's International Legal Scholarship', in Jean D'Aspremont and Jörg Kammerhofer (eds), *International Legal Positivism in a Post-Modern World* (Cambridge University Press 2014).

[27] Statute of the International Court of Justice, art 38(1)(d). Sondre Torp Helmersen argues that in practice, the court often invokes the 'official' positions held by leading publicists who are themselves former judges or state officials. Helmersen, 'Finding "the Most Highly Qualified Publicists": Lessons from the International Court of Justice' (2019), 30 *European Journal of International Law* 509. See also Oscar Schachter, 'The Invisible College of International Lawyers' (1977), 72 *Northwestern University Law Review* 217.

[28] Among others, the role of representatives of Indigenous nations in the negotiations leading to the Declaration on the Rights of Indigenous Peoples. See e.g. Claire Charters, 'The Sweet Spot between Formalism and Fairness: Indigenous People's Contribution to International Law' (2021), 115 *American Journal of International Law* 123.

[29] On judicialization of arbitration see Alec Stone Sweet and Florian Grisel. A discussion of the roles of foreign office lawyer appears in see Matthew Windsor, 'Consigliere or Conscience? The Role of the Government Legal Adviser', in Jean D'Aspremont et al., *International Law as a Profession* (Cambridge University Press 2017).

[30] Murphy, 'Law beyond the State' (n. 9) 210.

'who counts as' an official, but whether international law harbours a role of official of law at all.

b. A special role of 'official' of international law?

The challenge facing international officiality is not that there are no agents who are identified as core or peripheral international legal office-holders—clearly there are. The more foundational indeterminacy surrounds recognition of officiality as a special role within a legal system. On this view, the key feature of the idea of the official is not the 'rules of office' by virtue of which the official occupies her position, but the official's 'special position within the system'.[31]

The first concern about international law, therefore, is whether there is a system harbouring a special role of official. While Hart's use of the terminology of 'primitive law' to capture non-systemic law is often avoided or qualified in today's parlance,[32] and while there are many candidates to fill the set of secondary rules or even rules of recognition that Hart thought international law was lacking;[33] there is still some support for Hart's view that international law is law, but not a *legal system*. Theorists holding that view treat international law as a set (or sets) of rules, a non-systemic (or pre-systemic) 'legal order';[34] drawing a contrast (even if only one of degree), between a municipal 'structured' and an international 'unstructured' system of law.[35]

---

[31] Cf. Culver and Giudice (n. 4).

[32] Les Green, 'Introduction', in H. L. A. Hart, *The Concept of Law*, 3rd edn (Oxford University Press 2012), xvi. Hart himself did not appear inclined revisit the terminology or the argument. No changes were made to Chapter X between the publication of the first and second editions of *The Concept of Law*. The New College archive retains Hart's copy of his first edition, which is densely annotated throughout Chapters I–IX, while Chapter X on international law is almost entirely untouched. I do not wish to over-state the significance of that disparity, as there may be notes or annotations developed by Hart elsewhere.

[33] E.g. Payandeh (n. 3).

[34] Lefkowitz (n. 1) suggests that the absence of systematicity, at least in Hart's terms, is a 'claim that few of Hart's critics will deny'. Lefkowitz takes care to elaborate the ways in which a legal order may be a pre-*legal system*, but not pre-*legal*. See also Giudice, 'Hart and Kelsen on International Law', in Leslie Green and Brian Leiter (eds), *Oxford Studies in Philosophy of Law*, Volume 2 (Oxford University Press 2013).

[35] See e.g. Burazin on this distinction, in Luka Burazin, 'Legal Systems as Abstract Institutional Artifacts', in Luka Burazin, Kenneth Einar Himma, and Corrado Roversi (eds), *Law as an Artifact* (Oxford University Press 2018).

An important recent account from David Lefkowitz offers a fresh analysis of the importance of an official/subject distinction in the Hartian characterization of a legal system. Lefkowitz corrects common, excusable, but mistaken readings of Hart's scepticism about international law which, as Lefkowitz shows, doubted only that international law was a system, not that it was law. According to Lefkowitz:[36]

> Hart employs the contrast between a primitive and an advanced society to draw two distinctions: first, the absence or presence of a hierarchy of rules, and second, the absence or presence of a hierarchy of rulers, that is, of specialization in the performance of governance tasks.

Lefkowitz affirms that, for Hart, the distinction between systemic and non-systemic orders rests upon an official/subject distinction, and explains that this is no mere analytic categorization. The presence or absence of a differentiation 'between ruler and ruled' shapes different ways in which law contributes to social ordering: either through subjects governing themselves and each other directly, or through institutionalized roles of official generating rules to govern subjects (as well as themselves). A legal system, Lefkowitz explains, is "a social order characterized by a significant division of labor in sustaining the practice of holding accountable that constitutes a given society's law."[37] Where there is no such division of labour, participants must directly hold themselves and each other to account, operating law without a system. Lefkowitz effectively relocates the defect Hart diagnosed in international law's systematicity. The defect is not the absence of a rule or rules of recognition, nor even the mere absence/indeterminacy of officials, but the absence of a functional division of labour between officials and subjects.

A Hart-Lefkowitz account of undivided labour in international law can therefore be derived as an account of the absence of a social role of official of law, which undermines international law's systematicity.

---

[36] Lefkowitz, 'H. L. A. Hart: Social Rules, Officials, and International Law', in *Philosophy and International Law* (n. 1) 27.

[37] Lefkowitz, 'What Makes a Social Order Primitive?' (n. 1) 273. Cf. Leftkowitz, *Philosophy and International Law* (n. 1) 36.

Does that account accurately capture contemporary international law? It is hard to prove a negative. It is even harder to prove a point that, as a matter of method, requires deep sociological and interpretative engagement with the practices of such a diverse cast of actors and institutions. That is not the aim of the present work. Yet familiar concerns in international legal theory over (i) plurality and diversity of international offices; and (ii) plural and contested understandings of the role of states and state agents, suggest that any role of official of international law is murky, at best.

(i) Plural international offices fragmenting officiality

The proliferation and diversification of public international institutions and offices may dilute rather than serve recognition of a role of official, just as it may dilute rather than serve a notion of systematicity.[38] Within the broad scope of worries about international law's fragmentation lies a concern that office-holders in a heterarchical order are simply agents of their particular institutions. In the absence of general and comprehensive institutions with some offices empowered to structure the others, particular office-holders' competencies are in the mix with everyone else's. Particular office-holders carry out limited fragmented functions, rather than acting as occupants of a 'special role within the legal system'.

The issue is not simply the number of offices, but the ways in which their diversity, overlaps, and unstructured interactions suggests a diffusion of publicness. The influence of broader conceptions of the public realm (linked to governance rather than government, looser characterizations of law's authority understood to guide rather than bind, and the rise of emphases on transnational rather than international law), work against the recognition of official-subject distinctions. Even where scholars offer tighter accounts of publicness, legality, or constitutionalism in international law, work on the rules, principles, and practices through which institutions make and operate such public modes does

---

[38] As Murphy points out, the expansion of candidates for institutionalized public ordering may detract from the sense of a single systemic order. Murphy, 'Law beyond the State' (n. 2).

not treat these as instances of a more general recognition of officiality.[39] This is no criticism. The relative lack of direct conceptual work defending or simply explaining the role of the official may reflect practical scepticism about the recognition of such a role in international legal ordering.

(ii) Plural roles for states (and state agents)

An obvious rejoinder would argue that states operate as officials of international law. In the absence of centralized compulsory law-making, adjudicatory, or enforcement institutions, international legal orthodoxy treats states as both officials and subjects in international law.[40] That shorthand elides two different dualities: states as both officials and subjects of international law; and state officials as both officials of international law and state law, which further muddy rather than crystallize a role of official of international law.

The first duality—states as both officials and subjects of law—may seem unproblematic. After all, the subjection of states (or particular state organs) to laws that they make, apply, and enforce upon themselves is a structure familiar from domestic constitutional law. Domestically, operational problems arising from self-application are managed through separations and balances among the powers of state organs. In the case of international law, however, not only are such remedies for the defects of self-application more difficult to supervise and maintain, but international law's sovereign equality principle structures states to act as individual participants in law-generating practices (whether contractual, deliberative, customary or conventional), rather than as agents within an integrated official structure subjected to legal constraints, checks, and accountabilities.

---

[39] For example, Kingsbury's direct and detailed account of publicness in international law does not link publicity to an institutionalized hierarchy between officials and subjects, even though many of his notions (including principles of legality) might be thought to depend upon such a distinction. See Benedict Kingsbury, 'On the Concept of "Law" in Global Administrative Law' (2009), 20 *European Journal of International Law* 23; and Kingsbury, 'International Law as Inter-Public Law' (n. 14). An impressive recent collection elaborating key concepts for international law does not directly examine officiality, though there are practices of state agents and agents of international institutions littered through the book. Jean D'Aspremont and Sahib Singh, *Concepts for International Law: Contributions to Disciplinary Thought* (Edward Elgar Publishing 2019).

[40] See e.g. Besson (n. 12); d'Aspremont, *Formalism and the Sources of International Law* (n. 3).

The second duality—of state agents as officials of both state and international law—leaves open whether there is one integrated role of official of two separate legal orders, one integrated or unified order (in which the official role itself may be an integrating device),[41] two duplicate roles of officials of state and international order, or two alternate roles of official of state or international law.

The structure of plural roles for state agents presents perhaps the most important antidote to the Hartian view of an absence of an official/subject distinction, but it does so in a way that not only blurs, but arguably collapses, the role of the international official itself. In addition to Kelsen's monist treatment of states as 'organs' of international law, in which state institutions do much of the work of applying international law,[42] international legal theorists often invoke Scelle's classic formulation of 'role-splitting' (*dédoublement fonctionnel*).[43] Where Kelsen's monism turned on both the logic and the cognition of law's normativity, rejecting rather than relying upon a sharp official/subject distinction, Scelle seems to assume such a distinction in offering a broadly sociological and institutionalist explanation in which state officials, as individuals, perform dual functions as both state and international agents. As Cassese explains Scelle's formulation:

> For Scelle, national officials do not have double roles which are fulfilled simultaneously, but a dual role in the sense that they operate in a Dr. Jekyll and Mr. Hyde manner, exhibiting a split personality. In other words, although from the point of view of their legal status they are and remain national organs, they can function either as national or as international agents.[44]

---

[41] The most celebrated of the unified accounts is Kelsen's monism, but Kelsen's unity is an aspect of his account of norms and normativity, it does not turn upon an official/subject distinction. See n. 59.

[42] Hans Kelsen, *General Theory of Law and State* (Lawbook Exchange 1999), 351. See also Giudice, 'Hart and Kelsen on International Law' (n. 31).

[43] See George Scelle, 'Règles générales du droit de la paix' (1934), 46 *Collected Courses of the Hague Academy of International Law* 334.

[44] Antonio Cassese, 'Remarks on Scelle's Theory of "Role-Splitting" in International Law' (1990), 1 *European Journal of International Law* 210; and see Oliver Diggelmann, 'Georges Scelle', in Bardo Fassbender and Anne Peters (eds), *The Oxford Handbook of the History of International Law* (Oxford University Press 2012).

Leaving open whether this best captures Scelle's view,[45] it is important for the present purpose that, for Scelle, the dual roles of state officials exist in the absence of 'specifically international rulers and agents' (*gouvernants et agents specifiquement internationaux*).[46] State officials, when they act as agents of international law, are not duplicating functions attached to vacant international offices, they are performing a role that otherwise would not be performed. How then should we understand a state organ's role when there *are* such international institutions, replete with offices and office-holders, to perform those same functions?[47] What happens to supposedly dual functions when there are in fact many international institutional agents offering competing versions of those functions?[48] As scholarship post-*Kadi* has argued, a different account is needed to explain and indeed justify the roles of state and supra-state agents (such as judges) when these feature overlapping competencies and conflicting claims to supremacy.[49]

Different accounts on offer include treatments of both international and state office-holding agents (as well as states and international institutions) as trustees,[50] or more generically as fiduciaries,[51] drawing

[45] Scelle's apparent monism and commitment to the supremacy of international law casts doubt on the final sentence of Cassese's comment. It is also important that for Scelle, the state is a fiction, both the subject and the agent of law is the individual. For analysis see Martti Koskenniemi, *Gentle Civilizer of Nations* (Cambridge University Press 2001), 327–38.

[46] Scelle (n. 40) 358.

[47] See e.g. Yuval Shany, 'No Longer a Weak Department of Power? Reflections on the Emergence of a New International Judiciary' (2009), 20 *European Journal of International Law* 73.

[48] As Andre Nollkaemper puts it, "the fragmented nature of the international legal system also means that there is no longer (if there ever was) a singular meaning of *dedoublement fonctionnel*, but that different, and perhaps conflicting, approaches by domestic courts can be interpreted as good faith attempts to give effect to particular rules of the international legal order". Nollkaemper, 'The European Courts and the Security Council: Between Dédoublement Fonctionnel and Balancing of Values: Three Replies to Pasquale De Sena and Maria Chiara Vitucci' (2009), 20 *European Journal of International Law* 862, 869.

[49] See Iris Canor, 'The European Courts and the Security Council: Between Dédoublement Fonctionnel and Balancing of Values: Three Replies to Pasquale De Sena and Maria Chiara Vitucci' (2009), 20 *European Journal of International Law* 870. Post-*Kadi* literature responds to *Kadi and Al Barakaat International Foundation v Council of the European Union and Commission of the European Communities* [2008] ECR I-6411.

[50] Karen Alter, 'Agents or Trustees? International Courts in Their Political Context', *European Journal of International Relations* 14.1 (2008): 33–63; Eyal Benvenisti, 'Sovereigns as Trustees of Humanity: On the Accountability of States to Foreign Stakeholders' (2013), 107 *American Journal of International Law* 295; cf. Alec Stone Sweet and Thomas L. Brunell, 'Trustee Courts and the Judicialization of International Regimes' (2013), 1 *Journal of Law and Courts* 61.

[51] Evan J. Criddle and Evan Fox-Decent, *Fiduciaries of Humanity: How International Law Constitutes Authority* (Oxford University Press 2016).

upon principal-agent theories as well as broader work on public fiduciary theory. Fiduciary explanations might suffice for official agents of single orders, but are put to the test when the first and second dualities are placed back together. Could agents of both state law and international law, who are also (simultaneously) subjects of both state and domestic law, hold fiduciary roles or act as trustees within both systems, given their potential for practical conflicts? Even if conflicts are resolvable in theory or in practice, they may muddy a role of official of international law (and perhaps a role of official of law at all).

A different model of integration is generated by 'looking through' the state, retaining structural hierarchies between officials and subjects in ways that may support a version of officiality with at least a partial division of labour between social roles.[52] On this view, states sit in the middle of an integrated yet hierarchical structure of authority and/or legality. At the bottom of the structure, in the role of the subject, are not states themselves, but individuals. In Samantha Besson's view, individuals can be direct subjects of international law, but are also international law's 'ultimate subjects';[53] while for Jeremy Waldron, states act as administering agencies of the rule of law, for the benefit of such individuals.[54] Both accounts, though tendered around (respectively) theories of international law's authority and the international rule of law, operate with some concept of the official, locating state and international officials at different levels of an integrated yet hierarchical systemic structure. To some extent, this avoids the complications arising from the diversity of subjects in international law, understood to include individuals as well as states and international organizations.[55]

To operate and defend those accounts, however, as well as to either challenge or support views in which states occupy a role of official

---

[52] Besson (n. 37).   [53] Besson (n. 37) 377.   [54] Waldron (n. 12).
[55] The International Court of Justice in *Reparation for Injuries Suffered in the Service of the United Nations, Advisory Opinion: ICJ Reports 1949*, p. 121: "The subjects of law in any legal system are not necessarily identical in their nature or in the extent of their rights, and their nature depends upon the needs of the community". Anne Peters describes a 'paradigm shift' from treating individuals from objects to subjects of international, then as full agents (not mere protected rights-holders) bearing obligations, and having personality including standing to claim. Anne Peters, *Beyond Human Rights: The Legal Status of the Individual in International Law* (Cambridge University Press 2016).

through either integrated or bifurcated structures, requires a fuller account of what it is to be an official of law.

2. Officiality and Subjection

Accounts of the official of law and the official's relation to law's subjects are central to general jurisprudential debates over law's normativity, authority, and justification. Among key accounts, the most important to the present project are (a) Hartian accounts of officials holding internal points of view and generating rules of recognition at the foundation of a legal system, (b) Fullerian accounts of officials' responsibilities for upholding the rule of law and its protection for subjects; and (c) Razian accounts of officials making law's claim to legitimate authority.[56]

a. Officials and the customary rule of recognition

Hart's position (as nuanced and/or elaborated by subsequent theorists) argued that, for a legal system to exist, officials must have the internal point of view towards the rules of that legal system, seeing themselves and others as bound by both primary and secondary rules.[57] Subjects, meanwhile, must generally go along with the rules that are validated by that system's rule of recognition, which emerges from official practices

---

[56] Obvious omissions here include Dworkin and Kelsen, whose theories downplay or resist a distinction between law's (though not political) officials and subjects. The legal cognition that Kelsen sought to explain is that of lawyers generally, of law, and his key distinction between subjective and objective legal meaning of actions does not map on to an official/subject distinction (e.g. a contracting agent may be authorized, through the norms of private law, to bring about objective legal meaning and requirements upon another party). Dworkin, in contrast, emphasized the importance of official institutional acts, and the need to justify their use of coercion, but burdened all members of communities of principle (not just officials) with interpretive responsibilities. Dworkin is omitted here because international law is far from such a community of principle. Kelsen is omitted because of the distance his account sets up between cognition of law and social practices of recognition. Both are examined in the larger work.

[57] Hart's own expressions shift between ontological and epistemological versions of a rule of recognition. In the latter but not the former, the rule may entail broader practices of private persons identifying the law. See e.g. Hart (n. 5) 1: the rule of recognition exists as a "complex, but normally concordant, practice of the courts, officials, and private persons in identifying the law by reference to certain criteria".

of treating certain norms as valid norms of their legal system.[58] This rule
of recognition, though changing over time, constrains officials' recognition of sources of law, rule-hierarchies, and other secondary rules.

Although an official/subject distinction is at the heart of these conditions necessary for the existence of a legal system, and central to Hart's
effort to draw law's normativity out of social normativity, Hart moved
quickly past the question of what it is to be an official. Much jurisprudential elaboration and critique of Hart is also weighted towards the
more obviously philosophical insights around the normative character
of the rule of recognition, and the scope or content of the internal point
of view; rather than attention to what Perry describes as "those persons
in a society whom we would intuitively recognize as its officials."[59]

Among many key worries, interlocutors and Hartian defenders have
grappled with several versions of an apparent 'chicken and egg problem'
within Hart's position.[60] One surrounds the rule of recognition (how could
officials be bound by a rule that exists only as they attempt to follow it?).
A more basic chicken and egg problem surrounds officiality. If officials
are constituted by legal rules validated by a rule of recognition that
arises only from the practice of officials, then how can there be officials
at all? Gardner's explanation of the Hartian account resorts to custom to
resolve both problems together, arguing that:

[58] Hart (n. 5) 114–17.

[59] Perry, 'Hart on Social Rules and the Foundations of Law: Liberating the Internal Point of
View' (2006), 75 Fordham L Rev 1171. The voluminous work analysing and refining the rule of
recognition is rich in insights and contentions around officiality. To select just two examples,
see Grant Lamond, 'Legal Sources, the Rule of Recognition, and Customary Law' (2014) 59
Am J Juris; J. Dickson, 'Is the Rule of Recognition Really a Conventional Rule?' (2007), 27
OJLS 373. Among accounts examining officials more directly, see Stefan Sciaraffa, 'Two
Perspectives on the Requirements of a Practice', in Maksymilian Del Mar (ed.), New Waves in
Philosophy of Law (Palgrave Macmillan 2011); Matthew Noah Smith, 'The Law as a Social
Practice: Are Shared Activities at the Foundations of Law?' (2006), 12 Legal Theory 265;
Dimitrios Kyritsis, 'The Normativity of the Practice of Officials: A Philosophical Programme',
in Stefano Bertea and George Pavlakos (eds), New Essays on the Normativity of Law (Hart
Publishing 2011), 177l; Kenneth M. Ehrenberg, 'The Anarchist Official: A Problem for Legal
Positivism' (2011), 36 Australasian Journal of Legal Philosophy 89. Mikolaj Barczentewicz,
'The Illuminati Problem and Rules of Recognition' (2018), 38 Oxford Journal of Legal Studies
500. I discuss much of this literature in Nicole Roughan, 'The Official Point of View and the
Official Claim to Authority' (2018), 38 Oxford Journal of Legal Studies 191.

[60] Jules Coleman, The Practice of Principle: In Defence of a Pragmatist Approach to Legal
Theory (Oxford University Press 2001), 100–1; Neil MacCormick, H. L. A. Hart, 2nd edn
(Stanford University Press 2008), 136–40; Scott Shapiro, Legality (Harvard University Press
2011), 36–40; Culver and Giudice (n. 4) ch. 1; Collins (n. 10).

would-be officials of the legal system take each other already to be officials under the rule, and by conforming their conduct to the rule as they thus take it to be, they make that the rule, and anoint each other as officials of the legal system. That is why the ultimate rule of recognition cannot be legislated, but can only be customary.[61]

On this view, the circularity of the rule of recognition is explained as 'a benign self-referentiality in the customary rule of recognition (as in all customary rules).'[62] However, such a rule will be disturbed or even precluded if there is uncertainty about whose practices are recognized as 'official'. Even if would-be officials merely 'wish to do as others do'[63] as they conform their conduct to a customary rule of recognition, they need to figure out not only what others are doing, but which others to mimic. The prospect of plurality of conflicting claims to official status, in contexts of fragmented, heterarchical, as well as overlapping legal orders, further upsets the ease of Gardner's Hartian formulation in which officials' practices 'anoint' each other as officials.[64] Persons seeking to go along with other 'officials' behaviour may face choices between competing sets of agents claiming official or quasi-official status.

This concern supports a more foundational claim that it is not only officials whose recognitive practices matter for generating a *role* of official, whose occupants in turn have a special status within the legal system such that their recognitive practices can generate a *rule* of recognition. Instead of smoothing over the chicken and egg problem of officiality by relying upon a customary rule among officials who recognize themselves and each other as such, that problem is avoided altogether if the role of official is understood to be generated through

---

[61] John Gardner, 'Law as a Leap of Faith as Others See It' (2014), 33 *Law & Philosophy* 813, 817.

[62] John Gardner and Timothy Macklem, 'Book Review of Legality by Scott Shapiro' (2011), *Notre Dame Philosophical Review* (online).

[63] Hart (n. 5) 203 argues that the IPV need not be adopted for moral reasons. I have argued elsewhere that officials, on both conceptual and normative grounds do not hold a generic internal point of view, instead adopt an official point of view from their morally burdened standpoint as officials.

[64] See Roughan, 'Escaping Precedent: Interlegality and Change in Rules of Recognition', in Timothy Endicott, Hafsteinn Dan Kristjansson, and Sebastian Lewis (eds), *Philosophical Foundations of Precedent* (Oxford University Press 2023).

broader normative social practices of recognition. These practices recognize not the particular candidates who count as legal officials, but a social role of 'official of law'. The recognition of officiality underlies a rule of recognition among officials.

b. Officials and the commitment to legality

Broadening the recognitive practices at the foundations of legal ordering not only avoids the circularity in Hartian accounts, but also corrects what many have criticized as Hart's overemphasis on the official side of the stories of a legal system's existence and law's normativity.[65] Grounding the role of official on a collective's broader recognitive practices suggests some kind of connection between the role of the official and the role of the subject.

Hart's distinction between what is required of officials and subjects can be criticized not only for failing to provide adequate protections for subjects, risking authoritarianism while simultaneously discounting subjects' agency,[66] but also for splitting up law's normativity so that officials recognize law's claim to authority, while subjects feel law's force. This criticism rejects an account of law's normativity founded upon a narrow group of agents who recognize themselves and each other as officials, then impose the norms they generate and the decisions they make upon others.[67] To avoid the pitfalls of such self-referential normativity requires a justification for a self-recognizing role entailing normative powers over others.

This criticism lies at the core of broadly Fullerian accounts of legality.[68] Where Hart used an official-subject distinction to restrict the recognitive

---

[65] E.g. Gerald J. Postema, *Law's Rule: The Nature, Value, and Viability of the Rule of Law* (Oxford University Press 2022); Smith (n. 62); David Dyzenhaus, *Long Arc of Legality* (Cambridge University Press 2022).

[66] For critique of the unevenness of requiring only an official internal point of view, see Noah Smith (n. 61); and G. Postema, 'Law's Ethos: Reflections on a Public Practice of Illegality' (2010), 90 *BUL Rev* 1847; and see S. Perry, 'Holmes versus Hart: The Bad Man in Legal Theory' (Cambridge University Press 2009).

[67] Bratman offers a parallel criticism about planning for others, in Michael Bratman, 'Shapiro on Legal Positivism and Jointly Intentional Activity' (2002), 8 *Legal Theory* 511.

[68] This reading of Fuller owes much to Rundle's work on Fuller's account of reciprocity in Kirsten Rundle, *Forms Liberate: Reclaiming the Jurisprudence of Lon L. Fuller* (Bloomsbury Publishing 2012); its echoes in Postema's rich body of work including his most recent account

practices that count for the existence of a legal system and/or its normativity, Fuller emphasized that the distinct obligations of officials and subjects—obligations of fidelity to law—are owed reciprocally, within a relation they bear to each other. Fullerian accounts emphasize the vulnerability of subjects in the face of official powers, and directly link together the roles of officials and subjects in order to provide for the latter's protection, and the former's answerability to the latter.

For Fuller himself, officials are not mere creatures of legal rules constituting offices and appointing office-holders with special powers to bind subjects. Instead, subjects' obligations of obedience to law are contingent upon officials living up (more or less) to the aspirations of legality, typically understood as the ideals of the rule of law.[69] The official and subject roles are therefore not merely correlative positions, nor are 'official' and 'subject' merely contingent sociological labels springing from collective practices. It is not the mere distinction but the *relation* between officials and subjects that determines both what officials must do as agents of legality, and what they owe to persons qua subjects of legality.

It is important to the present project's concern for international legality, however, that Fuller's concern for the relation of reciprocity between subjects and officials sits within his broader interest in human interaction.[70] Fuller is not just the theorist who continues to teach generations of law students about the fabled King Rex's failings, with his secret, particular, discretionary, convoluted, incoherent, retroactive, and impossible pronouncements.[71] Fuller is also (and some argue predominantly) a theorist of horizontal and inter-personal legal relations.[72] Fuller's work on interactional law—in which horizontal interactions generate and stabilize meaning and expectations among persons—is

---

in Postema, *Law's Rule* (n. 63); and Dyzenhaus, *Long Arc of Legality* (n. 63). This is Fuller the theorist of hierarchy and reciprocity, which sits somewhat disjointedly with Fuller the theorist of private law interactionism.

[69] Lon L. Fuller, *The Morality of Law*, 2nd edn (Yale University Press 1969), e.g. at 39–40.

[70] See Lon L. Fuller, 'Human Interaction and the Law', in Kenneth Winston (ed.), *The Principles of Social Order. Selected Essays of Lon L. Fuller* (Hart Publishing 1981).

[71] Fuller (n. 68) 33–44.

[72] David Luban, 'Rediscovering Fuller's Legal Ethics' (1998), 11 *Georgetown Journal of Legal Ethics* 801—citing Owen Fiss, 'Foreword: The Forms of Justice' (1979), 93 *Harvard Law Review* 1, 39. I am grateful to David Lefkowitz for pressing me on this point.

invoked both by broadly pluralist accounts of legal ordering,[73] and by constructivist or interactional accounts of international legal ordering (to which I return below).[74] As Taekema argues, just as Fuller denied that enacted law is a one-way projection of authority in the public sphere, he rejected theories of one-dimensional top-down legality shorn of horizontal interactional law.[75]

Fuller's interests in both hierarchical and horizontal interaction are united by their concern for reciprocity. However, putting these two approaches together seems to depend upon a reasonably clear recognition of the roles of officials and subjects. While Fuller downplays the significance of mere 'offices' in order to emphasize the forms and constraints involved in legal processes (including those among non-officials),[76] some degree of officiality—some settled recognition of the role of official—seems necessary to the stabilization of what Fuller calls 'interactional expectancies' between actors.[77] Among the many failures of Fuller's King Rex in his efforts to make law, there was never doubt that he, his delegates (when he used them), and judges (when allowed to operate) addressed subjects of the purported legal order from a recognized official role. It is telling that Fuller brought his sorry saga to a close not by killing off the hapless king but by having his successor "announce that he was taking the powers of government away from the lawyers and placing them in the hands of psychiatrists and experts in public relations. This way, he explained, people could be made happy without rules."[78] King Rex II, not King Rex I, had the most spectacular failure, repudiating not only rules, but the very role of the legal official.

---

[73] Sanne Taekema, 'The Many Uses of Law: Interactional Law as a Bridge between Instrumentalism and Law's Values', in Nicole Roughan and Andrew Halpin, *In Pursuit of Pluralist Jurisprudence* (Cambridge University Press 2017); Wibren van der Burg, *The Dynamics of Law and Morality: A Pluralist Account of Legal Interactionism* (Routledge 2014), 19–32.

[74] Jutta Brunnée and Stephen J. Toope, *Legitimacy and Legality in International Law: An Interactional Account* (Cambridge University Press 2010).

[75] Sanne Taekema, 'Between or beyond Legal Orders: Questioning the Concept of Legal Order', in Jan Klabbers and Gianluigi Palombella (eds), *The Challenge of Inter-Legality* (Cambridge University Press 2010).

[76] See Fuller, 'Forms and Limits of Adjudication' (1978), 92 *Harvard Law Review* 353, 365–6.

[77] Fuller, 'Human Interaction' (n. 73).

[78] The fable of King Rex's violations of precepts of legality appears in Fuller, *The Morality of Law*, 33–44. The story of Rex II is examined at length in my full *Officials* project from which the present chapter draws.

Fullerian concerns for the protection of persons in the face of law's power suggests that, if legal ordering is understood to encompass both enacted and interactional law, it may be all the more important for persons to know when they interact in their own (inter-personal) capacities, and when they interact with (or are themselves) agents of official power. Recognized roles of official and subject allow persons to be both accountable and protected under the rule of law. Both self-recognition and recognition of others in these roles then allow persons to know whether they are interacting as subjects or as agents of law's power; whether their interactions are heterarchical or hierarchical; and whether they are direct or mediated through law's authority.

c. Officials making law's claim to authority

Important elements of officiality and subjection also inhere in Joseph Raz's argument that law necessarily claims legitimate authority, a claim that "is made by legal officials wherever a legal system is in force".[79] Work from Gardner elaborated this view, addressed criticisms that it oddly personifies the law, and fleshed out the concept of official of law beyond being a mere 'mouthpiece' of the law.[80] According to Gardner, "making the claim to authority is part of what it is to be an official," so that, when claiming law's authority, the official of the law speaks with law's "moral voice."[81] The official of law also owes moral obligations, Gardner argues, not because they have taken oaths nor signed employment contracts within particular institutions, but because these obligations fall out of the rationale for the official role.[82]

---

[79] Jospeh Raz, *Ethics in the Public Domain: Essays in the Morality of Law and Politics* (Oxford University Press 1995), 217: and see 215–16.

[80] John Gardner, *Law as a Leap of Faith: Essays on Law in General* (Oxford University Press 2012). I have examined these accounts in Roughan (n. 6).

[81] On the change from 'legal official' to 'official of the law' see Gardner, 'The Twilight of Legality' (n. 6) and Gardner (n. 75) 131. See also Gardner's reply to critics: law "cannot be understood except as issuing its requirements in a moral voice. There is no way to reduce this feature of law out. It is a defining aspect of the legal point of view", in 'Law as a Leap of Faith as Others See It' (2014), 33 *Law & Philosophy* 813, 826.

[82] Gardner, 'Criminals in Uniform', in R. A. Duff et al. (eds), *The Constitution of the Criminal Law* (Oxford University Press 2013). According to Gardner, among these obligations are special responsibilities to uphold the rule of law.

In Raz's own account, the claim to authority must satisfy non-moral conditions in order for authority to be able to serve subjects by helping them better conform to reasons that apply to them.[83] Key critics of Raz have argued, however, that this combination of non-moral criteria with an authority's substantive service of subjects' conformity to reasons is not enough; there must also be some role of authority from which the very claim to exercise the normative power of authority is made to subjects.[84] The insistence on some form of justified 'standing' of authority rejects unjustified efforts to claim authority, even if its substantive impact would serve the subject's conformity to reasons. If the standing objection succeeds, then claimants of authority must have justified standing, through either a valuably recognized role or relation, to claim authority over others.

This line of critique goes beyond the present concern for the role of the official (who claims law's authority), and into the prospect of a role of authority from which the normative power of authority is claimed. The critique is therefore only partially relevant. Not all roles of authority are also roles of official; and the claim to law's authority is only one of the claims made by the official of law. However, when the claim to law's authority is made by officials of law over subjects of law, it is made within a structure of roles that, if valuable, may be thought to satisfy demands for a particular justified role of authority.

d. A recognition model of legality

Three key claims can be drawn from these positions to capture a role of official of law that (i) emerges from collective social practices of

---

[83] Claimants of authority must be able to communicate their directives, and their authority must also be reasonably knowable. See the summary of Raz's account in 'The Problem of Authority: Revisiting the Service Conception' (2006), 90 *Minnesota Law Review* 1003.

[84] See Scott Hershovitz, 'The Role of Authority' (2011), 11 *Philosopher's Imprint* 1; Jeremy Waldron, 'Authority for Officials', in Lukas Meye, Stanley Paulson, and Thomas Pogge (eds), *Rights, Culture, and the Law: Themes from the Legal and Political Philosophy of Joseph Raz* (Oxford University Press 2003). In Roughan, 'The Recognition in Authority: Roles, Relations, and Reasons' (2022), *Jurisprudence* 14:2, 171–201. I build a variant of the standing objection into a justification for authority.

recognition, beyond those of the narrow class of officials themselves; (ii) is normatively connected to the role of the subject, so that officials and subjects are understood in a relation (not a distinction); and (iii) may satisfy demands for some form of 'standing' from which authority is justifiably claimed by some persons over others.

In other work I defend a fuller version of this role of official, from which institutional persons (the officials) have the moral standing to make claims to law's authority, claims to administer law's forms of justice, and claims to the use of justified coercion in the name of the law. That account relies upon two key types of recognition: collective recognition of the role of official, and recognition in relations between official and subject.[85] The first borrows (from work on social ontology and philosophy of social practices) ideas of recognition as the attribution and/or generation of an institutional status.[86] These invoke accounts of collective agency and various kinds of 'we-practices' or 'we-mode practices' that carry recognition's constitutive potential,[87] and examine the structure of recognitive practices by drawing distinctions between 'structured' and 'unstructured' systems for organizing practices of recognition.[88]

Such reliance on recognition differs from mere 'labelling' approaches in which an official is whoever a community counts as an official. If recognitive practices are regarded as constitutive of particular institutional statuses, then we leave behind the descriptive inquiry into who is in fact counted as an official, to analyse and evaluate such counting. A recognition approach emphasizes the normative status that is generated out of recognitive practices. Such practices are laden with normative potential

---

[85] Space precludes an engagement with the role of recognition in the critical political theories of recognition, or its resonance in international legal theory. See e.g. Axel Honneth, *The Struggle for Recognition* (MIT Press 1996).

[86] This is most familiar from the uses legal theory makes of constitutive rules; and their elaboration or extension into artefactual theories of law, including constitutive readings of Hartian rules of recognition and other customary foundations of law often drawing upon Searle's *X counts as Y (in domain Z)*. Compare Burazin (n. 32); Jonathan Crowe, 'Law as an Artifact Kind' (2014), 40 *Monash University Law Review* 737; Kenneth Ehrenberg, *Functions of Law* (Oxford University Press 2016); Dan Priel, 'Not All Law Is an Artifact: Jurisprudence Meets the Common Law', in *Law as an Artifact* (n. 32).

[87] See e.g. Raimo Tuomela, *The Philosophy of Social Practices: A Collective Acceptance View* (Cambridge University Press 2002); Raimo Tuomela, *Social Ontology: Collective Intentionality and Group Agents* (Oxford University Press 2013).

[88] Burazin (n. 32).

that is fully realized (so that standing is carried into the role) only when they are recognitions of value.[89] The value of the altered normative status of the official agent turns on its impact upon the agency on both sides of the official-subject relation. Recognition might be understood to 'temper' the agency on the official side of an official-subject relation.[90] Instead of power wielded by one person over another, official-subject interaction engages officials as constrained institutional agents.

The second contribution of recognition theories then explains the burdens of recognition within such interactions. Between law's officials and subjects there is not only a jural relation constituted and constrained by rules, but a moral relation requiring robust recognition. Officials making claims to law's authority (in contrast to the mere imposition of power) entails recognition of the role of subject, and the value of being subject to law's authority and not mere force. There is also a key element of self-recognition involved on the part of those who claim law's authority and wield its coercive and administrative powers, which entail recognition of themselves as officials, not simply powerful people manipulating or threatening others. Law's normativity can then be traced from the valuably recognized standing of officials into their relations with subjects, avoiding the objection that a group of self- and other-recognizing officials looks either like a group of powerful elites, or a gang of thugs.

Recognition of a role of official might therefore answer the concern about some persons being subject to the authority of others, by institutionalizing the relations of official and subject in order to ensure that law's protections, in the form of the ideals of legality, minimize the insult of subjection itself. A recognition account thus places the official-subject relation at the centre of an account of legality.[91]

---

[89] Depending on one's metaethical poison, recognition is conceived as responding to or generating value. See Roughan, 'The Role of Recognition: Persons, Institutions, and Plurality' (2022), 47 *Journal of Legal Philosophy* 53.

[90] Such tempering may be an aspect of the way in which the rule of law itself 'tempers' power. See Martin Krygier, 'Tempering Power' in Maurice Adams, Anne Meuwese, and Ernst Hirsch Ballin (eds), *Constitutionalism and the Rule of Law: Bridging Idealism and Realism* (Cambridge University Press 2017).

[91] Here the more robust claim differs from the place of the official/subject distinction in an austere concept of law, where it operates to demarcate and structure recognitive practices. I argue in the full project, however, that the distinction's protective implications place it among Hart's 'minimum content of natural law' that shape even the more austere concept.

3. Recognition of International Officiality and Subjection

The above account of official-subject roles and their relation suggests why it matters if international law is not a legal system harbouring a distinction between the roles of official and subject. On this view, the issue is less about a division of labour in holding power to account, but a relation of recognition that sets out what is required in order for there to be subjection to legality not mere force. If there is a problem here, it is a problem for international legality, not mere systematicity.

a. Recognition 'by whom, of what, as what?'

A theory of recognition does not even begin the sociological and interpretive tasks of mapping recognitive practices in international law. This limitation, however, highlights the importance of the relation between philosophical and sociological inquiry.[92] If the role of official is a social role—albeit one which is often recognized as involving quite technical forms of institutionalization, then the social practices acknowledging some agent as an official, as having a special normative status, contributes towards the very generation of that normative status. Yet if recognition is to be something other than mere labelling, there must be some account of the normative significance or status of what is recognized, and whose recognition contributes to generating that status. The 'by whom … as what' parts of the question are appropriate for philosophical explanation and argumentation.

Although an abstract recognition theory of legality does not provide a concrete answer to the question of whose recognition counts, and with what weight, it adds the key demand that the way to look for recognition of the role of official is not simply to count and collate international offices, or track only the practices of those who participate in practice as self-recognizing agents of the law.[93] This serves to frame the task of

---

[92] Julie Dickson, *Elucidating Law* (Oxford University Press 2022); Murphy, 'Law beyond the State' (n. 9) 225; and Roughan and Halpin, 'Promises and Pursuits of Pluralist Jurisprudence', in Roughan and Halpin (n. 71).

[93] Sciaraffa (n. 62).

examining recognitive practices in international law, a task that is complicated by the international context's contending visons of more cosmopolitan versus more sovereigntist structures for representation and participation of diverse agents.

A recognition theory also insists that the object of recognition is not simply the role of official or subject alone, but their relation. Here the difficulty for international law arises from the foundational commitment to sovereign equality. If states recognize themselves and each other as being bearing equal sovereign independence, how could they also see themselves as subjects of each other qua officials? If the dualities of states' official and subject roles undermines both their self- and other-recognition in a relation between official and subject, there will not be a relation of legality.

Here we can return to see how the promise of Besson's and Waldron's notions of ultimate subjection, coupled with intermediary or administrative conceptions of the official, turns upon the recognitive practices of those very individuals who would be ultimate subjects. Ultimate individual subjection to international law requires that individual subjects recognize their own states as (intermediary or administrative) officials of international law. However, the duality of the state officials' roles in such accounts may upset recognition in so as far as subjects' recognition of 'their' state officials (as agents of state law's claims to authority) makes it harder to recognise those same officials as 'administrators' of international legality.

b. Recognizing or rejecting officiality in international law

There may be avenues for rescuing the recognition of an official-subject relation in international law. One obvious strategy is to look for officiality and subjection within pockets of international law, to seek out regime-specific roles of officials, and relations of recognition between officials and subjects in those areas. Yet as Kingsbury argues, such fragmentation sits uncomfortably with juristic understandings of a more unified discipline bearing generality and publicness, and more integrated approaches to international legal practice.[94] The same factors that pressure the notion of publicness in general international law may also feed into doubts within more specialized regimes.

More promise might be found within work on the 'public' or 'constitutional' turns in international legal theory. However, as a compelling survey from Goldmann, von Bogdandy, and Venzke reveals, conceptions of international public authority, defences of constitutionality, and the development of international institutional law seek to defend different versions of robust public law frameworks, but then expand the category of their application beyond those who might be easily recognized as official agents.[95] Officiality is expressly downplayed. Such diffusion of publicness might weaken a sense of officiality even as it seeks to extend the reach of legality's constraints on governance and public power. Or it might go the other way, generating recognition of a role of official and its relations to subjects of law's power beyond the constraints of relatively impotent formal offices. Its overall impact might depend upon what the authors describe as the shape of "world public opinion," a demand for public frameworks of constraint as well as the pursuit of common interests. That may include a demand for robust officiality and subjection in international legal ordering, if publicness is linked not only to actions, forms, functions, and/or interests, but also to the status of agents or their agency.[96]

A more dismissive response to the recognition model of legality might insist that international law is not about persons and their recognitive practices at all. Instead, international law may be thought to be institutional all the way down, engaging only institutional actors and governing their interactions, so that there is no insult of subjection, no concern about the protection of persons from one another's power. Such a response is powerfully undermined by both Waldron's and Besson's accounts of the individual as direct or ultimate subjects of international law, and individuals' entitlements to the protection of the rule of law or

---

[94] Kingsbury (n. 14).   [95] See Goldmann et al. (n. 18).   [96] Cf. Kingsbury (n. 14).

the pursuit of law's legitimate authority.[97] The rise of the person as both an agent and subject of international law makes it hard to deny the importance of the protections associated with legality, including those that are built into relations of officiality and subjection.

A second dismissive response might downplay the seriousness of the blurring of official and subject roles by treating international law as primarily interactional law, in which institutions of international norm-generation and norm-application operate without central institutionalized hierarchies, but nevertheless support practices of coordination and transactional interactions, stabilize agents' expectations, and generate horizontal forms of legal accountability and enforcement.[98] On Collins's version of this view (among its strongest proponents), international law's primary functions and activities are not governance and constraints on power (the sorts of 'holding to account' that concern Lefkowitz), but support for interaction and co-existence. Collins argues that in international law, the dominance of transactional (rather than ruling) logics undermines the need for officials.[99]

However, as Collins himself notes, prioritizing a transactional functionalist understanding does not deny that international law may operate governance functions, too. Interactional accounts (including those drawing upon Fuller's work) explain not the absence of hierarchy, but the co-existence of both interactionally and hierarchically institutionalized aspects of legal ordering.[100] Gorobets effectively describes this as a 'peaks and valleys' model of international legal authority, in which high points of institutionality and 'mediated authority' are surrounded by more interactional and customary forms of legal ordering and 'unmediated authority.'[101] Interactionalism poses a complement rather than an

---

[97] Besson (n. 37); and see her reply to Waldron (n. 12) in Besson, 'Sovereignty, International Law, and Democracy' (2011), 22 *European Journal of International Law* 373.

[98] Collins (n. 10), Taekema (n. 71).

[99] Richard Collins, 'The Rule of Law and the Quest for Constitutional Substitutes in International Law' (2014), 83 *Nordic Journal of International Law* 87.

[100] See Taekema (n. 71), Fuller (n. 69), and Brunnée and Toope (n. 70).

[101] Kostiantyn Gorobets, 'Peaks and Valleys: Contemplating Authority of International Law', in Pauline Westerman, Kostiantyn Gorobets, and Andreas Hadjigeorgiou (eds), *Philosophical (De)Constructions of International Law* (Edward Elgar Publishing 2021). Doubts about the unmediated forms include the worry that unmediated authority looks more like guidance than authority. Cf. Roughan (n. 79).

alternative to hierarchical legal governance. Moreover, just as interactional law surrounds institutional law, institutional offices and their incumbent powers may be central to the smooth operation of interactional law. While the shadows of critical jurisprudence loom very large over any kind of idealization of protective hierarchies in international law, such hierarchies may provide frameworks for contesting if not resolving breakdowns of interaction, for protecting against its abuses, and for stepping in when practices of 'self-help' or 'auto-application' fall short of interactional standards in the relevant community of actors.

The aim is not to shoehorn an account of international legality into a hierarchically structured model that poorly fits the practice of international law, and which so much international legal theory rejects. The worry is that, even if a more interactional analysis frames philosophy of international law within a rich tradition of thinking about legal process and pragmatism,[102] international law is not all interactional, and not all about the interaction of states. The entanglement of public and private actors, and public and private statuses, makes it more difficult to defend an account of interactional international legality in the face of individuals feeling international law's force and seeking its tools or protections.

Finally, we can return to Lefkowitz's suggestion of the significance of the official/subject distinction for understanding law's role in social ordering. Blurred roles of official and subject may not upset a legal order where a generic internal point of view is widely and evenly shared, so that agents apply rules to themselves and others. Many customary legal orders take that form, having wider participatory institutions through which to 'hold accountable' persons' powers over others, contest legal claims, and protect the vulnerable. However, international ordering looks very unlike the ordering of customary communities in which there are widely shared and reciprocal understandings about mutual subjection to rules. When an internal point of view is held mainly by weaker agents needing law's protection, but not by stronger agents, the operation of legality (rather than force) will call for more protective divisions of labour.

---

[102] See e.g. Taekema (n. 71).

4. Conclusion

The recognition challenge facing international legality asks whether there is a recognized role of official of international law, understood to bear a moral relation to the role of subject of international law. This chapter has argued that recognition of a role of official, and recognition in an official-subject relation, are not simply necessary to the existence of a legal system, but are aspects of legality. If international law lacks a recognized role of official and both a distinction and relation between officials and subjects, the implications are more upsetting of international legality than is typically admitted.

The paper's frame, however, has bracketed the 'international' qualifier in its discussion of the official of law and official-subject relations. The brackets leave open that there may not be a distinctive category of international legal 'official' at all. This frame also suggests that the importance of recognition of (and between) officials and subjects is important for general jurisprudence, and not only a specialist interest for philosophers of international law. In this light, the question of what it is to be an official, and the resulting distinction and relation between officials and subjects, are not so much 'problematic' as productive. They invite a revision of key jurisprudential work on the official/subject distinction and a response to leading international legal theories that celebrate publicness but depart from officiality, or that characterize international law only along its horizontal axis of transactional interaction. Focusing upon an official/subject systemic distinction and relation restores some of the grounds for scepticism about international legality, by demonstrating the difficult and important challenge of putting publicness, officiality, interaction, and hierarchy back together.[103]

Nicole Roughan, *Officials, Subjects, and the Recognition Challenge for (International) Legality* In: *Oxford Studies in Philosophy of Law, Volume 5*. Edited by: Leslie Green and Brian Leiter, Oxford University Press.
© Nicole Roughan 2024. DOI: 10.1093/9780198919650.003.0003

[103] I am grateful for the support of a Rutherford Fellowship from the Royal Society Te Apārangi Fellowship, and a H. L. A. Hart Visiting Fellowship from University College, Oxford, which allowed me time and access to retrace echoes of Hart's work on international law. I thank Nadia Sussman and Kiraan Chetty for their expert research assistance, and Kostiantyn Gorobets, David Lefkowitz, Andreas Follesdaal, Ashwini Vasanthakumar, Steven Ratner, Fleur Johns, and other participants in an online philosophy of international law workshop, for their generous comments on an earlier version of this work.

Bulygin on Legal Gaps and the Normativity of Law

Ezequiel Monti

1. Introduction

In *Normative Systems*,[1] Carlos Alchourrón and Eugenio Bulygin provide an insightful account of normative legal gaps (i.e. gaps due to the absence of legal regulation), and argue for two claims, namely:

Possibility Thesis: It is possible for legal systems to have normative gaps.

Discretion Thesis: When faced with normative legal gaps, judges have legal discretion.

Over the years, Bulygin has further refined this view of normative legal gaps, defending it against a variety of objections.[2] Here I shall grant the Possibility Thesis but argue against the Discretion Thesis. The argument is based on considerations relating to the normativity of law. Thus, I shall distinguish between legal norms and the rights and obligations that obtain in virtue of them; and, correspondingly, between normative propositions (i.e. propositions about norms) and what I call genuinely normative propositions (i.e. propositions about rights and obligations).

---

[1] Carlos Alchourrón and Eugenio Bulygin, *Normative Systems* (Springer-Verlak 1971). See also the expanded Spanish edition: Carlos Alchourrón and Eugenio Bulygin, *Sistemas Normativos*, 2nd edn (Astrea 2012).

[2] See e.g. Eugenio Bulygin, 'En Defensa de El Dorado. Respuesta a Fernando Atria', in Fernando Atria et al., *Lagunas en el derecho* (Marcial Pons 2005); Eugenio Bulygin, 'The Silence of Law', in *Essays in Legal Philosophy* (Oxford University Press 2015); Eugenio Bulygin, 'Kelsen on the Completeness and Consistency of Law', in *Essays in Legal Philosophy* (Oxford University Press 2015).

This pair of distinctions allows me to distinguish between normative gaps (in Bulygin's sense) and what I shall call genuinely normative gaps. As I will show, Bulygin's arguments establish the possibility of the former but not of the latter. And if the latter are impossible, then judges have no legal discretion in cases of normative gaps. Or so I shall argue.

Here is how I shall proceed. First, I briefly outline Alchourrón and Bulygin's account of legal systems (Section 2) and of normative gaps (Section 3). Second, I reconstruct their defence of the Possibility Thesis against the argument that normative gaps are impossible in virtue of the so-called *Principle of Permission* (Section 4). Third, I reconstruct their argument for the Discretion Thesis (Section 5). Fourth, I shall elaborate the abovementioned pair of distinctions between norms and the rights and obligations that obtain in virtue of norms, on the one hand, and between propositions about the former (normative propositions) and propositions about the latter (genuinely normative propositions), on the other (Section 6). Fifth, I shall argue that interpreted as a genuinely normative proposition, the Principle of Permission is necessarily true and inconsistent with the Discretion Thesis (Section 7). Sixth, I briefly sketch some possible views one could adopt regarding the genuine deontic status of actions in cases of normative gaps, in line with the Principle of Permission so understood (Section 8). Finally, I shall close by reflecting on the theoretical and practical relevance of Alchourrón and Bulygin's account of normative gaps, even if they do not entail legal discretion (Section 9).

2. Legal Systems in Brief

2.1 Normative Systems, Norms, and Normative Propositions

In *Normative Systems*, Alchourrón and Bulygin provide an account of normative systems in general, and of legal systems in particular, and analyse some of their formal features, namely, completeness, consistency, and independence. Our focus here is completeness. However, before examining what it is for legal systems to be complete, it will be useful to give a brief overview of their more general account of legal systems.

Alchourrón and Bulygin characterize normative systems as a species of deductive systems. A deductive system is a set of (fully interpreted) sentences that contains all its logical consequences. A normative system is a deductive system that has *norms* amongst its logical consequences. Norms, in turn, are (fully interpreted) prescriptive sentences that correlate factual circumstances (i.e. *cases*) with deontic consequences (i.e. *solutions*). This characterization of norms requires some unpacking.

First of all, note that norms are characterized as *sentences*, that is, as linguistic entities. This might seem weird at first sight. But two clarifications should help to somewhat mitigate the perplexity. To begin with, norms are not bare linguistic expressions, but rather *fully interpreted* sentences, that is, sentences *together with* a unique and fixed associated meaning.[3] Furthermore, Alchourrón and Bulygin's motivation to so characterize norms was to remain aloof of controversies about the existence of abstract entities. Thus, they claim that their account 'does not pass judgement on the ontological status of norms', explaining that 'the treatment of norms as sentences (i.e. linguistic entities) is not incompatible with the view that they have extra-linguistic (ideal) existence. The only thing that is presupposed is that they can be expressed [...] by means of sentences.'[4] In fact, on their preferred ontological view, norms are abstract, proposition-like, entities. In a nutshell, according to this view, norms are the meaning of prescriptive sentences in very much the same way that propositions are regarded as the meaning of descriptive sentences.[5]

Second, note that norms are characterized as *prescriptive* sentences. Alchourrón and Bulygin observe that deontic sentences (i.e. sentences which contain deontic terms such as 'obligatory', 'prohibited', 'permitted', etc.) are generally ambiguous since they can be used descriptively as well as prescriptively. Consider the sentence 'Smoking in public places is

---

[3] In what follows, I shall no longer specify whether I am talking about fully interpreted sentences or bare sentences (without a unique and fixed associated meaning). Context should prevent any possible confusions.

[4] Alchourrón and Bulygin, *Normative Systems* (n. 1) 60.

[5] See what they call the *hyletic conception* of norms: Carlos Alchourrón and Eugenio Bulygin, 'The Expressive Conception of Norms', *Essays in Legal Philosophy* (2015), 149.

prohibited'. On the one hand, it can be used prescriptively to *thereby* prohibit smoking in public spaces (as would, say, a legislator). On the other hand, it can also be used descriptively to assert that a norm that prohibits smoking in public places belongs to a certain normative system. Consider, for instance, my Catalonian friend who reminds me that smoking in public places is prohibited in Barcelona as we enter a restaurant. My friend is not prescribing anything. She is just *informing* me about the deontic status of smoking according to, say, the legal order of Barcelona. In the first case, the deontic sentence 'Smoking in public places is prohibited' is or expresses a norm. In the second case, in contrast, it expresses what Alchourrón and Bulygin call a *normative proposition*, that is, a proposition about the existence of a norm or its membership to a given normative system. Normative propositions are, like any other propositions, either true or false, as the case may be. Norms, in contrast, are not truth-apt. They are (the meaning of) prescriptive sentences used to thereby enjoin, permit, or prohibit certain actions. They might be just or unjust, valid or invalid, efficacious or inefficacious, but, being prescriptive, they are neither true nor false. That is why we said that, when regarded as abstract entities, norms are proposition-*like* but not, strictly speaking, propositions.

You might be wondering, if norms are not truth-apt, then how come they feature in logical relations as Alchourrón and Bulygin's account of normative systems seems to presuppose? This raises what is known as Jørgensen's dilemma, according to which, in a nutshell, either norms are truth-apt or there can be no logic of norms.[6] Alchourrón and Bulygin's solution to this puzzle lies in rejecting the underlying assumption that the relation of logical consequence can only obtain between things that are truth-apt. Thus, for them, 'the scope of logic is wider than that of truth'.[7]

Finally, let us consider in more detail those things which norms are said to correlate, namely, factual circumstances (i.e. *cases*), on the one hand, and deontic consequences (i.e. *solutions*), on the other.

---

[6] Jørgen Jørgensen, 'Imperatives and Logic' (1938), 7 *Erkenntnis* 288; Alf Ross, 'Imperatives and Logic' (1944), 11 *Philosophy of Science* 30.

[7] Carlos Alchourrón and Eugenio Bulygin, 'Limits of Logic and Legal Reasoning', *Essays in Legal Philosophy* (Oxford University Press 2015), 268. For a concrete proposal along these lines with which Bulygin was sympathetic, see Carlos Alchourrón and Antonio A. Martino, 'Logic without Truth' (1990), 3 *Ratio Juris* 46.

Alchourrón and Bulygin distinguish between *individual* and *generic* cases. Individual cases are actual events with a determinate spatial and temporal location. Thus, we can refer to the case of the 9/11 attack on the World Trade Center, to the case of the 1992 bombing of the Israel Embassy in Buenos Aires, etc. In contrast, generic cases are characterized by a set of properties that can be instantiated in an indefinite number of individual cases. Thus, we can refer to the case of a terrorist attack, characterized as actions of violence against persons, designed to intimidate the public, to advance a political cause. It is generic cases that, on Alchourrón and Bulygin's account, norms correlate with deontic consequences or solutions.

Solutions, on their part, are deontically determined actions, that is, actions qualified as permissible, prohibited, obligatory or facultative. These deontic characters are interdefinable as follows:

ϕ-ing is prohibited $=_{df}$ ϕ-ing is not permitted (Phϕ $=_{df}$ ¬Pϕ)

ϕ-ing is obligatory $=_{df}$ not-ϕ-ing is not permitted (Oϕ $=_{df}$ ¬P¬ϕ)

ϕ-ing is permitted $=_{df}$ ϕ-ing is not prohibited (Pϕ $=_{df}$ ¬Phϕ)

ϕ-ing is facultative $=_{df}$ ϕ-ing is neither prohibited nor obligatory (Fϕ $=_{df}$ ¬Phϕ ∧ ¬Oϕ)

Here too we might distinguish between individual and generic deontic solutions, that is, between solutions that qualify as obligatory, prohibited, or permitted, individual actions (with a determinate spatial and temporal location); and solutions that qualify as obligatory, prohibited, or permitted, generic actions (i.e. actions defined by properties that can be instantiated by an indefinite number of individual actions). It is generic deontic solutions that norms correlate generic cases with. Thus, according to Alchourrón and Bulygin's account, norms are prescriptive sentences that correlate generic cases with generic deontic solutions.

2.2 Legal Systems

Normative systems, we said, are deductive systems that contain norms. *Legal systems* are normative systems that contain norms of a particular kind, namely, norms that establish the permission to impose sanctions for breach of other norms of the system.[8] Derivatively, a normative system that does *not* contain norms establishing sanctions can also be deemed legal in virtue of being a subset of one that does (in particular, in virtue of being a subset of a legal order; see below). Furthermore, all sentences that belong to a legal system are legal sentences, whether they are norms that establish sanctions or not, and even if they are not norms at all.

Now, the legal systems that usually concern jurists are those whose axiomatic basis is composed of *valid* legal sentences, that is, legal sentences that satisfy certain *identification or membership criteria*. These criteria allow us to determine the content of the law that governs a given society at a given time.

The (momentary) *legal order* of a given society (at a given time) is defined as the legal system that comprises all and only those sentences that are valid according to the corresponding criteria of identification.[9] Thus, the concept of a legal order 'is a special case—in a sense, a limiting case—of the more general concept of *legal system*'.[10] But jurists are not normally interested in the legal order as such but in subsystems of the legal order that are relevant for a particular issue. Thus, it is the more general notion of legal system (as any normative system whose basis is composed of valid legal sentences) that Alchourrón and Bulygin consider central for the 'rational reconstruction of the scientific practice of jurists'.[11]

3. Normative Gaps

Here we are interested in Alchourrón and Bulygin's discussion concerning the completeness of legal systems. A normative system is *complete* if

---

[8] Alchourrón and Bulygin, *Sistemas Normativos* (n. 1) 98.

[9] Alchourrón and Bulygin also provide an account of *persistent* legal orders, characterizing them as a sequence of momentary ones. See Carlos Alchourrón and Eugenio Bulygin, 'On the Concept of a Legal Order', *Essays in Legal Philosophy* (Oxford University Press 2015).

[10] Alchourrón and Bulygin, *Normative Systems* (n. 1) 74.   [11] Ibid. 75.

and only if (and because) it lacks normative gaps. Thus, to understand what it is for a legal system to be complete we need to understand what normative gaps are.

3.1 Legal Gaps: Recognitional vs. Normative

To begin with, normative gaps are to be distinguished from what Alchourrón and Bulygin call *recognitional gaps*, which can be character-ized as follows:[12]

Recognitional Gaps: A case (be it individual or generic) is a *recognitional gap* relative to a normative system α if and only if it is semantically indeterminate whether it is an instance of a generic case that a norm belonging to α correlates with a certain deontic solution.

Thus, recognitional gaps are explained by the vagueness of the language in which norms are formulated. Normative gaps, in contrast, are not explained by the existence of a norm formulated in a vague language but rather by the *absence* of a relevant norm. To use Raz's metaphor, we can say that recognitional gaps are cases where the law speaks with an inde-terminate voice, while normative gaps are cases where the law is silent.[13]

However, not every case that is not regulated by law is a normative gap. In fact, Alchourrón and Bulygin are interested in articulating an account of normative gaps such that normative systems being complete can plausibly be considered a rational ideal. But the mere fact that a normative system fails to correlate some case with a deontic solution concerning some action cannot plausibly be considered a rational fail-ure. Rather, on Alchourrón and Bulygin's account, a normative system has a normative gap only if a *relevant* case fails to be correlated with a *relevant* solution (i.e. a solution regarding the deontic status of the action

---

[12] Alchourrón and Bulygin identify two further kinds of gaps, namely, what they call 'knowledge gaps' and 'axiological gaps'. I won't discuss these here. See ibid. 33 and 107.
[13] Joseph Raz, *The Authority of Law*, 2nd edn (Oxford University Press 2009), 77.

in relation to which the case is relevant). Hence, to distinguish normative gaps from other, perfectly benign, instances of absence of normative regulation, we need to understand what it is for a case to be *relevant*.

3.2 Relevant Cases

To define the notion of relevant case, let us first introduce the notion of complimentary cases: 'two cases will be said to be *complimentary regarding a property p* if and only if *p* is present in one and absent in the other, and all the other properties remain constant'.[14] Against this background, we can say that:

Relevant properties: A property *p* is relevant for the deontic status of an action φ according to a normative system α if and only if there are two complimentary cases regarding *p* such that they are correlated by α with different deontic solutions regarding φ.

In turn, in a broad sense, we might say that a generic case is relevant relative to an action φ and to a normative system α if and only if it is defined by properties that are relevant for the deontic status of φ according to α. But, for our purposes, we are interested in a narrower notion, namely, what Alchourrón and Bulygin call *elementary* relevant cases. These are cases defined by the presence or the absence of *each* of the relevant properties. To illustrate, if the relevant properties are *p* and *r*, then the elementary relevant cases are the following four: $p \wedge q$, $p \wedge \neg q$, $\neg p \wedge q$, and $\neg p \wedge \neg q$. The case defined by *p* is a relevant case in the broad sense (it is defined by a relevant property) but is not an elementary relevant case. Here I shall use the expression 'relevant case' to refer to elementary relevant cases, unless I explicitly say otherwise. Thus:

Relevant cases: A case is a relevant case relative to a normative system α and action φ if and only if it is defined by the presence or the absence of each of the properties that are relevant for the deontic status of φ according to α.

---

[14] Ibid. 101.

3.3 Normative Gaps Defined and Contrasted with Other Cases of Absence of Normative Regulation

We are now in a position to provide a characterization of normative gaps, as follows:

Normative gaps: A case c is a normative gap relative to a normative system α and an action ϕ if and only if:

  i. c is a relevant case relative to α and ϕ.
 ii. α contains neither a norm according to which it is permitted to ϕ in c nor a norm according to which it is *not* permitted to ϕ in c (i.e. α does not contain a norm that correlates c with either a permission to ϕ or a prohibition to ϕ).

Thus, as we said, not every case that a normative system fails to correlate with a deontic solution regarding some action is a normative gap. Note, first, that for a generic case to be relevant relative to a certain action and a certain normative system, the action must be one that is regulated by the normative system in at least some cases. If the action is not regulated at all by the normative system, then all cases are correlated with the same deontic solution regarding that action, namely, none; and hence, there are no relevant properties or cases (relative to that action and that normative system). Thus, according to our characterization, normative gaps can only exist relative to actions that are regulated by the normative system in at least some cases. This is important for the following reason. For most normative systems, there will be a potentially infinite list of generic actions such that there is no norm either permitting or prohibiting them. Arguably, for instance, the Argentine legal order has neither a norm permitting nor a norm prohibiting people using two tea bags per cup. And likewise for all sorts of actions: writing a philosophy paper on New Year's Eve, drawing a tiger while having breakfast, etc. However, it would be absurd to claim that every case is a normative gap relative to such actions. As we said, Alchourrón and Bulygin are interested in articulating an account of normative gaps such that normative systems being complete can plausibly be considered a rational ideal. But for normative systems to have a norm permitting or prohibiting any conceivable generic action can hardly be considered a rational ideal. Thus, we should distinguish between complete normative systems (i.e. normative systems that lack normative gaps), and what we might call *total* normative systems, that is, normative systems that regulate all generic actions (at least in some circumstances or cases). On Alchourrón and Bulygin's account, a normative system can be complete without being total, and it is only completeness that can plausibly be regarded as a rational ideal.

Similarly, note that not every case that fails to be correlated with a deontic solution regarding an action that is regulated by the normative system in some cases is a normative gap either. It is only cases that are *relevant* relative to that action (according to the normative system) that can be normative gaps. Again, the reason is that it would be absurd to consider it a rational ideal for normative systems to correlate every possible case with a unique deontic solution concerning the actions it regulates. Suppose a normative system contains a norm prohibiting smoking in public places and another permitting doing so in non-public ones. What about, someone could ask, places owned by millionaires? Well, the normative system does not say anything about that. If the place owned by a millionaire is a public space, then it is prohibited to smoke in it, while if it is not a public space, it is permitted to do so. Thus, the case of places owned by a millionaire is not correlated with a unique solution. However, it would be absurd to claim that it constitutes a normative gap. In fact, all individual cases are correlated with a unique deontic solution regarding smoking. The generic case of places owned by millionaires is not correlated with a unique solution for the simple reason that the system does not deem it relevant, for the deontic status of smoking, whether a place is owned by a millionaire or not. Thus, we should restrict our attention to relevant cases, that is, to cases that are defined by properties that are relevant for the deontic status of the action according to the normative system.

3.4 An Example

Someone could worry that normative gaps so understood are impossible by definition. Because it might seem that if certain properties are relevant for the deontic status of an action according to the system, then that is because the system correlates the cases characterized by those properties with a solution that qualifies that action as permitted or prohibited. Thus, either a case it is not relevant and so condition (i) is not satisfied, or it is relevant, but then it is correlated by a norm of the system with a solution that qualifies the action as permitted or prohibited, so that condition (ii) is not satisfied. To show why this is not the case, consider the following example. The old Argentinian Civil Code had two norms regulating the recovery of real estate from third parties. The problem arises when someone in possession of a real estate, but who lacks a valid title to it, transfers it to a third party. The question is whether the third party has an obligation to restore it to the actual owner ($O\phi = \neg P\neg\phi$) or she is allowed to keep it ($\neg O\phi = P\neg\phi$). Simplifying a little bit, the two norms that regulated the issue established the following:

> N1: If the transfer was made with consideration (i.e., roughly, in exchange for something), the third-party who is currently in possession of the real state acted in good faith (i.e. without knowing that the transferor lacked a valid title), but the transferor did not act in good faith, then the third-party has the obligation to restore the real estate to the original owner.
>
> N2: If the transfer was made without consideration, then the third-party has the obligation to restore the real estate to the original owner.

Thus, the relevant properties relative to the action of restoring the real estate according to the legal system constituted by these two norms are the following: the existence of consideration (C), the good faith of the current possessor (GFP), and the good faith of the transferor (GFT). Hence, the relevant cases, and the solutions they are correlated with by the system, can be represented in the following matrix.

As it can be seen, there are three relevant cases relative to the action of the third-party restoring the real estate that are not correlated by the system with a solution determining its deontic status (1, 3, and 4). The third-party failing to restore the real state to its original owner in such cases is neither permitted nor prohibited by a norm of the system. But these are still very much relevant cases (relative to such action and to

	C	GFP	GFT	N1: (GFP, ¬GFT, C) → Oφ	N2: ¬C → Oφ
Case 1	Yes	Yes	Yes		
Case 2	Yes	Yes	No	Oφ	
Case 3	Yes	No	Yes		
Case 4	Yes	No	No		
Case 5	No	Yes	Yes		Oφ
Case 6	No	Yes	No		Oφ
Case 7	No	No	Yes		Oφ
Case 8	No	No	No		Oφ

the normative system in question). Thus, they are, according to Alchourrón and Bulygin, normative gaps.

4. The Principle of Permission and the Possibility of Normative Gaps

Thus far I have reconstructed Alchourrón and Bulygin's account of normative gaps. It is a separate issue whether legal systems can actually have normative gaps so understood. Many legal philosophers, like Hans Kelsen[15] and Joseph Raz,[16] seem[17] to deny this possibility. They seem to argue that, necessarily, all legal systems are complete in virtue of what might be called the *Principle of Permission*,[18] according to which:

Principle of Permission: For every action φ, if φ-ing is not prohibited, then φ-ing is permitted.

Alchourrón and Bulygin show that this argument is misguided. The Principle of Permission, they argue, is doubly ambiguous. As we saw, deontic sentences can be prescriptive, expressing a norm, or descriptive,

---

[15] Hans Kelsen, *Introduction to the Problems of Legal Theory* (Oxford University Press 1992), 84; Hans Kelsen, *Pure Theory of Law*, tr. Max Knight, 2nd edn (University of California Press 1967), 245.

[16] Raz (n. 18) 76.   [17] I will later suggest an alternative reading of their views.

[18] Alchourrón and Bulygin refer to it as the 'Principle of Prohibition'. The only reason they refrain from calling it the 'Principle of Permission', which is arguably more intuitive, is to avoid confusion with another principle which had been so named by von Wright. Here there is no room for such confusion.

expressing a normative proposition. Correspondingly, the Principle of Permission could be read as expressing either a norm or a normative proposition.

Furthermore, a normative proposition according to which a certain action, say, double parking, is permitted can also be ambiguous. On the one hand, it might mean that a norm permitting double parking belongs to the normative system at issue. Here the normative proposition informs about the presence of a permissive norm. On the other hand, it might mean that a norm prohibiting double parking does not belong to the normative system at issue. Here it informs about the absence of a prohibitive norm. Thus, Alchourrón and Bulygin distinguish between weak and strong permissions:

Weak Permission: ϕ-ing is *weakly* permitted (in a case c) according to a normative system α if and only if α does not contain a norm that prohibits ϕ-ing (in c).

Strong Permission: ϕ-ing is *strongly* permitted (in a case c) according to a normative system α if and only if α contains a norm that permits ϕ-ing (in c).

Thus, a deontic sentence according to which 'It is permitted to ϕ' can express (i) a norm permitting to ϕ; (ii) a normative proposition according to which ϕ-ing is weakly permitted by a given normative system; or (iii) a normative proposition according to which ϕ-ing is strongly permitted by a given normative system. How should we interpret the Principle of Permission?

A first possibility is to interpret it as a norm. As a first approximation, it could be reconstructed as follows:

The Principle of Permission as a Closure Norm (first draft): For every action ϕ and every case c, if no other norm of this system prohibits ϕ-ing in c, then it is hereby permitted to ϕ in c.

This norm, however, would have disastrous consequences for all systems that prohibit some action in certain cases but not in others. For suppose there is a norm that prohibits to ϕ in circumstances $p \land q$ and another one that permits to φ in ¬(p∧q). Now consider the generic case p. This case is not correlated by a norm of the system with a prohibition to φ. Consequently, the closure norm as formulated establishes that it is permitted to φ in p. But then the case p∧q will now be correlated with both the prohibition to φ and the permission to φ. To prevent this, the Principle of Permission must be relativized to relevant cases. This can be done as follows:

The Principle of Permission as a Closure Rule or Norm (revised): For every action φ:

i. If φ-ing is not prohibited *in any case* by other norms of this system, then it is hereby permitted to φ in all cases.
ii. If φ-ing is prohibited in some cases by other norms of this system, but there are relevant cases such that they are not correlated by other norms of this system with its prohibition, then it is hereby permitted to φ in those relevant cases.

However, it is contingent whether this norm actually belongs to a given legal system or not. In fact, such a norm presupposes that at least *some* legal systems are incomplete. Preliminarily, note that clause (i) is sufficient for the normative system to be total, but it is not sufficient for it to be complete. In virtue of (i) any conceivable action would be regulated in some way in some circumstances. But this is consistent with some actions being regulated in some but not all relevant cases. In contrast, (ii) is, indeed, sufficient for the normative system to be complete. Thus, it is (ii) that concerns us here. But consider the alternative legal system that could be constructed by jettisoning (ii) while retaining all the other norms of the system. Let us call it α. Now, either α is complete and adding (ii) would be redundant, or it is incomplete. Hence, if there are legal systems where (ii) is not redundant, then there are also incomplete legal systems. Someone could grant that legal systems in Alchourrón and Bulygin's idiosyncratic sense can be incomplete, but still deny that *legal orders* (i.e. the set of *all* valid legal sentences) can be so. The idea would be that the Principle of Permission, understood as a closure norm, necessarily belongs to every legal order. But it is hard to see what the motivation for such a view could be.

A second possibility would be to interpret the Principle of Permission as a normative proposition according to which if ϕ-ing is not prohibited, then it is weakly permitted. This normative proposition is analytically, and thus necessarily, true. In fact, given the definition of weak permission, it simply means that:

Principle of Weak Permission: For every action ϕ and for every normative system α, if α does not contain a norm prohibiting ϕ (in a case c), then α does not contain a norm prohibiting ϕ (in c).

Obviously, this trivial truth does not rule out the existence of normative gaps. On the contrary, the fact that a case constitutes a normative gap relative to ϕ *implies* that ϕ-ing is weakly permitted in that case.

A third possibility is to interpret it as a normative proposition according to which if ϕ-ing is not prohibited, then it is strongly permitted. This proposition could be formulated as follows:

Principle of Strong Permission: For every action ϕ and for every normative system α:

i. If α does not contain a norm prohibiting ϕ in any case, then it contains a norm permitting ϕ in all cases.
ii. If α contains a norm prohibiting ϕ in some cases, but there are relevant cases that are nor correlated by α with the prohibition to ϕ, then α contains a norm permitting ϕ in those relevant cases.

However, this proposition is arguably false. (ii) implies that all legal systems are complete. But, as we have seen, this is surely not the case (otherwise closure norms of the sort examined previously would be redundant). Again, we could consider a weaker version, according to which it is not true of all legal systems but just of all legal orders. But this weaker version is not necessarily true. It is not a logical or metaphysical truth: from the mere fact that a certain norm does not belong to a legal order, it does not follow that a different norm belongs to it. The principle could be true if all legal orders were complete due to the craftsmanship of legal authorities or to the fact that they happen to contain closure norms of the kind we examined above. But both these facts are contingent: legal authorities are often sloppy and, as we saw, it is hard to see what the motivation would be for the view that, whatever societies do, legal orders necessarily contain a closure norm.

To sum up, the argument that purports to establish that legal orders are necessarily complete by appealing to the Principle of Permission faces the following trilemma:

1. The Principle of Permission is either (i) a norm; or (ii) a normative proposition according to which if an action is not prohibited, it is weakly permitted; or (iii) a normative proposition according to which if an action is not prohibited, it is strongly permitted.
2. (i) does not necessarily belong to all legal orders, so it does not preclude the possibility of legal orders having normative gaps.
3. (ii) is trivially true but does not preclude the possibility of legal orders having normative gaps.
4. (iii) is not necessarily true, so, again, it does not preclude the possibility of legal orders having normative gaps.
5. Therefore, the Principle of Permission does not preclude the possibility of legal orders having normative gaps.

5. Normative Gaps and Judicial Discretion

We have established that normative legal gaps are possible. But it is not clear what their legal implications are for judicial decisions. Suppose that *Plaintiff* files a claim against *Defendant*, demanding the court to order her to φ. However, this individual case is an instance of a normative gap. There is no norm establishing that people in the defendant's circumstances have an obligation to φ or are permitted not to φ. What is the court legally bound to do? As anticipated, Alchourrón and Bulygin argue that:

Discretion Thesis (refined): If an individual case is an instance of a normative legal gap, then judges have legal discretion, that is, they are not legally bound to decide either in favour or against the defendant.

The argument is the following. Normally, judges have a legal obligation to decide the cases submitted to them (as long as they are within their competence) by relying on the relevant pre-existing legal norms that apply to the parties. This implies that (i) if there is a legal norm that establishes that the defendant has an obligation to φ, then the court is legally bound to rule against her; and that (ii) if there is a legal norm that permits the defendant not to φ, then the court is legally bound to rule in her favour. However, this obligation cannot be met where the legal order has a normative gap relative to φ. By hypothesis, in such a case there are no relevant pre-existing legal norms that apply to the parties. Thus, the court will have to justify its decision by appealing to non-legal norms or to legal norms created ex post facto. In any case, it will not be legally bound to decide either way.

A common line of resistance to this argument runs as follows.[19] Judges have an obligation to decide the cases within their competence in a way that is justified in light of the relevant pre-existing legal norms that apply to the parties. However, there is an asymmetry in this regard between judicial decisions that rule against the defendant and judicial decisions that rule in her favour. The former are legally justified only if there is a norm that applies to the defendant's case and requires her to φ. The latter, in contrast, can be legally justified even if there is no norm that explicitly permits the defendant not to φ. Thus, for the decision to rule in favour of the defendant to be legally justified it is sufficient for there to be no norm that requires her to φ. Therefore, if an individual case constitutes a normative legal gap judges have no discretion but are legally bound to decide in favour of the defendant. Call this *the asymmetry view*.

Alchourrón and Bulygin argue that such view should be rejected. Its appeal is based on a failure to distinguish between norms and

[19] See Fernando Atria, 'Creación y Aplicación del Derecho: Entre Formalismo y Escepticismo', *Lagunas en el derecho* (Marcial Pons 2005); Juan Ruiz Manero, 'Algunas Concepciones del Derecho y Sus Lagunas', *Lagunas en el derecho* (Marcial Pons 2005); Juan Carlos Bayón, 'Sobre el Principio de Prohibición y Las Condiciones de Verdad de las Proposiciones Normativas', *Problemas lógicos en la teoría y práctica del Derecho* (Fundación Coloquio Jurídico Europeo 2009).

normative propositions. When judges decide a case, they are not merely *describing* how the legal order solves the individual case submitted to them. They are thereby *solving* it. Thus, when a judge rules in favour of the defendant, she is not merely stating that the defendant is strongly or weakly permitted not to φ; she is thereby permitting her not to φ. However, such individual norms cannot be justified by normative propositions. An individual norm can only be justified by general norms, that is, by showing that the individual case is an instance of a generic case that a legal norm correlates with a generic solution that corresponds to the solution prescribed by the individual norm, be it an obligation to φ or a permission not to φ. Thus, the ruling that thereby permits the defendant to φ is justified only if there is a general norm that permits the defendant not to φ. The mere fact that there is no norm that requires her to φ is not sufficient.

6. Neither Norms nor Normative Propositions

My criticism of the *Discretion Thesis* begins with the observation that Alchourrón and Bulygin's analysis of the Principle of Permission is not exhaustive. In fact, their argument presupposes that it expresses either a norm or a normative proposition. There is no third option. But this presupposition is, I think, unwarranted. Thus, I would like to suggest that deontic sentences can also express claims about rights and obligations.[20]

6.1 Claims about Rights and Obligations

To convey what I have in mind, consider the following example. Suppose you are telling me a story about your childhood. When you were five your aunt promised she would take you to the cinema to see a newly released film and kept her promise. I then observe that 'She acted as she had the obligation to act'. How should we understand this deontic sentence?

---

[20] For brevity, I am here using the expression 'rights' capaciously to refer not only to claim-rights but to other normative incidents as well, namely, permissions, normative powers, and immunities, whether they are rights in a strict sense or not.

Quite clearly, it does not express a norm. I am not purporting to thereby impose your aunt an obligation to take you to the cinema or anything of that sort.

But it does not seem plausible to consider that it expresses a normative proposition either. That would imply that I am asserting that there was a norm according to which your aunt had an obligation to take you to the cinema (or that such a norm belonged to some normative system) and that your aunt conformed to that norm. But what norm or normative system could I be talking about?

Your aunt's promise could be regarded as a norm in Bulygin's sense. In the same way that when a legislature enacts a norm, it is, roughly, purporting to thereby impose an obligation on citizens, when someone promises to do something, she is, roughly, purporting to thereby acquire an obligation to do it. But, in the example, I am not *merely* asserting that your aunt acted as she had promised. That assertion would have been consistent with me adding 'but she had no obligation to do so' while, arguably, what I said is not.

It could also be suggested that my deontic sentence expresses a normative proposition about moral norms. Thus, I would be asserting that there is a norm that establishes the obligation to keep our promises that belongs to the system of moral norms (or something like that), and that your aunt conformed to that norm. But that presupposes a rather legalistic view of morality, according to which morality is a system or set of norms.[21] Maybe some people do hold such a view. Maybe Kant thought that morality is the set of universal norms that a fully rational agent would enact as a law-making member of a merely possible kingdom of ends or some such. Maybe some rule consequentialists believe

---

[21] Remember that here we are talking about norms understood as prescriptions, that is, as prescriptive sentences or as what is expressed by such sentences. The expression 'norm' is used in a variety of ways, and there are perfectly legitimate uses in which talk of moral norms is sensible and not at all legalistic in any pejorative sense. Just to give an example, sometimes people talk about moral norms to refer not to prescriptions but to something analogous to laws of nature for the moral domain, i.e. very roughly, necessary truths stating that agents in such and in such circumstances, have such and such rights and obligations. On my vocabulary, these would be genuinely normative propositions of a distinctive kind rather than norms or normative propositions. Furthermore, I am not denying that there are moral norms (understood as prescriptions) nor that, in some relevant sense, they are metaphysically fundamental. I am just suggesting that we can intelligibly speak about rights and obligations independently of any norms (prescriptions).

that morality is the set of norms that would be optimific for all of us to follow. But these are idiosyncratic views. I, for one, find such legalistic conceptions of morality implausible. When I said that your aunt acted as she had an obligation to act, I was not, I hope, presupposing any such thing. Furthermore, even on those views, it would make sense to ask whether we are actually bound by, say, those universal norms that a fully rational being would enact as a law-making member of a possible kingdom of ends. Here, as in the case of promises, we could also distinguish between a normative proposition about such norms, and a claim about the right and obligations, if any, that obtain in virtue of them. And in the example, I am not *merely* asserting a normative proposition about moral norms (whatever those are). That would have been consistent with me adding 'but she had no obligation to act as she did' while, arguably, what I said is not.

This example suggests that, besides norms and normative propositions, deontic sentences can also express claims about rights and obligations. Furthermore, I believe that claims about rights and obligations are in a relevant sense conceptually more fundamental than norms and normative propositions. In fact, norms would be unintelligible for someone who lacked a minimal grasp of the notion of rights and obligations. Let us consider what Bulygin regards as a, if not the, paradigmatic case of a norm, that is, enacted norms. As far as I am aware, Bulygin never provided any detailed account of what it is to enact or issue a norm. Here is, in a nutshell, what I consider to be one of the most plausible accounts. For someone to enact or issue a norm, say, one according to which citizens have an obligation to wear black to funerals, is, very roughly, for her to communicate the intention to thereby impose on them the obligation to wear black to funerals by that very act of communication. Thus, when we refer to what such norms require or establish we are normally referring to the content of the thus communicated intention, that is, to the rights and obligations that the person or institution purported to bring about by that very act of communication (independently of whether she succeeded or not). If this account is more or less on the right track, then to be able to enact norms and to understand other people's actions as amounting to the enactment of a norm we need to have some grasp of what rights and obligations are. And analogous considerations could be made, I believe, regarding customary norms and precedents.

6.2 Rights and Obligations and Genuinely Normative Propositions

Thus far I have suggested that some deontic sentences do not express norms or normative propositions but rather claims about rights and obligations. However, I haven't said much about what claims about rights and obligations positively amount to. In particular, I have tried to remain neutral regarding whether we should be cognitivists or non-cognitivists about them.

According to cognitivism, claims about rights and obligations express belief in a proposition about deontic facts (i.e. facts about rights and obligations), and are therefore apt for robust[22] truth or falsity. This is often coupled with the view that there are deontic facts in virtue of which some such claims are true (rejection of error theory). Here I shall further assume that such deontic facts are to be understood in terms of irreducibly normative facts, that is, in terms of facts about what people have reason to do, feel, and believe, which cannot be reduced to natural, non-normative, facts (non-naturalism). To distinguish propositions about rights and obligations (understood as irreducibly normative facts) from Bulygin's normative propositions (i.e. propositions about enacted or customary norms), I shall refer to the former as *genuinely normative propositions*. And sometimes I will refer to rights and obligations as *genuine* rights and obligations just to highlight that I am referring to the reason-implying, irreducible normative, phenomena, rather than to what norms prescribe.

According to non-cognitivism, in contrast, claims about rights and obligations do not express belief in genuinely normative propositions but rather conative or non-cognitive mental states (emotions, attitudes of approval and disapproval, attitudes of norm-acceptance, etc.) and, thus, they are not apt for robust truth or falsity.

---

[22] The relevance of this qualification will be explained shortly.

My sympathies, as you might have noted, lie with cognitivism. Bulygin's, in contrast, lie with non-cognitivism. However, my argument in what follows does not depend on the truth of cognitivism. All that I will go on to say should be perfectly consistent with a sufficiently sophisticated version of non-cognitivism. Unlike old-fashioned emotivists, contemporary non-cognitivists do not claim that the surface of moral discourse is mistaken. Thus, they do not deny that there is a sense in which it is perfectly appropriate and meaningful to say, e.g. that it is true that your aunt had an obligation to do as she promised, that it is a fact that your aunt had such an obligation, and so on and so forth. They just provide a non-cognitivist account of what that means, that is, an account consistent with the insistence that the function of claims about rights and obligations is not to describe some putative deontic reality, so that they are not *robustly* true or false (i.e. true or false in the same way that claims about non-normative facts are). Thus, although in what follows I will talk of deontic facts, of propositions about such facts, of claims about rights and obligations being true or false, etc, sophisticated non-cognitivists should feel free to read these seemingly realist claims in their preferred non-cognitivist way.

7. Again on the Principle of Permission

The distinctions I have drawn in the last section also apply, *mutatis mutandis*, to *legal* deontic sentences. Thus, we should distinguish between legal norms and the legal rights and obligations that obtain in virtue of them in the appropriate way; and, correspondingly, between normative legal propositions (i.e. propositions about legal norms) and genuinely normative legal propositions (i.e. propositions about legal rights and obligations).[23]

On the assumption that those distinctions are sound, we can now see that there is a fourth possible reading of the Principle of Permission,

---

[23] Very roughly, legal rights and obligations are the rights and obligations that obtain in virtue of legal norms in the appropriate way. However, as I will highlight next, for an action to be legally permitted is for it to be the case that it is not legally prohibited, so that legal permissions need not obtain in virtue of a permissive of legal norm; it is enough for there not to be a genuine legal prohibition to ϕ that obtains in virtue of legal norms in the appropriate way.

not as a norm or a normative proposition, but as a genuinely normative proposition about legal rights and obligations. Thus:

Principle of Permission as a Genuinely Normative Proposition: For every action φ, if φ-ing is not genuinely legally prohibited then φ-ing is genuinely legally permitted.

Contra to what Alchourrón and Bulygin suggest, I think this is the reading that Kelsen and Raz had in mind. Thus understood, the Principle is, I believe, necessarily true. And Alchourrón and Bulygin should agree. In fact, as we saw, they explicitly claim that, as *norm-characters*, 'permission' and 'prohibition' are, interdefinable.[24] This implies that a norm that establishes that φ-ing is not prohibited is equivalent, by definition, to a norm that establishes that φ-ing is permitted. On my reconstruction, this means that for someone to communicate her intention of thereby making it the case that it is not genuinely prohibited to φ is equivalent to someone communicating her intention of thereby making it the case it is genuinely permitted to φ. Thus, an action not being prohibited in the genuinely normative sense must be equivalent, by definition, to its being permitted in the genuinely normative sense. Furthermore, given the interdefinability of obligation and permission, it also follows that an action not being obligatory in the genuinely normative sense is equivalent, by definition, to it being genuinely permitted not do it.

We should note that, on this interpretation, the Principle still doesn't rule out the possibility normative gaps as Alchourrón and Bulygin define them. Normative gaps are relative to a system of norms, and their existence or inexistence is completely independent of whatever genuine legal rights and obligations obtain in virtue of them. However, it does imply the impossibility of what we might call *genuinely* normative gaps, so that:

Genuinely Normative Gaps: There is a genuinely normative (legal) gap relative to an action φ if and only if φ-ing is neither genuinely (legally) prohibited nor genuinely (legally) permitted.

---

[24] Alchourrón and Bulygin, *Normative Systems* (n. 1) 123.

The impossibility of genuinely normative gaps has at least two import-ant related consequences. First, given the possibility of run of the mill cases of absence of legal regulation and of (non-genuine) normative gaps, the impossibility of genuine normative gaps implies that at least one of the following is possible: (i) there is genuine legal permission to φ (in a certain case) without there being a legal norm that permits φ-ing (in that case) in virtue of which that genuine permission obtains; or (ii) there is genuine legal prohibition to φ (in a certain case) without there being a legal norm that prohibits φ-ing (in that case) in virtue of which that prohibition obtains. The former possibility should be readily granted. In fact, at least normally, actions that are not regulated at all by a given legal system (like, say, writing a philosophy paper on New Year's Eve), will be actions that people have a genuine legal permission to do. Whether we should also acknowledge the latter possibility is something we will consider shortly.

The second important consequence is that, as I anticipated, the Discretion Thesis defended by Alchourrón and Bulygin must be false. Alchourrón and Bulygin are surely right in observing that rulings can-not be justified by appealing to normative propositions. But it does not follow that they can only be justified by appealing to norms. Rather rul-ings are to be justified by appealing to genuinely normative rights and obligations. Norms matter, to the extent that they do, because they give rise to genuinely normative rights and obligations. And, given the Principle of Permission, for every action φ, it is either genuinely obliga-tory to φ or genuinely permitted not to φ. In the former case, the judge is legally bound to rule in favour of the plaintiff. In the latter, she is bound to rule in favour of the defendant.

However, this argument does not commit us to accepting the asym-metry view, according to which ruling against the defendant requires a norm while ruling in her favour does not. The Principle of Permission implies that judges lack legal discretion in cases of normative gaps. But it says nothing about what it is that judges are legally bound to do in such cases. That depends on whether the defendant is genuinely permit-ted not to act as the plaintiff demands or not. But whether it is one or the other depends on what is the correct view about the way in which legal norms change our genuine rights and obligations. The asymmetry view assumes that only a legal norm that prohibits φ-ing (in c) can give rise to a genuinely normative prohibition to φ (in c), and thus concludes that the relevant action is always genuinely permitted in cases of normative gaps. But this is not implied by the Principle of Permission and would require independent justification. I will examine this issue in more detail in the next Section.

8. Legal Rights and Obligations in Cases of Normative Gaps

Here I cannot defend a complete account of the normativity of law that would help us determine the genuine deontic status of the relevant actions in cases of normative gaps. But let me at least briefly sketch two possible alternatives to the asymmetry view. For that purpose, let us consider once again the normative gaps in the old Argentine Civil Code concerning the recovery of real estate from third parties. Remember that, according to N1 and N2, three properties are relevant to determine the deontic status of the action of restoring the real estate, namely, whether the transfer was made in exchange for something, whether the transferor acted in good faith, and whether the transferee (i.e. the current possessor) acted in good faith. However, not every relevant case, built out of these properties, is correlated by a norm of the system with a relevant solution. There are, indeed, three normative gaps (viz, cases 1, 3, and 4). Now, given the impossibility of genuine normative gaps, we know that, even in such cases, the current possessor must either have a genuinely normative obligation to restore the real state or a genuinely normative permission not to do so. But, by itself, the Principle of Permission says nothing about which one is the case.

To make some progress, let us start by observing that for each of the relevant properties, the authority must have considered that there was some reason for the issue of whether the current possessor is obligated to restore the real estate or not to depend on its presence or absence. In fact, its reasoning here is not hard to grasp. The fact that the transfer was made in exchange for something, that the transferor acted in good faith, and that the transferee acted in good faith, were each considered by the authority to be a reason *against* imposing the latter an obligation to restore the thus acquired real estate. Furthermore, at the very least, it must have considered that these three reasons were jointly sufficient to defeat the main reason for imposing that obligation, namely, the fact that the transferor lacked a valid title. Otherwise, it wouldn't have gone into all this trouble, and would have simply established that the current possessor is always obligated to restore the real estate. Thus, the authority must have considered that in *Case 1* (which is characterized by exactly those three properties) it was justified to permit the current possessor not to restore the real state.

By an analogous reasoning, we should also conclude that the authority must have considered that it was justified to impose the current possessor the obligation to restore in *Case 4*. In fact, in *Case 2* the authority considered that it was justified to impose the current possessor the obligation to restore (see N1). But the only difference between *Case 2* and *Case 4* is that the current possessor acted in good faith in the former but not in the latter, and the fact that the current possessor acted in good faith was considered by the authority to be a reason *against* imposing her the obligation to restore the real estate to the original owner. So, if the authority considered that the balance of reasons favoured imposing her the obligation to restore the real estate to the original owner in *Case 2* (despite her good faith) then, *a fortiori*, it also should have considered the balance of reasons to favour imposing her the obligation to restore in *Case 4*.

Thus, to sum up, although *Cases 1* and *4* are normative gaps, we can conclude, given what we know about the authority's motivating reasons to enact norms N1 and N2, that it would have been irrational for her not to judge that it was justified to permit the current possessor not to restore the real estate in the former, and not to judge that it was justified to obligate her to do so in the latter.

Now, it would not be implausible for the correct theory of the normativity of law to deem these facts relevant to determine the genuine rights and obligations that obtain in virtue of the enacted norms. Thus, the idea would be that in *Case 1* the current possessor has a genuine legal permission not to restore the real estate in virtue of the fact that it would have been irrational for the authority not to judge that it was justified to so permit her or, simplifying, in virtue of the fact that it was irrational for the authority not to enact a norm so permitting her. And that, likewise, in *Case 4* the current possessor has a genuine legal obligation to restore it to the original owner in virtue of the fact that it would have been irrational for the authority not to judge that it was justified to impose such obligation or, simplifying, in virtue of the fact that it was irrational for the authority not to enact a norm so obligating her.

Note that the relevant irrationality judgements are not normative but rather concern the consistency of some of the authority's beliefs and attitudes with others. Thus, in principle, a legal positivist could accept this suggestion.

Case 3, however, is different. Like the other cases, it is characterized both by properties that the authority considered to be reasons in favour of imposing the current possessor an obligation to restore (i.e. lack of a valid title) and by properties that she considered reasons against doing so (i.e. consideration, transferor's good faith). But, in contrast with cases that are not normative gaps, there is no authoritative norm settling the conflict. And, in contrast with *Cases 1* and *4*, it would have been rational for the authority to solve such conflict one way or the other. This is what we might call a *troublesome* normative gap, that is, a normative gap such that there are at least two inconsistent norms that it would have been rational for the authority to enact to solve it.

One option here is to claim that, in cases of troublesome normative gaps, the relevant action is genuinely permitted. Thus, in our example, the current possessor would be genuinely permitted not to restore.

But another option, an antipositivist one, would be to claim that, in cases of troublesome normative gaps, whether the relevant action is genuinely obligatory or not, turns on whether it would be best for it to be so. Thus, in our example, if it would be better for the current possessor to have the obligation to restore, then she is genuinely obligated to restore. Otherwise, she is genuinely permitted not to do so. Note that this does not imply that people always have the legal rights and obligations that it would be better for them to have. That would be an absurd theory of law. The claim is much more limited: in cases of troublesome normative gaps, the issue of whether the relevant action is genuinely legally obligatory or not turns on whether it would be best for it to be so.

Thus, if we were to conclude that the current possessor is genuinely legally obligated to restore in Case 3, that fact would be grounded not only in the fact that it would be best for that to be the case, but also in the fact that the case has features that the legal authority judged to be reasons to impose that obligation and the fact that it wouldn't have been irrational for her to judge that it was justified in doing so.

We can summarize these three views concerning the genuine deontic status of actions in cases of normative gaps as follows:

Asymmetry View: In cases of normative gaps, the relevant action is always genuinely legally permitted.

Rationality View: In cases of non-troublesome normative gaps, the relevant action has the genuine deontic status that it would have had had the legal authority enacted the norm that it was irrational for her to not to enact. In cases that are troublesome normative gaps, the relevant action is genuinely permitted.

Antipositivist View: As the *Rationality View* in cases of non-troublesome normative gaps. But in cases of troublesome normative gaps, the relevant action has the genuine deontic status that it would be best for it to have.

These alternatives are obviously not exhaustive. And any of these views would need to be defended by appealing to an underlying account of the distinctive mechanism by which legal norms give rise to rights and obligations. But I hope that sketching these alternatives gives you a sense of the range of possibilities, and of how the discussion would have to proceed.

9. On the Importance of Normative Gaps

I have argued that although Alchourrón and Bulygin are right in claiming that it is possible for legal orders to have normative gaps, they are wrong in claiming that judges have legal discretion as a result. The explanation is that, as Kelsen and Raz had argued before, there are no *genuinely* normative gaps. Someone might argue that once our attention

is drawn to such a distinction, then it is obvious that it is genuinely normative gaps that really matter, and since those are impossible, then there
is not much interest in the notion of normative gaps developed by
Alchourrón and Bulygin. However, this would be a serious mistake for
at least three reasons.

First, although in cases of normative gaps the relevant action must be
either genuinely permitted or genuinely prohibited, it is not easy to
determine which one it is. Those who, like Kelsen and Raz do not
adequately distinguish between normative gaps and other cases of
absence of legal regulation, tend to hastily conclude that whenever the
law is 'silent' the action at issue must be genuinely permitted, thus
adhering to the asymmetry view. But, as we saw, such solution is far
from being obvious, even for legal positivists, at least in cases of non-
troublesome normative gaps.

Second, if one were to accept the Asymmetry View or the Rationality
View, there would be reasons to explicitly grant judges legal discretion
in cases of normative gaps that are not present in run of the mill cases of
absence of legal regulation. Let us put ourselves in the legislative authority's shoes. We know that, even if we are diligent, there will likely be
some troublesome normative gaps, that exhibit features we deem reasons
for imposing a legal obligation to φ, and reasons against doing so,
without us having settled the conflict. We also know that, in such cases,
the agent will be legally permitted not to φ independently of the relative
weight of such reasons. Sometimes we will regard this as a regrettable
circumstance. But there is something we could do about it. We could
explicitly grant courts legal discretion in such cases, so that they can
decide as they see fit, according to their view of the relative merits of the
applicable reasons.[25] Normally courts are legally bound to rule by relying on the pre-existing legal rights and obligations of the parties. But
there is no obstacle for the law to grant courts the authority to decide
some cases in ways that are not dictated by the parties pre-existing legal
rights and obligations. Arguably, the law cannot grant them such authority
in all cases, and there are normally very good reasons not to do so. But
in cases of troublesome normative gaps, the reasons for conferring such

---

[25] See e.g. Article 1 of the Austrian Civil Code.

discretion will be weightier, other things being equal. In fact, these are cases where, although it is legally permitted not to ϕ, there are also features that a legal authority deemed to be reasons to impose a legal obligation to ϕ. The relevance of this fact is twofold. On the one hand, that reason normally doubles as a reason for courts to impose such an obligation, and so for legislative authorities to confer them the ability to do so. On the other hand, it weakens the force of what Hrafn Asgeirsson has called the *No Violation!* objection that defendants have against courts ordering them to do something they had not ex ante legal obligation to do.[26] These considerations are missing in run of the mill cases of absence of legal regulation.

Third, if one were to accept the Rationality View or the Antipositivist View, legislative authorities will sometimes have reasons to enact closure norms (of the sort considered in Section 4). In fact, it is often better for people to have a legal permission to ϕ that is relatively easy for judges and citizens to establish, than them having the rights and obligations regarding ϕ that it would be better for them to have, or that it would be irrational for the authority not to grant them, but with a higher probability of those being misidentified.

These brief considerations show that, even if normative gaps as Alchourrón and Bulygin understand them do not entail legal discretion, we still have reasons to single them out, both in virtue of the distinctive way in which our rights and obligations are established in such cases, and in virtue of having normatively relevant features that can constitute reasons for legislative authorities to (i) explicitly grant courts the authority to decide in ways that are no dictated by the parties' legal rights and obligations; as well as ii) to pre-emptively eliminate them by enacting permissive closure norms.

Ezequiel Monti, *Bulygin on Legal Gaps and the Normativity of Law* In: *Oxford Studies in Philosophy of Law, Volume 5.* Edited by: Leslie Green and Brian Leiter, Oxford University Press. © Ezequiel Monti 2024. DOI: 10.1093/9780198919650.003.0004

[26] Hrafn Asgeirsson, 'A Puzzle about Vagueness, Reasons, and Judicial Discretion' (2022), 28 *Legal Theory* 210.

Legal Realism in France

Michel Troper

I. Introduction

Realism in France is not part of a general philosophical doctrine like, for example, pragmatism or empiricism, nor was it created within one of the dominant doctrines of legal philosophy, like natural law or legal positivism, simply because, until the 1980s, legal philosophy was almost non-existent in France. It was not part of the curriculum of most law schools, except for two, one in Paris, one in Strasbourg, where it was optional. The same was true in the philosophy departments, where scholars had little interest in the law, in great part because of the influence of Marxism or phenomenology. In any case, the law schools were institutionally cut off from the rest of the university, in particular from the philosophy and social science departments; the faculty, the students, and the curriculum were completely separate.

Another symptom of the weakness of legal philosophy in France was the scarcity of publications: there was only one journal with the title *"philosophie du droit"* and it was a yearly; law reviews rarely published articles related to the field; there were very few books, whether textbooks or monographs, and very few translations of foreign books. French academics were cut off from debates going on in other countries, as they were, for institutional reasons, from departments of philosophy. Before 1962, when Charles Eisenmann published his translation of the 2nd edition of Kelsen's *Pure Theory of Law*, Kelsen had only been known through a few articles, mostly on constitutional review and a defective translation of the 1st edition, published in Switzerland, with very little circulation; H. L. A. Hart was only translated in Belgium in 1976.[1] Those very rare scholars with an interest in legal philosophy were either Thomists, like Michel Villey, or Kelsenians, like Charles Eisenmann, and no reference was ever made to realism, whether American or Scandinavian. It was not until the 1970s that a few scholars, mostly at the University of Paris at Nanterre, became aware of realist theories under the influence of American, Scandinavian, and above all Italian literature,

I will first outline the general context that can help explain the development of Realism in France at this particular moment; secondly, I will situate French realism within the tradition of legal positivism and other and more ancient schools of realism; and thirdly, I will describe a few features that distinguish French from other schools of realism, especially the Italian.

II. The context

The new developments that took place in the 1970s can be explained by several factors: new research on legal and constitutional history, especially history on the Revolution; the constitutional changes in the Fifth Republic; and, finally, a reinterpretation of Kelsen's Pure Theory.

The main character of legal realism in France is its focus on the theory of interpretation. Indeed, it is sometimes described, by scholars who are not realists, as TRI ("Théorie Réaliste de l'Interprétation"), but this should not be surprising since the question whether judges merely apply law or produce law has been central in French legal and political history and depends on theories about the nature of legal interpretation. Judges in France have often been at odds with political power. There were periods when they confronted the sovereign, others when they were strictly restrained, and the conflict depended to a large extent on diverging theories of interpretation, with judges pretending that interpretation is the discovery of the true meaning of

---

[1] KELSEN, Hans. *Théorie pure du droit*, trad. Charles Eisenmann (Paris: Dalloz, 1962); HART, H. L. A. *Le concept de droit*, 1re édition, trad. Michel Van De Kerchove et al. (Bruxelles: Presses de l'Université Saint-Louis, 1976).

the rules, which they can apply without imposing their own political, religious, or moral preferences—while the king's lawyers assert that only he could know (or decide) what the true meaning was. Legal interpretation is thus a highly charged political issue in France, central to the question whether there is or ought to be an independent judicial power.

French constitutional history, going back to the "Ancien Régime", shows the importance and the dangers of a powerful judiciary. Before the Revolution, the Parliaments, which were sovereign courts of appeal, had resisted the King's power, whose laws they reviewed against some "fundamental laws of the realm", before "registering" them and making them applicable. The fundamental laws were for the most part unwritten principles, which courts constructed freely and often used to refuse registration. Resisting the absolute monarch was not perceived as a defense of liberty, but rather as a defense of privileges, because judges were necessarily members of the nobility who had bought or inherited their position, and this in a country where the nobility already enjoyed enormous privileges, such as tax exemptions and the exercise of certain feudal powers over the peasantry. Moreover, the French intellectuals did not resent sovereignty, but only that it was lodged in a monarch. The obvious conclusion was that judges ought to be subject to the law, i.e. to general laws enacted by representatives of the sovereign people.

In Montesquieu's words, "the judiciary is, in some measure, next to nothing"[2] and one of his first disciples, Beccaria, held that adjudication ought to be conducted by means of syllogisms, so that the sentence would be a mere deduction from legislation, i.e. statutes.[3] This implied that judges should be prevented from manipulating the major premise, the rule derived from the text of the statute, especially by means of interpretation. The overwhelming majority of members of the National Assembly that drafted the first French constitution between 1789 and 1791 were deeply influenced by these ideas. They developed a

---

[2] MONTESQUIEU, Charles. *Complete Works*, vol. 1, *The Spirit of Laws* (T. Evans, 1748), Book XI, Chap. 6. He adds that "the national judges are no more than the mouth that pronounces the words of the law, mere passive beings, incapable of moderating either its force or rigour".

[3] BECCARIA, Cesare, *An Essay on Crimes and Punishments* (1764), chap. IV.

conception of legal interpretation very close to the modern realist views and wanted to resist allowing the courts to do any interpretation. They held that interpretation of the law was a re-creation and thus a usurpation of the legislative power, which ought to be exercised solely by the representatives of the sovereign people. Interpretation of statutes ought therefore to be reserved to the law maker—not, as in the case of the King, because having enacted the law in the first place, he knows what his intention was and thus the meaning of the text—but because the power to interpret is a form of legislative power. It is remarkable that this was a mere repetition in a different context of the old formula "*ejus est interpretari legem cujus est condere*".

The National Assembly drew the same conclusions as the King's lawyers from this idea about interpretation and, even before the constitution was finally enacted, they passed a law on the judiciary, which is still in force.[4] The law presumed that the law is always clear and that no interpretation is necessary. Thus, for judges to interpret would amount to attempting a usurpation of the legislative power; hence, the law strictly prohibited judicial interpretation, attaching very severe penalties. In the rare case when the text was really obscure, the judge had an obligation to refer the matter to the legislature.[5] The prohibition of judicial interpretation was repeated in the Civil Code and has been maintained, at least formally, to the present day.

However, since it is absolutely impossible to avoid interpretation, judges not only continued *surreptitiously* to interpret the laws, but the official prohibition had the perverse effect of reinforcing their power.[6] First, the Constituent Assembly itself, recognizing in fact the necessity to interpret, distinguished between interpretation *in abstracto*, which was prohibited, and interpretation *in concreto*, which was not only permitted but mandatory. Interpretation *in abstracto* consists in determining the

---

[4] Loi des 16–24 août 1790 sur l'organisation judiciaire.

[5] Article 10: «Les tribunaux ne pourront prendre directement ou indirectement aucune part à l'exercice du pouvoir législatif, ni empêcher ou suspendre l'exécution des décrets du Corps législatif, sanctionnés par le Roi, à peine de forfaiture»; article 11: «Ils ne pourront point faire de règlements, mais ils s'adresseront au corps législatif toutes les fois qu'ils croiront nécessaire, soit d'interpréter une loi, soit d'en faire une nouvelle».

[6] TROPER, Michel. «La forza dei precedenti e gli effetti perversi del diritto», *Ragion pratica* (juin 1996), p. 65.

meaning of a text in general, independently of the facts, even before a case has been brought before the judge; indeed, it determines the category under which the facts of an actual case will be subsumed. Because it is general, this interpretation, according to the Constituent Assembly, amounts to changing the rule or making a new one, and thus constitutes an impermissible exercise of legislative power. Interpretation *in concreto*, by contrast, consists in assuming that the meaning of the text is clear, that this meaning is the rule and thus involves merely subsuming the facts under that rule.[7]

The latter was mandatory, because refusing to make a decision on the grounds (or the pretext, as the civil code would later say) that the law is obscure or incomplete would amount to a denial of justice and was also a crime.[8] Interpretation *in concreto* was simply disguised as mere "application" of the law, but, because one could not tolerate diverging interpretations, judicial decisions could be referred to a national "tribunal of cassation" in case of "false application". The tribunal of cassation did not review the case but only the legal reasoning. In case of a very serious difficulty involving a problem of interpretation, the tribunal ought to refer the case to the legislature, but this has never happened. Since the tribunal was national and the lower tribunals were de facto constrained by its decisions, it was able to produce in a centralized manner interpretations it labelled the "correct application of the law", when actually the tribunal was offering interpretations *in abstracto*, i.e. a new statement of the general rule. In fact, after the enactment of the civil code in 1804, the "tribunal de cassation", later renamed "cour de cassation" was able to produce a vast body of judge-made law. For example, today the law of torts is still the result of the interpretation by the cour de

[7] The distinction is still being used to day, without using the word "interpretation." It is customary to oppose two forms of review of legislation, one that is abstract and *a priori*, which is exercised by the Constitutional Council immediately after Parliament has adopted a new law, when the Council evaluates the law in light of the constitution; the other, that is a *posteriori* and concrete, which is exercised by ordinary courts when they confront a law already in force with international treaties; cf. DUTHEILLET DE LA MOTHE, Olivier. «Contrôle de constitutionnalité et contrôle de conventionnalité», in *Juger l'administration, administrer la justice: Mélanges en l'honneur de Daniel Labetoulle* (Paris: Dalloz, 2007). Often, interpretation *in concreto* is not called "interpretation" but "qualification des faits"; cf. infra n. 24.

[8] Civil code, Article 4: "A judge who refuses to give judgment on the pretext of legislation being silent, obscure or insufficient may be prosecuted for being guilty of a denial of justice."

cassation of only three articles of the code. Yet the denial that interpretation takes place persisted and, while the civil code had a few articles regarding interpretative methods for contracts, there was no such provision regarding statutory interpretation.

The official prohibition on interpretation had a second unexpected effect: since the courts had to disguise interpretation as mere application of the law, they just claimed that the text was clear and there was no need to justify the interpretation that was actually imposed on the text. Thus, decisions were kept very brief, sometimes only one or two paragraphs and neither the court of cassation nor the lower courts were constrained by any methods of interpretation, nor any previous reasoning.

Judges were also prohibited from interfering not only with the legislative power, but also with public administration. This was interpreted as a prohibition to decide cases between public administration and private parties. It would indeed have been difficult for them to decide such cases, because there were very few laws in administrative matters that could be applicable by way of syllogistic reasoning. Administrative authorities were not given precise directives, but most often general objectives such as the defense of public order or the general interest, and were necessarily left with wide discretionary powers. If civil judges had been given jurisdiction over these cases, they would inevitably themselves have exercised discretion and controlled public administration.

But again, this latter prohibition contributed to the emergence and the growth of a jurisdictional power. Since ordinary judges were prohibited from deciding these cases, a separate court system was established with exclusive jurisdiction over administrative matters, with a distinct supreme court, the Conseil d'Etat. Because there were no administrative codes or applicable laws, the Conseil d'Etat had to produce a whole body of case law, using methods resembling those of the Common Law. Formally, administrative courts are not part of the judiciary and judges on these courts have a different status, but they also present their decisions as mere application of pre-existing law, albeit not statutory law, but general principles that the Conseil d'Etat pretends to discover and that have the same status as statutes. In theory, statutes can override them, but since constitutional review has been introduced during the Fifth Republic, the Constitutional Council, whose legal doctrines have been to a great extent imported from the Conseil d'Etat, tended to preserve the general principles by granting them constitutional status.

Thus, not only did the prohibition of judicial interpretation not limit the power of the courts, it actually played a major role in increasing that power. The development of this power has been greatly facilitated by the prevalent legal scholarship, which helped to conceal it by refusing to classify "jurisprudence" (the French word for case law) among the sources of law. Only statutory law and perhaps customary law were considered sources of law, but "jurisprudence", along with legal scholarship, had mere persuasive authority.[9] When it became impossible to deny that judges do interpret, the prevailing view was that they discover the "true" meaning of the text using specific methods of interpretation. It was thus possible to accept the idea that interpretation does take place without acknowledging that judges, in fact, enjoy discretion and create law.

This conception of the judicial power as inferior and subsidiary to the general will as expressed in statutes had yet another consequence: it was incompatible with any form of review of legislation, much less with judicial review. One notable attempt, most probably inspired by the councils of censors that had been created in a few American states,[10] was made in 1795 by Emmanuel Sieyes under the name "jury constitution-naire". Sieyes's proposal was far from what would later be called "judicial review," because his "jury" was a body of representatives of the people, composed not of judges, but of former members of the legislature. They would not be able to strike down statutes, but only decisions taken separately by one or the other section of the legislature, and this mostly for violations of procedural rules. In any case, it was unanimously rejected by the National Convention, which argued that it was useless because the constitution provided sufficient internal guarantees and also dangerous because "who would guard the guardians?".

In 1921, Edouard Lambert, a professor of comparative law, published a very influential book with the title "le Gouvernement des juges"

---

[9] See the foremost manual on civil law: CARBONNIER, Jean. *Droit civil. 1: Introduction.* 17. éd., mise à jour. Thémis Droit (Paris: Pr. Univ. de France, 1988), pp. 136–42.
[10] *See the Constitution of Pennsylvania*, September 28, 1776, Sect. 47, https://avalon.law.yale.edu/18th_century/pa08.asp.

(government by the judiciary).[11] Lambert criticized the American institution of judicial review that gave judges too much power, in virtue of their capacity to invalidate laws by interpreting the constitution and to decide cases effectively according to their political preferences in a manner that was incompatible with the supremacy of law enacted by representatives of the people. However, the book's success was not due to this view of legal interpretation, but mostly to the expression "gouvernement des juges" which was used as a slogan to reject every suggestion by scholars or (rarely) by politicians to allow some sort of review of legislation by the judiciary. Thus, the classical theory of legal interpretation continued to prevail.

Suggestions by legal scholars to allow for judicial review or to create a constitutional court had been made in Europe, even in France, towards the end of the nineteenth century due to the development of the German ideology of the *Rechtsstaat* or its Anglo-American equivalent, the rule of law: consistency seemed to demand that the submission of public administration or the judiciary to higher norms be matched with a similar submission of the law maker to judicial review. In this respect, Kelsen's proposal in the twentieth century to establish a specialized constitutional court did spark a debate. All these suggestions presupposed that constitutional review is a neutral process, a mere confrontation of a statute with the constitution, whose meaning is normally clear and, in the rare case when it is not, the meaning will nonetheless be reliably retrieved by the judge.

In the end, none of these suggestions were successful, but not because scholars or politicians rejected the theory of interpretation that they had assumed all along. The reason was always the same: the law is the expression of the general will, i.e. the will of the sovereign, and by definition, the sovereign cannot be limited, not even by a rule whose meaning can be applied in a neutral and impartial manner. It must be stressed that in the legal tradition of the French revolution, there cannot be a real

---

[11] LAMBERT, Edouard. *Le gouvernement des juges et la lutte contre la législation sociale* (Paris: 1921; new edition Paris: Dalloz, 2005); HEUSCHLING, Luc. «Edouard Lambert. Le gouvernement des juges et la lutte contre la législation sociale aux États-Unis. L'expérience américaine du contrôle judiciaire de la constitutionnalité des lois». *Revue internationale de droit comparé* 59, no. 4 (2007), 958–61.

hierarchy between constitution and statute, since both are the expression of the general will: thus, a statute conflicting with the constitution is only a change of will. As Sieyes used to say "let us not be afraid to repeat it; a nation is independent of any form, and in whatever way it wills, it suffices that its will appear for all positive right to yield before it, as before the source and the very master of all positive right".[12]

Things finally began to change with the constitution of the Fifth Republic in 1958, which introduced a new type of authority, the Constitutional Council. Originally, the Council was far from resembling a constitutional court and it was not established with the intention that it would eventually become one. On the contrary, the writers declared explicitly that the Council would not be empowered to invalidate statutes for a violation of human rights, because that would amount to a "gouvernement des juges". In fact, the reason for the creation of this new institution was that the constitution had divided the "domains" of legislation and made two lists: one consisted of domains that were to be regulated by statutes, i.e. acts of Parliament, the other of domains to be regulated by decrees of the Executive. It was, therefore, necessary to create an authority (the Constitutional Council) to decide on the inevitable conflicts of jurisdiction, at least with regard to possible infringements by Parliament over the jurisdiction of the Executive. After a statute has been enacted by Parliament, but during the short period of two weeks until promulgation by the President of the Republic, a statute can be referred to the Council, i.e. *a priori*, by the President himself, the Prime Minister, or one of the chair persons of the houses of Parliament. The Council then reviews it against the text of the constitution and in case it decides that it is unconstitutional, the President may not promulgate it.

In the constituent's view, the constitution was understood *stricto sensu as composed only of those provisions that had a number*, i.e. without the Preamble or the Declaration of the Rights of Man. Since the constitution in this sense did not mention fundamental rights, the Council was

---

[12] «Ne craignons pas de le répéter; une nation est indépendante de toute forme, et de quelque manière qu'elle veuille, il suffit que sa volonté paraisse pour que tout droit positif cède devant elle, comme devant la source et le maître même de tout droit positif»; *Reconnaissance et exposition raisonnée des droits de l'homme et du citoyen*, in E.-J. SIEYÈS, *Ecrits politiques*, R. Zapperi éd. (Paris: Éditions des archives contemporaines, 1985), 198–9.

not expected to review the constitutionality of the contents of statutes, but mostly to check on procedural defects, especially infringements by Parliament on the domains of the Executive. But in 1971, in a case acknowledged as the French *Marbury v. Madison*, the Council in a bold decision, based on a very broad interpretation of the text of the constitution, extended its own powers to invalidate statutes that were substantially unconstitutional, not only because they violated the numbered articles of the constitution, but also because they infringed principles mentioned in the preamble.[13] The preamble itself is very brief and vague, but refers to the Declaration of the Rights of Man and the Citizen of 1789, which until 1971 had not been considered legally binding, and also to the Preamble of the Constitution of 1946. The latter Preamble itself enumerates a number of new principles of economic and social rights. It also referred to the "fundamental principles recognized by the laws of the Republic". The Preamble of 1946 did not give a list or a definition of these fundamental principles, but in its 1971 decision, the Constitutional Council chose to construe that expression as referring to principles that pre-existed statutes. Allegedly, when enacting certain laws, Parliaments of the past had not posited these fundamental principles but merely "recognized" them. Since the Preamble of the Constitution had mentioned them, they possessed constitutional status and a new statute that contradicted these principles would be unconstitutional. In 1971, the statute that had been referred to the Constitutional Council brought some restrictions to freedom of association. Associations were regulated by a very liberal statute of 1901. Since there was no provision regarding associations in the text of the constitution *stricto sensu*, the Council used the Preamble. Neither the Declaration of the Rights of Man nor the Preamble of 1946 mention the freedom of association. Therefore, the Council's only choice, if it was bound to invalidate the 1971 statute, was to confront it to the statute of 1901, but since a new statute can freely derogate an older statute, it could only be declared unconstitutional if the older statute had constitutional status. This was only possible if it was assumed that the 1901 Parliament had not expressed its will but had "recognized" freedom of association as a

---

[13] Décision no. 71–44 DC du 16 juillet 1971, Loi complétant les dispositions des articles 5 et 7 de la loi du 1er juillet 1901 relative au contrat d'association.

fundamental principle, akin to those that had been "declared" in 1789. Since 1971, the Constitutional Council has identified ten other principles, that only the constituent power could derogate.[14] The Council had thus acquired not only a new power to review the constitutionality of statutes, but also the power to change the hierarchy of norms and, by promoting statutes to the constitutional level, to fill the constitution with new principles.

At this point, it became difficult to maintain the fiction that adjudication does not require interpretation, or that interpretation was a mere discovery of the "real" meaning of the law. The time was now ripe to challenge these fictions. Thus, in the 1990s a few scholars became aware of legal realism, first through the question of legal interpretation and developing from there other ideas, some common to other and more established forms of realism, some more specific to the French context. Among the former are the ideas that there is no natural law, that law exists only as a social fact, the product of human behavior and human discourse, and that legal interpretation is central to the functioning of the legal system. Among the latter, there was a particular attention to the substance of French law, to legal history and, to an effort to find causal explanations for the social facts about law.

III. French realism as an instance of positivism

Norberto Bobbio famously distinguished between three meanings of the term positivism:[15] as a methodological approach to the law, as a theory about the nature of law, and as an ideology. The first approach to the law

---

[14] In addition to freedom of association, the rights to defend oneself in court, individual freedom, freedom of education, freedom of conscience, the independence of a separate administrative court system, the independence of university professors and lecturers, the exclusive jurisdiction of administrative courts for the annulment or reform of decisions taken in the exercise of the prerogatives of public power, the exclusive jurisdiction of judicial courts for cases related to private real estate property, the existence of specialized criminal courts for minors, the use of local laws on religion in Alsace and Moselle. Naturally, the Constitutional Council could always identify more "fundamental principles recognized by the laws of the republic"; see SENAC, Charles-Edouard. «Y a-t-il encore place pour la découverte de nouveaux principes fondamentaux reconnus par les lois de la République? Conseil constitutionnel», https://www.conseil-constitutionnel.fr/publications/titre-vii/y-a-t-il-encore-place-pour-la-decouverte-de-nouveaux-principes-fondamentaux-reconnus-par-les-lois-de.

[15] BOBBIO, Norberto. *Giusnaturalismo e positivismo giuridico* (Roma: Laterza, 2011).

maintains a strict distinction between the law as it is and the law as it ought to be, remaining ethically neutral in order to treat the law as an objective phenomenon, that can be described by methods akin to those of the empirical sciences. The second meaning of legal positivism is closely connected to the emergence of the modern state: it emphasizes the idea that law is a system of rules posited by the state, that court decisions are mere applications of pre-existing rules, that interpretation is a description of the true meaning of a legal text, however different the views about the nature of these rules may be.[16] Finally, legal positivism as an ideology is the view that positive law is just, by the mere fact of being posited by the will of a political authority, something that ought to be obeyed, whatever its content. No legal positivists, including Bobbio, actually accepted this last view. Bobbio was also very careful to stress that there is no necessary or logical connection between these three ways of understanding legal positivism and that they may even be incompatible. For example, legal positivism as a scientific approach is characterized by a commitment to neutrality and a refusal to prescribe, while legal positivism as an ideology involves precisely a prescription, namely, to obey the law.

In France, legal positivism in Bobbio's first sense was never very strong.[17] Most scholars who identified as positivists used the label to claim neutrality, while disguising as a description of the law what was in reality an expression of their preferences about the law that ought to be. Realism, by contrast, obviously belongs to positivism in the first sense. Not only do realists want to construct a legal science distinct from the law itself and refrain from prescribing or formulating value judgments, but they want that legal science to be as close as possible to the empirical sciences.[18] For the French realists, as for the Scandinavians and the

---

[16] In the Anglophone world, this tends to be described as "formalism" rather than "positivism." H. L. A. Hart, however, does note a similar sense of the term, for example in Positivism, Law and Morals, in HART, H. L. A. *Essays in Jurisprudence and Philosophy* (Oxford: Oxford University Press, 1983), 57 note 25, ("it may help to identify five meanings of positivism (the contention that laws are commands…2 the contention that there is no necessary contention between la and morals…").

[17] TROPER, M. (2021). "The French Tradition of Legal Positivism". In T. SPAAK and P. MINDUS (eds.), *The Cambridge Companion to Legal Positivism* (Cambridge: Cambridge University Press), 133–51.

[18] ROSS, Alf. «Validity and the Conflict between Legal Positivism and Natural Law», *Revista Jurídica de Buenos Aires*, V (1961), reproduced in *Normativity and Norms: Critical Perspectives on Kelsenian Themes*, ed. Stanley L. PAULSON (Oxford: Oxford University Press, 1999), 146–63.

Italians, the connection to positivism and the empirical conception of science presupposes a non-cognitivist and relativist philosophy of values,[19] as well as an ontological thesis: that "law is fact" to put it in a slogan. What in the law is a fact still remains to be discussed.

What may be specific to the French realists is that the factual character of law arises from an analysis of the process of interpretation. The meaning of a legal text is not inherent in the text, but rather ascribed by an authorized interpreter. Non-realists also believe that the interpreter has been authorized, empowered by a norm expressed in a legal text, but realists argue that, since this legal text is being interpreted, it is the interpreter who decides that the legal text gives him the power to interpret. The interpreter, in other words, is that person or group who is in a position to successfully claim that he has been authorized to interpret and exercise a monopoly of the power of interpretation. Thus, the facts of the law are, indeed, the expressions of will: either the will of the legislator who by adopting a text enacts a law or, crucially, the will of the interpreter. These are empirical facts that can be studied as such and assertions about these facts can be true or false.

IV. Some features of French realism

A. Radical skepticism

It may seem strange that the most important influence on French realism has been that of Kelsen, but this can be explained by the conjunction of two factors. One that has already been mentioned was the growth of the Constitutional Council only a few years after it had been created at the beginning of the Fifth Republic. Because Kelsen had been very influential in the creation of the Austrian constitutional court in 1920—which had served, before 1958, as a model for the constitutional courts of Italy, Germany, and Spain—French scholars turned to Kelsen and to his main representative and translator, Charles Eisenmann, to find a justification for the institution of constitutional review, which was so

---

[19] It is "non-cognitivist" in denying that value judgments have truth-values; and it is relativist in recognizing that value judgments vary with social and cultural context.

contrary to the traditional French hostility towards the "gouvernement des juges".[20] The second factor was the apparent contradiction between the theory that courts do not interpret and merely apply the law (including the constitution) and the fact that the growth of the Constitutional Council was due to an extremely audacious interpretation of the text of the constitution of 1958, a contradiction that required at least a careful examination of Kelsen's theory of interpretation.

This contradiction mirrors a contradiction within Kelsen's view of constitutional review, a contradiction that is twofold. First, there is a contradiction between Kelsen's justification for the democratic character of the constitutional court and his theory of democracy. One of his arguments for the democratic character of the court is that it does not decide on the merits of an act of Parliament, but only on the procedure, because finding that an act is unconstitutional means that it should have been adopted not by the legislature but by the constituent power, by way of an amendment to the constitution. Kelsen believes that this procedure is democratic because the amending procedure requires a qualified majority, i.e. the consent of a larger part of the elected representatives. In so arguing, he apparently forgot his own argument that a procedure requiring a qualified majority is not more but less democratic than a simple majority since it allows a minority to block a proposal willed by the majority.

Secondly, there is a contradiction between this justification and his own theory of legal interpretation that he develops in the last chapter of the *Pure Theory*. The argument that the court decides on the procedure and remains politically neutral is based on the presupposition that it is not really a decision, but a mere "confrontation" between the text of the law and the constitution in order to check whether the substance of the law came within the jurisdiction of Parliament. But, again, Kelsen seems to forget that this confrontation requires an interpretation of both texts and that, according to his own theory, interpretation does not involve knowledge (in a sense I will explain in a moment). Because the

---

[20] EISENMANN, Charles. *La justice constitutionnelle et la Haute Cour Constitutionnelle d'Autriche: édition de 1928* (nlle édit. Paris: LGDJ, Paris: Economica, 1986); TROPER, Michel. «Kelsen et la théorie de la justice constitutionnelle», in *Kelsen, Hans. Autobiographie*, ed. Eric MILLARD (Paris: Dalloz, 2023), 143–62.

Constitutional Council had been able to extend dramatically its own powers by means of an interpretation of the constitution, and because that extension clearly happened in a heavily political context (when the Council acted as an opponent to the President of the Republic), it became hard to keep the fiction that interpretation is politically neutral and consists merely in the discovery of the true meaning of a text. A new reading of Kelsen's theory of legal interpretation was required.

In the last chapter of the *Pure Theory*, Kelsen makes a sharp distinction between "scientific" and "authentic" interpretation. The former, which is an epistemic act, consists in identifying all possible meanings of a norm, thus creating a "frame"; the latter, which is an act of the will, is a choice within that frame of the meaning that will be ascribed to the norm. The norm is then valid in the sense determined by the authentic interpreter, who has thus created law. Although illuminating, Kelsen's presentation is defective in several ways and does not go far enough. Yet, we can draw several consequences from these defects.

Kelsen contends that a norm has multiple meanings. However, according to his own definition, a norm *is* the meaning of an act. Since a norm is a meaning, it cannot have a meaning. Therefore, since one cannot determine the meaning of a meaning, the real object of interpretation cannot be a norm but rather a text, and the meaning of the text is the norm. If authentic interpretation is an act of will, it follows that the interpreter is the real producer of the norm.

On the other hand, the distinction between scientific and authentic interpretation has no practical consequence, because only an authentic interpretation has legal consequences. Ultimately, the law only validates or sanctions behavior in accordance with the text as interpreted by the authentic interpreter; any other meaning within the "frame" discovered by scientific interpretation becomes irrelevant. A court interpreting a statute does not really apply the statute, but rather the norm it has itself created by means of interpretation. Even if a statute has never been interpreted by a court, people who comply with the law have to interpret it and since their interpretation is subject to review by an authentic interpreter, they have to base their behavior on the most probable interpretation by a court.

One may certainly object that there is at least one norm that such a court must apply: the norm that has created the court and defined its power, in particular the power to give an authentic interpretation. However, this norm has necessarily been expressed by a text and this text is also subject to interpretation. The court is therefore in a position to decide on its own powers. This is precisely what happened in *Marbury v. Madison* in the United States; or in France in 1971, when the constitution was construed to mean that the Council had the power to review the constitutionality of legislation; or again in Israel when the Supreme Court gave itself the power of judicial review although there is no constitutional text in Israel.[21] It is thus true that the court's power is based on an empowering norm, but that norm has been produced by the court itself.

This preceding form of rule skepticism is close to that of John Chipman Gray and also of the Italian realists, who deeply influenced the French. There are however some differences. In this paper I will consider here only the most significant differences with Guastini.[22]

Guastini favors a more moderate version of legal realism and criticizes the radical skepticism of French realism, on two main grounds. Firstly, he contends that the French view rests on the assumption that legal texts, until they have been interpreted, have no meaning whatsoever, not even a *prima facie* meaning, so that anything goes. However, for French realists, the idea that legal texts have no meaning is not a point of departure but a point of arrival.

Naturally, every text has meaning, even several meanings, since we can understand them. The skeptical thesis rests on a distinction between the meaning of a text in ordinary language and its meaning in the law. In case of a conflict between the two, it is only the latter that matters because, once the authentic interpreter has decided on a meaning, i.e. what

---

[21] CA 6821/93 Bank Mizrahi v. Migdal Cooperative Village. Decided: November 9, 1995.

[22] I discussed Guastini's views more extensively in TROPER, Michel, «Sur la théorie guastinienne de l'interprétation. La distinction entre text-oriented et fact-oriented interpretation». Pierluigi CHIASSONI, Paolo COMANDUCCI, and Giovanni Battista RATTI (eds.), Marcial Pons Madrid, *L'arte della distinzione. Scritti per Riccardo Guastini*, vol. i (2018), 57 s., with Guastini's reply in the same volume.

norm is expressed by the text, the law then prohibits it from applying any other norm. Sometimes, this prohibition is expressed in a text. For example, one provision of the constitution says that the Constitutional Council's decisions are binding for every court and public authority; the Council then itself interpreted that provision to mean that not only the decisions themselves but also the interpretations that it has given are binding. But if there is no text, the prohibition arises from the fact that all behavior based on a different interpretation or all decisions by a court are bound to be sanctioned by a higher court acting as the authentic interpreter. It is therefore true that the text has no *legal* meaning until it has been interpreted. This remains true even for texts that are not subject to adjudication and so not "interpreted" by a court, because Courts are not the only authentic interpreters. Any authority who can give an interpretation that cannot be sanctioned or overridden is, for purposes here, an authentic interpreter (for example the President of the Republic interpreting the constitution to justify the 1962 referendum, against the views of a majority of jurists, which is discussed below).

On the other hand, Guastini insists on distinguishing interpretation from creation of the law, and presents a mixed theory between what he calls, following Hart, the noble dream (the idea that interpretation is the discovery of the true meaning of a text) and the nightmare (radical skepticism). According to Guastini's theory, which closely resembles Kelsen's, a legal text has neither one single meaning nor an infinite number of meanings such that anything goes and the interpreter can decide arbitrarily. The text has a finite number of possible meanings, which form a frame that can be known by observing the usual practice of the legal community. Interpretation is the choice that courts make within the frame. When they decide on a meaning outside of the frame, the process should not be called interpretation, but rather creation of law. A norm has indeed been produced, and it is in force, but it is not valid according to Guastini.

Several objections must be raised against this theory, in particular, against the distinction between being in force and being valid, which rests on Guastini's specific conception of validity. True, when Guastini talks of validity he does not refer to some kind of mystical quality of the law that would make it binding, but only to a prescription by the legal system itself that another prescription is indeed a norm of the system. By contrast, "in force" means for Guastini that the behavior prescribed or permitted by some norm is, in fact, being followed. However, the distinction fails for two reasons.

On the one hand, what the text prescribes is, according to Guastini, its meaning in the language of the law as understood by the legal community, i.e. by scholars and by jurists who practice the law. However, not only are scholars often divided, but it is also possible that a majority of scholars agree that a text has one meaning while the authentic interpreter ascribes another. In the latter case, the lack of validity of a norm that is nevertheless in force, has no consequence at all, since behavior prohibited by the "invalid norm" cannot be sanctioned and the invalid norm can still be the basis for the validity of subsequent norms.

One such situation occurred in France in 1962, when De Gaulle as President of the Republic decided to submit a constitutional amendment to referendum in order to change the mode of election of the president, so that from then on, the president would be elected by direct popular suffrage. The vast majority of jurists considered De Gaulle's decision as a clear violation of the constitution on the ground that the text seemed to allow either for a referendum on a constitutional amendment (but only after the amendment had been approved by both houses of parliament), or on legislative bills. Thus, De Gaulle could be accused of violating the constitutional provisions on the amending procedure. However, since the decision was not justiciable, De Gaulle asserted that he was the authentic interpreter of the constitution, and the referendum took place and the amendment was adopted by a clear majority. Subsequently, De Gaulle was reelected and all presidents after him were elected by direct popular suffrage. In Guastini's terms, the amendment was in force but invalid. One is at pains to grasp the significance of "invalidity" in this context, since neither this supposedly invalid norm nor its author can be sanctioned, and it can still be the basis for the validity of other norms. Here the "invalid" constitutional norm expressed in a new provision inserted in the constitution is indeed the basis for validity of all the presidential elections that followed 1962; it would obviously be an absurd conclusion that Emmanuel Macron's election to the presidency is not valid. The distinction is therefore void of consequences.

Let me add—and this is a second argument against the distinction between being valid and being merely in force—that accepting the term "nightmare" reflects a value judgment that seems inconsistent with the positivist commitment to neutrality and its conception of legal science as purely descriptive. In fact, the thesis that judges have complete discretion to create law is a nightmare only in relation to an ideal of legal stability and certainty, or of democracy, i.e. in relation to the law as it ought to be. The realist theory of interpretation may be considered a nightmare by lawyers and judges and from an external point of view we could very well describe the empirical fact that they hold this view, but if the object of a theory of legal interpretation is not a set of beliefs but the nature of the process and the extent of judicial discretion, it is no more a nightmare or a noble dream than a theory about hurricanes or earthquakes.

B. Authentic interpreters and the hierarchy of norms

Another feature that is perhaps specific to French realism is that it seeks to go beyond the debate on the law-creating power of judges and recognizes that there are other authentic interpreters: all those authorities that are able to give a final interpretation, i.e. one that cannot be successfully challenged, either because no court has jurisdiction or because the costs of going to court are too high. Such authorities include the President of the Republic, as in the case of the 1962 referendum described above, but also Parliament, ministers, or police authorities.[23]

Simultaneously, the court is able to manipulate the hierarchy, promoting some norms to higher level or demoting some other norms. In the 1971 decision, it decided that the Preamble and the Declaration of the Rights of Man, which had been considered until then to be philosophical statements or mere political rhetoric that were not legally binding, were true legal norms and were part of the constitution with the same status as all of the provisions. These norms therefore have super legislative value. Furthermore, with the doctrine of the fundamental

---

[23] LE PILLOUER, Arnaud. «Les pouvoirs non-constituants des assemblées constituantes: essai sur le pouvoir instituant.» Nouvelle bibliothèque de thèses 47 (Paris: Dalloz, 2005).

principles recognized by the laws of the republic, the Constitutional council gave itself the power to promote a principal from the statutory to the constitutional level. It is with similar tactics that the Council has faced the perils coming from the European Court of Justice, claiming that European law prevails over national law. The Council, without directly confronting the European court, has interpreted EU law's supremacy as existing over statutory law only, but not over the constitution, and thus was able to promote to a constitutional level certain principles in order to protect them from EU law. At this point, the EU treaty was modified by the treaty of Lisbon, which explicitly declared the supremacy of European law over national law, including the constitution. Nevertheless, the French constitutional council, starting from the idea that the European treaty is only binding because the French constitution makes it binding, was able to argue that the constitution could not have contradicted itself to the point of allowing EU law to prevail on its own most important principles. Hence the supremacy of EU law is necessarily limited and does not prevail over those principles that are constitutive of the constitutional identity of France.[24] Therefore, only the national constituent power could abolish such principles or derogate them.

Thus, the hierarchical structure of the legal system appears to be essentially mobile, depending on decisions made by the courts. Contrary to the Kelsenian model, which rests on the presumption that a norm is valid when it has been produced according to a higher norm emanating from another authority, we see that the various norms at different levels are being produced by the same court. The Constitutional Council applies a constitutional norm that forms the basis for the validity of its decision, but this constitutional norm has been produced by means of an interpretation of the text of the constitution by the Constitutional Council itself. The hierarchy of norms is therefore internal to the jurisprudence of the court.

This conclusion allows for a new solution to a classical problem among French legal theorists regarding the hierarchy of norms. Some

---

[24] Centre d'études et de recherches internationales et communautaires, et Institut Louis Favoreu (ed.). *L'identité à la croisée des États et de l'Europe: quel sens ? Quelles fonctions ?* À la croisée des droits 14 (Bruxelles: Bruylant, 2015).

claimed that, since the French Revolution, because of the principle that the people exercises its sovereignty through representatives, the law's supremacy reflects the supremacy of Parliament and the hierarchy of norms reflects a hierarchy of organs of the state. By contrast, Kelsenians maintain that since organs of the state have been created and empowered by norms, the hierarchy of organs follows and reflects the hierarchy of norms.[25] According to the French realist position, the hierarchy of norms simply reflects the structure of argumentation by an authentic interpreter and determines the respective positions of the organs of the state. As long as the courts refused to review the constitutionality of legislation, there was no supremacy of the constitution, as Kelsen himself acknowledged.

C. Legal constraints and attention to substantial concepts

Naturally, the realist theory of interpretation has faced several objections.[26, 27] According to one of the most difficult, if the theory were true, the interpreter could act arbitrarily and there would be no such thing as the jurisprudence of a court: the interpreter would only follow his personal preferences, whether political, moral, or religious, and the legal reasoning in the opinion would simply amount to window-dressing. However, such is not the case since we can observe continuities in the practice of interpreters, to the effect that lawyers do not make their cases by appealing to the feelings and political opinions of judges

[25] KELSEN, Hans. *Théorie pure du droit, op. cit.*; CARRÉ DE MALBERG, Raymond, *Contribution à la Théorie générale de l'État (1920)*, new edition (Paris: Dalloz, 2004); *Confrontation de la théorie de la formation du droit par degrés: avec les idées et les institutions consacrées par le droit positif français relativement à sa formation (1933)*, new edition (Paris: Dalloz, 2008); BÉCHILLON, Denys de, *Hiérarchie des normes et hiérarchie des fonctions normatives de l'État* (Paris: Economica, 1996).

[26] TROPER M., CHAMPEIL-DESPLATS V., and GRZEGORCZYK C., éd. *Théorie des contraintes juridiques* (Paris: LGDJ, 2005); PAOUR, Raphaël. «Les contraintes juridiques de la hiérarchie des normes». *Revus. Journal for Constitutional Theory and Philosophy of Law* 21 (10 December 2013), p. 201.

[27] PFERSMANN, Otto. «Contre le néo-réalisme juridique. Pour un débat sur l'interprétation», *Revue française de droit constitutionnel* 50, no. 2 (2002), 279–334. And my reply TROPER, Michel. «Réplique à Otto Pfersmann», *Revue française de droit constitutionnel* 50, no. 2 (2002), 335–53.

but by using specific arguments related to specific legal theories. A theory of legal constraints can help confront this objection.

If legal science is viewed as an empirical science and if law is viewed as fact, then we ought to be able to explain facts about law according to the principle of causality. For example, it is a fact that interpreters have the power to create law, that they do not use this power capriciously, and that they do not openly act out of sheer political preferences; these facts have to be explained. American and Scandinavian realists typically look for psychological or sociological explanations, i.e. one that relates a legal fact, such as the creation of a norm or a legal concept, to psychological or social facts. Yet we can also appeal to other social facts: for example, that judicial discretion can cause other authorities to retaliate by using their normative powers. The creation or transformation of some legal concepts can also be explained by the function that it will exercise in the legal system: for example, during the writing the 1795 constitution, a new concept of "citizen" was forged in order to justify a restriction of the right to vote. In the previous 1793 constitution a citizen was a man born or residing in France and all citizens who were of age could vote, but the writers of the new constitution, who were more conservative, wished to restrict the right to vote to those men who paid a certain minimum amount of taxes. In order to avoid possible resistance from those who were deprived of their political rights, they redefined the citizen as: a man who is of age and who pays a certain amount of taxes. They were thus able to claim that since all citizens had the rights to vote, they had sustained the democratic principle of universal suffrage.

Let me illustrate such a constraint by a metaphor taken from the game of chess. In any given situation on the board, a player has a choice between several moves that are equally valid according to the rules of the game. However, some of these moves are bad moves and it may happen that only one of all the possible valid moves can prevent immediate defeat. The player who chooses that one move will say "I was forced" to do it. Here the constraint results from the situation on the board, i.e. from the system formed by all the rules of the game and by all the preceding moves. We explain it not by the player's ideology or the psychology of the player, because any rational player in the same circumstances would have acted in the same way. Of course, there is no absolute necessity. A less competent player would not make that same move, or people playing with their children who want them to win, but if the move has been made, we can still say that what explains it is the player's perception of the situation on the board. The explanation is still causal, albeit in a weak sense: without the fact that is mentioned as a cause, the event to be explained would not have happened.

This type of reasoning can be used as a tool to explain certain moves in the game of law, such as court decisions or some non-decisional changes in the substance of the law. Take, for instance, the 1971 decision by the Constitutional Council, already mentioned, which radically changed the French legal system by instituting constitutional review of legislation and promoting some pieces of ordinary legislation to the constitutional level. We cannot be certain of the real psychological or political motives behind the decision, but we can make a reasonable guess. If the purpose was that of invalidating a statute adopted by Parliament limiting freedom of association, and since there was no provision dealing with freedom of association either in the constitution, the preamble or the declaration of the Rights of Man, the best, if not the only, means to achieve that result was to promote a statute to the constitutional level, by deciding that by enacting the statute Parliament had not willed but merely recognized a prior and fundamental principle of constitutional value.

Several years later, the Conseil d'Etat made a similar move to defeat a constitutional provision that gives international treaties supremacy over statutes, by deciding that since they are superior to statutes only and not to constitutional norms, they are not superior to statutes that have recognized fundamental principles of constitutional value.[28]

V. Conclusion

French realism, as other varieties of legal realism, is an endeavor to construct legal science as both a normative and an empirical science.

[28] CHAMPEIL-DESPLATS, Véronique. «L'arrêt Koné, produit et source de contraintes», in TROPER, CHAMPEIL-DESPLATS, and GRZEGORCZYK, eds., Théorie des contraintes juridiques, supra n. 26.

Obviously, it is not normative in the sense that it would create norms or formulate binding propositions, but only that it deals with a complex discourse that presents the law as a set of norms. It is empirical because it attempts to treat this object as a social fact; subject to causality. Yet this social fact has certain particularities, which have to be taken into account, by legal science, in defining its object: not the norms but the discourse and reasoning of jurists, a discourse understood as a system of facts, in which internal constraints can bring about important changes within its own formal structure and provoke the emergence of new concepts, essential to its coherence.

Michel Troper, *Legal Realism in France* In: *Oxford Studies in Philosophy of Law, Volume 5*. Edited by: Leslie Green and Brian Leiter, Oxford University Press. © Michel Troper 2024. DOI: 10.1093/9780198919650.003.0005

Justification and Duty

James Edwards and A.P. Simester

1. Pros and Cons

Justifications are bound up with reasons. This much, at least, is fairly uncontroversial. Disagreement breaks out when we begin to investigate the binding. The disagreements that most occupy philosophers of criminal law are disagreements about reasons *in favour*. Imagine P φs. She claims to have been justified in φing. P's claim is true, some say, if and only if P had undefeated reasons to φ.[1] Whether P is aware of those reasons, or motivated by them, is beside the point. A rival view has it that this conflates the justifiable with the justified. While undefeated reasons make φing justifi*able*, more is required for justification. Those reasons must also figure in P's practical reasoning. And they must figure in the right way.[2]

These views sit at the heart of one debate about the connection between justifications and reasons. Our principal interest here is in a second such debate. It is a debate not about reasons in favour but about reasons *against*. Consider a distinction drawn by John Gardner.[3] In a looser sense, Gardner writes, justification is always a live issue. We can evaluate φing against the tests set out above whatever φing may be. In a stricter sense, justification has presuppositions that are not always met. Something calls for justification only if it is in some way objectionable:

---

[1] See, among others, P. Robinson, 'Competing Theories of Justification: Deeds vs. Reasons', in Simester and Smith (eds.), *Harm and Culpability* (Oxford University Press 1996); H. Hurd, 'Justification and Excuse, Wrongdoing and Culpability' (1999), 74 *Notre Dame Law Review* 1551.

[2] Defences include J. Gardner, *Offences and Defences* (Oxford University Press 2007); A.P. Simester, *Fundamentals of Criminal Law* (Oxford University Press 2020).

[3] Gardner (n. 2) 95.

only if, that is, there are reasons that countervail. If P has no reason not to φ, P has nothing to justify. The question of justification, in the stricter sense, does not arise.

Philosophers of criminal law tend to take it for granted that they are dealing with justification in the stricter sense. The obvious explanation for this is that their interest is in justificatory *defences*. There are loose and strict senses in play here, too. In the loose sense, a defence is anything that precludes criminal liability. In the strict sense, to plead a defence presupposes, at least *arguendo*, that one has satisfied the defining elements of a criminal offence: absent the latter, one has no need of the former. Criminal offences, almost everyone agrees, are legal wrongs. Paradigmatically, they are moral wrongs too. Where this is so, a justificatory defence—in both law and morality—is a justification *of* wrongdoing. The debate of interest to us here concerns how best to make sense of this thought.

2. Concession and Denial

Let us begin by distinguishing between two views. According to the first, to plead a justificatory defence is to *concede* wrongdoing. To be clear from the outset, the idea here is not evidential. As Gardner writes,

> To say that an action was prima facie wrongful normally signals, to the legal mind, that there is some reason to believe that a wrong was committed, but that it may yet, once more evidence is presented, turn out not to be so. But in the sense which matters for an understanding of the demarcation between offences and justificatory defences, to identify a prima facie wrong is to identify an *actual* wrong, not just an apparent or putative wrong.[4]

Let us call this *the concession view*. It is a view that generates an apparent contradiction when placed alongside a familiar account of the distinction between justifications and excuses. On that account,

[4] Gardner, ibid., 96.

justifications *deny* wrongdoing. Excuses concede it, while denying blameworthiness.[5] In Michael Moore's words,

> When an action is justified, any prima facie wrongfulness is eliminated by the other (and good) attributes of the action; when an action is excused, it is still wrongful but the actor cannot be held responsible for it because she is not culpable.[6]

Must we choose between the familiar account and the concession view? It may seem obvious that we must. In truth, however, the contradiction is only apparent. The two views can be rendered consistent by disambiguation. When we claim that φing is wrong, one thing we may mean is that φing breaches a duty. Alternatively, we may mean that φing is something that ought not to be done. Since duties can be overridden, these claims need not conflict. Acts that breach a duty can be acts we ought to perform. When Gardner endorses the concession view, in the quotation set out above, he is using the language of wrongdoing in the first sense: his claim is that a justification of φing concedes that P breached a duty when she φed.[7] What justifies the breach is the fact that P's act was not wrong in the second sense: that it was not the case that the duty ought not to have been breached. So "a justified wrong" is not an oxymoron.

Does a justification concede so much as this? Not everyone thinks so. On a rival view, to claim a justification is to deny wrongdoing in both senses: it is to deny both that one breached a duty and that one ought not to have acted as one did. Call this *the denial view*. It does not follow, if we endorse this view, that justificatory defences are justifications in the looser sense only. It is one thing to deny that justified actors breach a duty in doing what they do. It is another to deny that there is any reason for them not to do it. In later work, Gardner shifts from the concession view outlined above. He claims that—at least in the criminal law—it is countervailing reasons, not breaches of duty, that the justified concede:

---

[5] Mitch Berman describes this account as standard. See M. Berman, 'Justification and Excuse, Law and Morality' (2003), *Duke Law Journal* 1.

[6] M. Moore, *Placing Blame* (Oxford University Press 1997), 483.

[7] For Gardner, a wrong 'is no more and no less than a breach of duty'. See Gardner (n. 2) 356.

'the effect of a justification is to leave intact the reasons for not committing the wrong apart from the mere fact that it is a wrong'.[8] Put another way, a 'justification defence does not cancel the reasons not to do what the criminal law would have one not do'.[9] Rather, it cancels the duty the criminal law would otherwise impose requiring one not to do it. So there is something to justify, but ultimately no wrong.

These preliminary remarks put two views on the table. One—the concession view—tells us that the justified breach a duty. The second—the denial view—tells us that they do not. On both views, the relationship between wrongdoing and justification is univocal: all justifications are in this respect alike. Here, we argue for a different position. We argue that, while some justifications concede a breach of duty, others deny the breach. On this bifurcated view, the relationship between justification and wrongdoing depends on which justification is at issue. This is the case, we contend, in both morality and law.

One further preliminary point before we proceed. It might be said that the distinction drawn above—between justifications that concede versus deny wrongdoing—is a familiar distinction unnecessarily clothed in unfamiliar garb. The familiar distinction is that between *prima facie* and *pro tanto* wrongs. When we say that justification concedes wrongdoing—it might be said—what we are really saying is that justified acts are *pro tanto* wrongs. When we say that justification denies wrongdoing, we are saying that justified acts are only wrong *prima facie*. The difficulty with this terminology, for our purposes, comes of the different ways in which the familiar distinction is drawn. *Pro tanto* wrongdoing is itself sometimes understood in terms of countervailing reasons: it is *pro tanto* wrong to φ if there is a reason not to φ which is or can be overridden. *Prima facie* wrongdoing is then contrasted with *pro tanto* wrongdoing: it is *prima facie* wrong to φ if any reason not to φ turns out to be no more than apparent. If this is so, both the concession *and* denial views hold that justified acts are *pro tanto* wrong. Denials of *prima facie* wrongs, in contrast, are not justifications in the stricter sense at all.

[8] J. Gardner, 'In Defence of *Offences and Defences*' (2012), 4 *Jerusalem Review of Legal Studies* 110, 118.
[9] Ibid.

Since our own distinction falls within the category of justifications *stricto sensu*, the two distinctions are not one and the same. Not everyone, of course, distinguishes the *pro tanto* from the *prima facie* in the same way. In order to avoid confusion, we eschew the familiar terminology altogether.

3. Protection and Justification

We are bound by duty, whether we like it or not. This is not to claim that all duties are absolute. Neither is it to claim that duties are necessarily unavoidable. To say that duties bind *whether we like it or not* is to say that duties are categorical. They are reasons we cannot escape merely by changing our projects or goals. To say that duties *bind* is to say that they are mandatory not advisory. Part of what it is for a norm to be mandatory is for it to drive a wedge between two propositions: (i) that φing is what one ought to do; (ii) that the reasons that favour φing are the weightier reasons. To have a duty to φ is for occasions to exist on which (i) is true but (ii) is false. The puzzle of how this can be so was famously solved by Joseph Raz.[10] It can be the case that one ought to φ—despite having weightier reasons not to do so—because one's duty is no mere first-order reason to φ. It is also a second-order reason: a reason not to act for at least some countervailing reasons. These countervailing reasons, in Raz's terminology, are excluded from consideration. They are reasons for which one should not act. One ought to φ if the remaining reasons against φing—those unexcluded by one's duty—are less weighty than the reasons for one to φ. This is so, crucially, even if the excluded reasons are weightier still—even if, were all first-order reasons placed in the balance, the scales would tilt decisively against φing. One's duty binds in part by making it the case that one ought to φ despite there being weightier reasons to refrain from φing.

A reason to φ is a protected reason if it is (also) a reason not to act for at least some countervailing reasons. On the view just sketched, duties are reasons of this kind. Call this *the protected reasons view* for short. If sound, the protected reasons view identifies conceptual conditions for

---

[10] The *locus classicus* is J. Raz, *Practical Reason and Norms* (Oxford University Press 1975).

the existence of a duty. Duties count as such in virtue of the fact that these conditions are met. A legal duty to φ is a legal reason to φ that (also) excludes at least some reasons against φing. A moral duty is a moral reason to φ that (also) excludes at least some countervailing reasons. And so on. Note that this leaves open a variety of views about material conditions—the conditions, that is, in virtue of which duties of each type exist. Some claim that—as a matter of necessity—what makes it the case that P has a legal duty to φ is the fact that P has a (particular type of) moral duty to φ.[11] Others claim that—as a matter of necessity— the existence of (any type of) moral duty to φ fails to make it the case that P has a legal duty to φ.[12] There are, of course, intermediate possibilities. The point here is just that this disagreement about the material conditions for the existence of (legal) duties is compatible with agreement about the corresponding conceptual conditions.[13] We set the former aside here and focus on the latter.

Let us assume, aligning with Gardner and Raz, that the protected reasons view is the correct one. Whether those who benefit from a justificatory defence nonetheless breach a duty then depends on whether their action is one they have a protected reason not to perform. If they do have such a reason, the concession view is right about justificatory defences. If they do not, it is the denial view that is correct. We already noted a shift in Gardner's own views.[14] Having initially endorsed the concession view, he later embraced the denial view. The shift might be thought to be necessitated by two other claims Gardner makes. The first is that, if it is a criminal offence to φ, the default position is that all reasons to φ are legally excluded reasons—they are not reasons for which, in the eyes of the law, one may φ.[15] The second is that,

> when the law grants a justificatory defence it *unexcludes* some otherwise excluded reasons, and allows them once again to punch their weight in an ordinary rational conflict with the law's ordinary

---

[11] See e.g. M. Greenberg, 'The Moral Impact Theory of Law' (2014), 123 *Yale Law Journal* 1288.

[12] See e.g. J. Raz, *The Authority of Law* (Oxford University Press 1979).

[13] It presupposes such agreement, at least, if it is a genuine disagreement.

[14] Gardner notes the shift in a reply to Leora Dahan Katz. See Gardner (n. 8) 118.

[15] Gardner (n. 2) 106.

(now unprotected) reasons for not offending. At this point, everything depends on the comparative weight of the reasons.[16]

If (i) breaches of duty are acts that fail to conform to protected reasons, and (ii) we have unprotected reasons not to offend when we benefit from a justificatory defence, then (iii) acts which benefit from justificatory defences breach no duty. It seems that the denial view is the correct one, as Gardner came to think.

But that's too fast. Consider again Gardner's claim in the above passage. The claim, to repeat, is that the legal effect of a justificatory defence is to unexclude some otherwise excluded reasons for offending. P benefits from such a defence if and only if P offends for an unexcluded reason, and that reason is not outweighed by the legal reason(s) against. Unexcluding some reasons is not unexcluding all of them. Neither does Gardner claim that justificatory defences have so dramatic an effect. Some reasons for offending, he repeatedly implies, remain legally excluded reasons.[17] Recall too that P has a protected reason not to offend—despite benefiting from a justificatory defence—if P's reason not to offend continues to exclude some reasons for offending. If (i) those who benefit from a justificatory defence do something they have a protected reason not to do, and (ii) acts contrary to protected reasons are breaches of duty, then (iii) those who benefit from a justificatory defence do breach a duty. Which suggests that the concession view, not the denial view, is correct.[18]

4. Self-Defence, Cancellation, and Exception

Should we accept that those who benefit from a justificatory defence nonetheless breach a duty? Our own view, advertised earlier, is that this

---

[16] Ibid., 148.   [17] See Gardner (n. 8) 118–19 for one example.

[18] It is worth emphasizing that, on the protected reasons view, duties need not be (and often are not) absolute. On that view (which we will qualify later) the test of whether P breaches a duty by φing is not whether the reasons against φing defeat the reasons in favour. The test is whether P has a reason not to φ that excludes at least some reasons for φing. The words 'at least some' are crucial. Where reasons to φ are not excluded by P's duty, they are reasons for which P is permitted to φ. The unexcluded reasons may yet be outweighed. Where they are not, however, P has undefeated reason to φ despite having a duty not to do so.

is sometimes the case. Sometimes, but not always. On the bifurcated view we favour, some justifications concede a breach of duty. Others, however, deny the breach. The aim of this section is to make the case for the second half of the conjunction.

Consider a paradigmatic case of self-defence.[19] V attacks P for a defeated reason. She does so culpably. P uses lethal force against V to repel the attack. P's resort to such force is reasonable in the circumstances, given both the gravity of V's threat to P and P's alternatives. Two things, we argue here, are true of this example. First, although P satisfies the offence-elements of murder, she also benefits from a justificatory defence to that offence. Second, P breaches no duty—moral or legal—by using lethal force against V in self-defence.

Self-defence and breach of duty

Take the second claim first. This claim is false if P has a duty not to kill others—or not to kill others intentionally—that admits of no *exception*. Let us begin, then, by noting two indications that no such duty exists. The first is that breaches of duty have normative consequences for the duty-bearer. Where the duty is directed, these consequences typically include duties to apologize, and to compensate those to whom the duty is owed for harm caused. No such duties arise in paradigmatic cases of self-defence. We need not apologize for using reasonable force to defend ourselves against those who culpably place us under attack. Neither need we make them as well off as they would have been had we not used such force. The point holds true in law as well as in morality. P is not liable in tort if V is an attacker and P uses reasonable force against V to thwart her attack.[20]

This first indication that P breaches no duty is provided *ex post*—by the normative position that obtains in the wake of P's actions. A second such indication is provided *ex ante*—by P's deliberative position prior to

---

[19] In what follows, when we talk of self-defence *simpliciter* we have in mind the paradigm case.

[20] *Ashley v Chief Constable of Sussex Police* [2008] UKHL 25.

any such breach. We claimed earlier that a duty not to φ is a norm that binds the duty-bearer. Its binding character is owed in part to its exclusionary force: to the fact that at least some reasons to φ are excluded from consideration. Duties, however, are not mere exclusionary reasons. A duty not to φ is not only a norm that rules out φing for at least some reasons. It is also a norm that counts against φing—that provides us, that is, with a reason not to φ—and that ought to figure as such in our practical deliberations. Implicit in this is a converse aspect of the mandatoriness of duty. A norm does not mandate that we refrain from φing if φing is something that norm does not count against. Neither does it mandate that we refrain from φing if the reason it gives us not to φ is a reason we are permitted to exclude when we deliberate about φing.

Why does all this matter here? It matters because, if P has a duty not to kill V in self-defence, P has a reason not to kill V which P ought to weigh in the balance. The reasons against which that reason ought to be weighed, of course, are reasons P has to prevent V from causing her harm. The crucial point here is that, if the pro and cons of using defensive force were (first-order) reasons P ought to weigh against one another, P would lose her justification for using such force as the number of attackers went up. To see the point, imagine that P's reason to prevent V from harming P—by using defensive force—is slightly weightier than P's reason not to kill V in self-defence. Now imagine we increase the number of attackers from one to five. Grant that all five attackers are culpable for the attack, and that if P does not kill all five, one or more will kill P. Faced with a threat of this magnitude—and under the assumptions just stated—P's reason not to kill all five is surely the weightier reason. As such, if P ought to weigh that reason against her reason to use defensive force, P is not justified in defending herself against it. The problem, of course, is that this conclusion is counterintuitive. If five culpable attackers will otherwise kill P, she can justify defending herself by killing all five if that is the only way to save herself from her attackers. What drives us towards the contrary conclusion— the conclusion we take to be counterintuitive—is the notion that we have a duty not to kill in self-defence. This is a second indication that, *pace* our opponent, there is no such duty.

So far, of course, these are just indications. Further argument, however, is on offer. Let us begin by drawing out two features of our paradigm case. First: by the time V attacks P, harm is unavoidable. If the (would-be) self-defender does not harm the attacker in self-defence, the attacker will harm the (would-be) self-defender. If P does not harm V, V will harm P. Second: the first feature is V's doing. Harm is unavoidable *because* V culpably attacked P. Had V not violated P's autonomy in this way, there would be no need for one of them to suffer harm.

Now suppose that, as our opponent claims, P has a duty not to harm V in self-defence. Given the first feature, the existence of this duty presents P with a dilemma. Either P conforms to her duty not to harm V or she does not. To do the former is to refrain from defending oneself, and to suffer harm at V's hands. To do the latter is to defend oneself, become a wrongdoer, and incur secondary duties as a normative consequence. Both horns of the dilemma leave P worse off than she otherwise would have been. Given the second feature, the dilemma is one with which V saddles P by culpably attacking her. P can legitimately object to P's having the power to put her in this position. V has no comparable objection, by contrast, to P's benefiting from a liberty to defend herself against attack. V could—and should—have refrained from attacking P in the first place. The liberty in question obtains only because V did so.

To say this is not to claim that V's interests—to the extent that they compete with P's—are of lesser significance. P's dilemma arises because those competing interests are now incompatible. In such cases, the challenge for both morality and law is to determine whose interests, if either's, take priority. Our point in the paragraph above is that the exception to P's duty not to kill V is warranted because the competition itself is under V's control—and so, therefore, is the triggering of the exception. P's action is justified, in part, because it is a *response to V's wrong*. Were we not to acknowledge an exception to P's duty, we would in effect give V an *ex ante* power to place P under a duty to self-sacrifice.[21] Such a power should not lie in V's hands.

---

[21] Because P would breach a duty by harming V, and because the only way for P not to breach that duty would be for P to refrain from defending herself.

We conclude that P does no wrong by forcibly defending herself against V's attack. V's wrongful attack upon P crystallises a liberty for P, a liberty carved out of P's duty not to use force against her.

Two kinds of denial

The concession view, it may seem to follow, must be rejected. Alas, things are not so simple. The concession view cannot stand, assuming our arguments are successful, *if* self-defence is properly regarded as a justificatory defence. But the claim that self-defenders benefit from a liberty might already be thought to point in a different direction. Rather than supporting the denial view, it might be thought to imply that no defence in the strict sense is in play at all—that those who use reasonable force in self-defence do not satisfy the defining elements of the offence. It might be thought to imply, in short, that self-defence is not a justification but an *offence-denial*. If this is so, the conclusion with which we ended the last paragraph casts no doubt on the correctness of the concession view.

Is self-defence properly regarded as an offence-denial?[22] We think not. To see why, we can usefully draw a further distinction. Imagine that P would have a duty not to φ were it not for some fact *f*. One possibility is that *f* makes it the case that P's duty not to φ is *cancelled*. A second is that *f* brings φing within an *exception* to P's duty. Here is the difference as we see it. Where *f* serves to cancel P's duty not to φ, the rationale for P's duty no longer speaks against P φing. Where *f* brings φing within an exception to P's duty, that rationale continues to provide reason for P not to φ. As an example of cancellation, imagine Q is the owner of a clock. Part of what it is for Q to be the clock's owner is for P to have a duty not to take the clock from Q. Now imagine Q bequeaths the clock to P. Here, P's duty not to take the clock is cancelled. Q's ownership right provides no reason, in the wake of the transfer, for P not to take the

---

[22] Gardner's views shifted on this point too. Having initially treated self-defence as a prime example of a justificatory defence, Gardner came to think that it was better seen as an offence-denial. See Gardner (n. 8) 113.

clock from Q. So, absent other reasons, P need not appeal to a reason in favour of taking it to show that the taking is permissible.

Things are different when P kills V in self-defence. V does not become an *outlaw*—somebody outside the protection of the law—by placing P under attack. The value of V's life—the rationale for P's duty not to kill her—continues to speak against acts that would cause her death.[23] It follows that, although P breaches no duty by killing V in self-defence, this is not because V's attack cancels P's duty. Rather, it is because P's actions fall within an exception to her duty not to kill. One upshot is that, if she is to show that her actions are permissible, P *does* need to appeal to a reason in favour of acting as she does. P must show that the reason she has to defend herself is undefeated by the reason she continues to have not to take V's life. This countervailing reason, in our view, is no mere first-order reason. P would not act permissibly if, say, P killed V in order to eliminate the competition for a lucrative promotion. The value of V's life continues to exclude such reasons as permissible reasons for P to kill V.

If we are right about all this, self-defence is no offence-denial. To offer an offence-denial is to deny that φing is contraindicated by the norms of the criminal law. No such contraindication exists, we have argued, when P's duty not to φ is cancelled. Matters are otherwise when P benefits from an exception to that duty. Where this is so, P perpetrates the elements of an offence—though she breaches no duty—because the norms of the criminal law continue to make a rational case against her actions. Unlike taking the clock, P's actions cause a significant and regrettable set-back to V's interests—the very interests that warranted, and continue to warrant, protection by law as well as morality. In not treating P's duty as cancelled, the law signals ongoing respect for V and her interests, while simultaneously paying attention to V's agency. P is nonetheless properly acquitted, in our paradigmatic case of self-defence, because her reason for acting is undefeated by the reasons against. It follows that self-defence is indeed a justificatory defence. Here, at least, the concession view is mistaken.

---

[23] This is true, we claim, in both law and morality. On this point, we agree with Antony Duff. See R. A. Duff, *Answering for Crime* (Hart 2007), 213–14.

Exclusionary permissions

It might be said in response that we have now made three claims which cannot all be true. The first is that duties are protected reasons. The second is that those who use lethal force in self-defence act contrary to such a reason. The third is that, when they kill in self-defence, self-defenders fall within an exception to the duty not to kill. The first two claims seem to entail that those who kill in self-defence breach a duty. The third, however, entails the contrary.

In truth, the trilemma is merely apparent. We need not deny that, if one has a duty not to φ, one has a protected reason not to φ. We need only deny that, if one has a protected reason not to φ, one necessarily breaches a duty in φing. In order to effect such a denial, we must supplement the analysis so far. We need to add that one has a duty not to φ only if one lacks an exclusionary permission. A protected reason not to φ, recall, is a first-order reason not to φ that is also an exclusionary reason. It is a reason that both weighs against P φing, and makes it the case that some reasons to φ are reasons for which P should not act. All else being equal, when P has such a reason, P should refrain from φing if her first-order reason not to φ is weightier than the unexcluded reasons that favour φing. Where P benefits from an exclusionary permission, all else is not equal. P is permitted to exclude her first-order reason not to φ from her deliberations. She need not weigh that reason against the unexcluded reasons that favour φing. In a case of self-defence, P need not weigh her reason not to harm V, by using reasonable force to ward off V's attack, against her reasons to protect herself against V. This gloss on the protected reasons view may appear *ad hoc*. In fact, it is implicit in what we have already said about the mandatoriness of duty. Part of what is for duties to bind, we claimed above, is for the reasons they provide to be reasons we ought to weigh against countervailing (unexcluded) reasons. Duties provide us with first-order reasons of this kind only if we do not benefit from an exclusionary permission.[24]

---

[24] We leave open whether all wrong-denying justifications—those that fall within an exception to a duty—are cases where the justified actor has an exclusionary permission. We claim only that this is true of self-defence.

Do self-defenders indeed benefit from an exclusionary permission to harm attackers by using reasonable force in self-defence? We have already encountered two reasons to think they do. One is the fact that, as the number of attackers goes up, P's justification remains. Were P required to weigh reasons not to harm attackers in the balance, this would not be the case. A second is the fact that, as a matter of both morality and law, self-defenders lack a duty to compensate attackers.

Recall our claim that P has a protected reason not to harm V. Gardner argues that such reasons are not extinguished by our failure to conform to them. According to his well-known continuity thesis, they survive as reasons to do the next best thing.[25] All else being equal, where those reasons give us a duty not to cause harm *ex ante*, they also give us a duty to compensate *ex post*. Obligation in. Obligation out. All else being equal.

That self-defenders do not incur compensatory obligations can be explained by extending Gardner's reasoning in the following way. All else being equal, a reason not to harm V which P is permitted to disregard *ex ante*, is a reason P is permitted to disregard *ex post*. Grant that P's reason to compensate V is that this is the best P can do to conform to her original reason not to harm V. If P is permitted to disregard that original reason *ex ante* when defending herself against V's attack, P is also permitted to disregard that surviving reason once she has harmed V in self-defence. If P is permitted to disregard her reason to compensate V, she lacks a duty to pay compensation. Exclusionary permission in. Exclusionary permission out. All else being equal.

One might fairly worry that our analysis here proves too much. Imagine that V attacks P with a soggy lettuce leaf. P can only ward off the watery assault by killing V. Does the claim that V benefits from an exclusionary permission entail that V has a justification for the killing? No. Recall our claim that P's conduct falls within an exception. This is to say that V's right to life continues to speak against the use of lethal force. In turn, the circumstances in which P can avail herself of the exclusionary permission are limited in several respects. One such limitation is that P must have a reason to use lethal force that V's right does not

---

[25] See J. Gardner, 'What Is Tort Law For? The Place of Corrective Justice?' (2011), 30 *Law and Philosophy* 1.

exclude. Compare reasons to ward off the threat of soggy lettuce with reasons to ward off threats to life. Part of the (continuing) significance of V's right to life is that it excludes the former but not the latter. It follows that, however large the number of lettuce leaves may grow, P lacks a justification for using lethal force in self-defence. Not so if one's own life is under threat. Since P has an unexcluded reason to use lethal force in self-defence, it is a live question how that reason fares in competition with P's reason not to use it. To claim that P benefits from an exclusionary permission is to claim that P need not weigh the two reasons against one another to work out whether she may resort to lethal force. She need not lay down her life if she faces five attackers rather than one.

These remarks help to explain how three claims we have made can stand together. First: that P has a duty not to φ only if P has a protected reason not to φ. Second: that killing in self-defence falls within an exception to the duty not to kill. Third: that self-defence is not an offence-denial but a justificatory defence. The second and third claims are reconciled by the thought that, where P φing falls within an exception to a duty, the rationale for that duty continues to speak against P φing. This is what makes P's plea a defence in the strict sense rather than an offence-denial. The first and second theses are reconciled by the thought that, although self-defenders retain a protected reason not to kill attackers, they also benefit from an exclusionary permission to defend themselves against attack. This explains why self-defenders breach no duty by defending themselves. It follows that, as the bifurcated view claims, not every justificatory defence concedes a breach of duty.

5. Necessity, Agency, and Compensation

We therefore reject the concession view. This leaves open the possibility that the denial view is correct: that all cases of justification are like self-defence, in as much as none of them concedes a breach of duty. Our argument in this section is against that possibility.

To make our case, we turn to the defence of necessity. It is worth observing at the outset that cases of necessity are not all alike. In some, it is necessary to harm V to protect V's own interests. In others, it is P's own interests that are in need of protection. In yet other cases, neither P nor V is at risk. P must harm V for the sake of one or more third parties. Here, we focus on cases of the second kind—cases in which P will suffer harm if P does not harm V. For convenience, we describe them as cases of *private necessity*.

Private necessity cases have at least one thing in common with our paradigmatic case of self-defence: if V's interests are not set back, P's will be. Harm to one of them is now unavoidable. What sets private necessity apart is that this is not V's doing. Unlike in our self-defence case, is not *because* V wrongs P that P's interests compete with V's. They compete only in virtue of being incompatible. If P does not harm V, P will be harmed, but not by V. Here, we argue, the concession view gets things right: P does breach a duty by harming V. Yet, assuming the harm caused is proportionate, she does so with justification. If this is right, and if the argument of the previous section is sound, the bifurcated view is the correct one.

Is it right? Let us start by considering the two indicia we identified earlier. First: that duties are mandatory. They are reasons we are not permitted to exclude from consideration.[26] A duty not to φ is a reason against φing that must be weighed against unexcluded reasons to φ. Second: that breaches of duty have normative consequences for the duty-bearer. Where the duty is owed to V, these consequences typically include duties to compensate V for harm caused by the breach.

Both indicia suggest that P breaches a duty in cases of private necessity. The first is evidenced by the fact that P's justification is lost as the harm done increases. Imagine that P damages V's property in order to prevent a fire from damaging her own. This isn't like self-defence, where P retains her justification as we increase the amount of harm done. P cannot burn down V's house to prevent fire damage to her car. The implication is that, in cases of private necessity, P lacks the exclusionary permission from which she benefits in cases of self-defence. Put differently: P's reason not to damage V's property has to be weighed against P's reasons to cause the damage. It might be objected, of course, that this shows only that the former is a first-order reason not to cause damage.

---

[26] And that exclude at least some countervailing reasons.

But that seems wrong. P is not permitted to damage V's property for any old reason (say, to improve her own view or to get revenge on V). If so, all three features of a duty are present: (i) a first-reason not to cause damage, that (ii) excludes at least some countervailing reasons, and that (iii) is not itself permissibly excluded from consideration.

So much for the first indicium. Now consider the second. Where P harms V in self-defence, we have claimed, P owes V no compensation. This is so in both law and morality. Things are different in cases of private necessity. As a matter of law, P is obligated to compensate V for harm done. In *Vincent*,[27] P tied its boat to V's dock during a storm, thereby saving the boat from sinking. P was held liable for damage caused to the dock as the boat banged into it. It is widely claimed that, on this point, law reflects morality. Joel Feinberg's famous *Cabin* example illustrates:[28]

> Suppose that you are on a back-packing trip in the high mountain country when an unanticipated blizzard strikes the area with such ferocity that your life is imperiled. Fortunately, you stumble onto an unoccupied cabin, locked and boarded up for the winter, clearly somebody else's private property. You smash in a window, enter, and huddle in a corner for three days until the storm abates. During this period you help yourself to your unknown benefactor's food supply and burn his wooden furniture in the fireplace to keep warm.

Feinberg continues: "almost everyone would agree that you owe compensation to the homeowner for the depletion of his larder, the breaking of his window, and the destruction of his furniture." We share that intuition (and would add that you also have a duty to apologize to the owner). The duty to compensate is of a next-best kind; it reflects our obligation to make the cabin owner, like the dock owner, as well off as they would have been had their property rights not been infringed.

---

[27] *Vincent v Lake Erie Transportation Co* 124 NW 221 (1910).
[28] J. Feinberg, 'Voluntary Euthanasia and the Inalienable Right to Life' (1978), 7 *Philosophy and Public Affairs* 93, 102.

Duty and compensation

Not everybody is convinced that there is a duty of compensation in such cases. Some would concede that something is owed to V, but object to the notion that it is owed by way of *compensation*. P incurs a duty to pay V, they would claim, because P benefits from her harmful action. P's obligation does not arise from the fact that she has wronged V by harming her. Rather, it arises because, having benefited at V's expense, P will otherwise be unjustly enriched. The obligation to pay V, then, is an obligation to *repay*. It is restorative without being compensatory.

A reply to this objection starts with the observation that we often benefit at the expense of others without owing them compensation. Fair competition is like this. Suppose that P Ltd runs a successful advertising campaign and thereby tempts customers of V Ltd to switch their loyalty, with the result that P's profits increase and V goes out of business. On these facts, P owes V nothing. For restoration to be owed, there must be some additional feature. In both *Vincent* and *Cabin*, we contend, that additional feature is a wrong.[29]

Even admitting that, of course, our objector may contend that the wrong alone doesn't generate the obligation that falls upon P. P must also benefit. But then, on an unjust enrichment analysis, P's obligation to repay the transferred value should be limited to the lesser of P's benefit and V's loss. Only that lesser quantum represents a benefit that is *transferred* and thus eligible to be restored. By contrast, in law and, we think, in morality, V is entitled to recover the full amount of the loss even if P's benefit turns out to be less. Unless one holds that V should not be entitled to recover the whole of her loss, its measure is necessarily compensatory.[30]

Two kinds of justification

A more radical response is also available. It might be claimed that, in cases of private necessity, P owes V neither restoration nor compensation.

[29] By which, to repeat, we mean a breach of duty.
[30] Feinberg (ibid.) thinks so too. One worry about our response here is that in private necessity it is always, in principle, the case that P's gain exceeds V's loss. However, that need only be true *ex ante*. It might turn out (given vagaries of causation) that the actual quanta of benefit and harm are different from their expected values.

Perhaps P has a reason to pay V, given the loss V has suffered at P's hands. P nonetheless has no duty to do so. The facts which justify P's actions, this second objector contends, are facts which also negate any such reparative duty.

Why should this be so? The natural answer appeals to the denial view. P lacks a duty to compensate V for her losses because P lacks a duty not to cause those losses in the first place. The facts that justify P's actions successfully negate the former duty by successfully negating the latter. No obligation in. No obligation out. At least in cases of private necessity.

This line of thought harbours an ambiguity exposed in the previous section. Understood one way, our second objector is claiming that P's duty is cancelled.[31] Understood another way, she is claiming that P's conduct falls within an exception. We already rejected the former possibility in the paradigmatic case of self-defence. P is justified in using reasonable force against V to defend herself against V's attack. But V's interests—the very interests that would otherwise ground P's duty not to cause V harm—continue to speak against P's actions. V does not become an outlaw, legally or morally, merely because she is an attacker. Neither, however, is V merely in the wrong place at the wrong time. P's justification for harming V is within V's control. All V need do to deny that justification to P is refrain from attacking her. In our paradigmatic case of self-defence, V chooses otherwise: she places P under attack, and does so culpably. P's liberty to harm V, we argued, follows from this fact. To deny P that liberty—to hold that P has a duty not to harm V—would to be to confer upon V a power she should not possess: a power to require P, by culpably attacking her, to choose between self-sacrifice and becoming a wrongdoer.

In making these claims about the paradigmatic case of self-defence, we occupy a middle ground. On the one hand, we deny that P's duty not to harm V is cancelled. On the other, we deny that P's duty is breached. Things are different, we claim, in cases of private necessity. But they are different in the latter respect, not the former. In both cases of

---

[31] This, in substance, is the position argued for by John Oberdiek. For Oberdiek, cases in which P is justified in causing V some harm are cases in which no right of V's speaks against P's actions. Our argument in this section confronts Oberdiek's view. See J. Oberdiek, 'Specifying Rights out of Necessity' (2008), 28 *Oxford Journal of Legal Studies* 127. For an instructive response, see H. Liberto, 'The Moral Specification of Rights: A Restricted Account' (2014), 33 *Law and Philosophy* 175.

self-defence and private necessity, the rationale for P's duty continues to speak against what P does. Neither is like the case, considered in section 4, in which Q bequeaths a clock to P. There, Q's ownership right provides no reason for P not to take the clock. *Ceteris paribus*, P need not appeal to a reason to take it to show that the taking is permissible. Neither does the permissibility of P's taking the clock depend on why P takes it. Things are different when P eats V's food, or burns V's furniture, without gaining V's consent. P is not permitted to cause such damage unless she has a sufficiently weighty reason to cause it. Nor, we have claimed, is she permitted to cause the damage for any old reason. P's permission is limited in both respects precisely because V's property rights continue to speak against P's actions. They do so even as P is justified in acting as she does.

It is tempting to think the resemblance we have identified goes deeper: that, like self-defence, private necessity involves an exception to the duty owed by P to V. That, however, would be a step too far. Recall our contention that, in cases of self-defence, P benefits from an exclusionary permission. In cases of private necessity, by contrast, no such permission obtains. P's protected reason not to harm V must be weighed in the balance. The possibility of justification arises because P's duty is not absolute. There are countervailing reasons it neither excludes nor outweighs. Where P has (and acts for) such a reason, her duty is overridden. She has a justification despite committing a wrong.

We have already seen why private necessity is unlike self-defence in this respect. In the paradigmatic case of the latter, to repeat, V controls P's justification. She can secure herself against being permissibly harmed by refraining from attacking P. That V declines to avail herself of that security, by choosing to attack P, explains why P benefits from the exclusionary permission—why P's actions fall within an exception to her duty not to cause V harm. This must be so, we have claimed, if both law and morality are not to confer on V a power over P that V should not possess.

When it comes to private necessity, the picture is markedly different. V has no control over P's justification. There is nothing she can do to secure herself against being permissibly harmed. She lacks such security because the ground of P's justification is not an exercise of V's agency. Imagine that a fire breaks out. Ploughing up some of V's crops proves necessary to create a fire break and thereby save P's house. P may be justified, we take it, in ploughing up the crops. It is true, of course, that no justification would have obtained had V not chosen to farm where she did. But the fact that V did so is not the ground of P's justification. The ground of P's justification is the fact that V's farm happens to be in the path of the fire, plus the fact that ploughing part of the land is the only effective means of saving the house. None of this, obviously enough, is V's doing. Here, V *is* in the wrong place at the wrong time. Ultimately, P is justified because the causal levers arrange themselves so as to make V a convenient victim. This, however, is no reason to deny that P owes it to V not to cause her harm. That P continues to have a duty not to harm V acknowledges that V is no mere resource for solving P's problem—that she is a person whose rights and interests demand respect. Those rights and interests continue to speak against P's actions even as the duty they justify is overridden.

Two kinds of defence

If we are right so far, P has an *ex ante* duty not to harm V in cases of private necessity. P's *ex post* duty to compensate V is a normative conse-quence of P's having breached this duty.[32] It may seem to follow that the denial view must also be rejected. In truth, this does not quite follow. The denial view cannot stand, assuming our arguments are successful, *if* private necessity is properly regarded as a justificatory defence. But the claim that a wrong is done in cases of private necessity might be taken to point in a different direction. Rather than confronting the denial view, it might be thought to imply that no justification is in play. It might be

---

[32] On an alternative analysis, this is not so. In cases of private necessity, P incurs a duty to compensate V for harm caused. This duty is not owed, however, to P's breach of a duty not to harm V. As in cases of self-defence, P has no such duty. If this alternative analysis is correct, private necessity and self-defence are alike when it comes P's duties *ex ante*. They differ when it comes to P's duties *ex post*. One way to explain this difference is to appeal to an idea we intro-duced earlier. Perhaps P has a duty to compensate V because, though P's problem is not of V's making, P nonetheless chooses to solve that problem by causing V harm. We think this analysis gets the *ex post* picture right. We disagree, however, when it comes to the *ex ante*. In cases of private necessity—unlike in self-defence—V is a convenient victim. Though V proves to be the resource P needs to solve her problem, P nonetheless has a duty not to use V as such. This is a duty P breaches by harming V in order to protect herself. P's duty remains intact even though, since her conduct is justified, P has an undefeated reason to cause V harm.

thought, instead, to imply that *Vincent* and *Cabin* are properly regarded as cases of *excuse*. That is to say: P's action is an unjustified breach of duty, one for which she must pay compensation, yet one for which she is not culpable.

Legal support exists for the alternative reading. In *Perka*, the Canadian Supreme Court endorsed the view that private necessity excuses rather than justifies.[33] To be sure, from an *ex post* standpoint, private necessity exhibits features similar to those of an excuse. It generates secondary duties for P, including a duty of compensation. Crucially, however, it does not share the same *ex ante* features. By contrast with cases of excuse, the guiding reasons favouring action taken in private necessity are undefeated. As such, those reasons operate also to guide V and others. V is not permitted to resist P's efforts to plough her crops. Neither is T, an onlooker perceiving events, permitted to join V in resisting P. Quite the opposite: T is permitted to help P. Should she choose to do so, T's intervention would not be *excused*. It would be justified. Looking at the case from an *ex ante* perspective reveals this difference.

6. Closing Remarks

The bifurcated view for which we have argued is possible because, in private necessity cases, the *ex ante* and the *ex post* come apart. Between P and V, *ex post* P ought to pay for the harm done to V. P chose to cause that harm, and did so for her own benefit. She imposed costs upon V for reasons that arose outwith V's control. Morally and legally, however, it is permissible *ex ante* for P to harm V. She has undefeated reasons for doing so. The harm P causes is, thus, justified. Others may help P to plough V's crops; and V may not take self-protective measures to resist them. Yet P's reasons do not respond to an exercise of V's agency. In that sense, there is no dialogue, no mediation between the two agents. V's interests are merely subordinated to those of P. The concession view is right about private necessity.

---

[33] Partly for rule of law reasons: 'To go beyond [the Criminal Code] and hold that ostensibly illegal acts can be validated on the basis of their expediency, would import an undue subjectivity into the criminal law.' *Perka v The Queen* [1985] 13 DLR (4th) 1, 14.

P acts permissibly, too, when she uses reasonable force in self-defence. Here, however, the *ex ante* and the *ex post* are aligned, because P chooses to harm V for reasons of V's own making. That additional feature is and should be liberating for P. No longer is V simply a victim. Rather, she controls the permissibility of P's response. To hold that action taken in self-defence constitutes a wrong would be to give V a power over P—a power to require P to choose between self-sacrifice and becoming a wrongdoer. This would be to make law and morality an instrument of oppression. To reject that possibility, and deny that P is a wrongdoer, is to respect the agency of both P and V. The denial view is right about self-defence. And so the bifurcated view is the correct one.[34]

James Edwards and A.P. Simester, *Justification and Duty* In: *Oxford Studies in Philosophy of Law, Volume 5.* Edited by: Leslie Green and Brian Leiter, Oxford University Press. © James Edwards and A.P. Simester 2024. DOI: 10.1093/9780198919650.003.0006

[34] An earlier version was presented at the Michaelmas Hearings in October 2022 at King's College London. Thanks to the audience on that occasion, and to Andrew Halpin for written comments.

The Trouble with Trespass

John Oberdiek

I. Introduction

Private property is a fundamental feature of nearly every well-developed legal system, and in common law jurisdictions it is protected first and foremost by the tort of trespass: one is not permitted intentionally to enter or even touch property belonging to another without authorization, and one who does is liable to the owner.[1] The protection offered by the tort of trespass is, moreover, robust. For in addition to being an intentional tort, trespass is a strict liability tort. This means that even one who enters another's property *with justification* is liable to them for trespass. In this way, the tort of trespass is indifferent to the circumstances surrounding the entry; what matters is that it was not authorized. This conception of the tort of trespass, and thus of property, seems to be settled as a matter of positive law. The Restatement (Fourth) of Property, now underway, for example, has confirmed that even justified entries onto another's property are trespasses and subject to liability. It is my aim in what follows to challenge the normative cogency of this apparent fact of positive law.

I argue that trespass acquires whatever normative significance it has, ultimately, from the tort of battery. People's *things* matter because *people* matter. It follows from this that property should not be more protected than people. And yet, in a basic sense, the common law does protect

---

[1] "Owners" is a simplification; tenants and others with lesser property interests count for these purposes as well. "Possessors" would be more accurate, but also more cumbersome. I use "owners" in what follows as a shorthand for anyone with a relevant possessory interest. My focus here is on trespass to land, not trespass to chattel/personal property, which also requires that the personal property be damaged.

property more than people insofar as the *prima facie* case of battery is rebutted if a would-be battery is justified while the *prima facie* case of trespass is *not* rebutted even if a would-be trespass is justified. Put another way, although a justified battery is not in fact a battery, a justified trespass is nevertheless still a trespass. This asymmetry, I argue, reveals that the common law of trespass is conceptually and morally misguided.

I begin in Section II by explicating the tort of trespass and the right to exclude at its heart. In Section III, I focus on the limits of the right to exclude, making special reference to the famous necessity cases of *Ploof v. Putnam* and *Vincent v. Lake Erie*. In Section IV, I locate the tort of trespass within the wider firmament of tort law, and make the case that it is conceptually and normatively subordinate to the tort of battery. Section V illustrates the trouble with trespass as presently conceived by contrasting its exceptions, or lack thereof, with the exceptions to the tort of battery. If trespass answers to battery, then things should not enjoy greater protection than persons, and yet that inversion is precisely what we find in the law. I conclude by noting and defending a revisionary implication of my criticism of the tort of trespass, namely, that one who enters another's property under circumstances of necessity should not be liable to them.

II. Trespass and the Right to Exclude

Fundamental to property is the right to exclude. This right lies at the center of the ascendant "architectural" or "new essentialist" approach to property[2], but it is also valorized in the competing bundle-of-sticks

---

[2] See e.g. Thomas W. Merrill, "Property and the Right to Exclude," 77 *Nebraska Law Review* 730 (1998), Henry E. Smith, "Exclusion versus Governance," 31 *Journal of Legal Studies* 453 (1998), and Thomas W. Merrill and Henry E. Smith, "The Architecture of Property," in Hanoch Dagan and Benjamin C. Zipursky (eds.), *Research Handbook on Private Law Theory* (Edward Elgar Publishing 2020), 134–54 . For discussion, see Katrina Wyman, "The New Essentialism in Property," 9 *Journal of Legal Analysis* 183 (2017). Though Merrill and Smith offer a broadly economic explanation of the right to exclude, the centrality of the right to exclude to property need not depend on an economic explanation. It also does not follow from the centrality of the right to exclude that property revolves exclusively around that right on such an approach; license and alienation also are crucial. For example, James Penner defends a theory making

approach insofar as the right to exclude is "one of the most essential sticks in the bundle of rights that are commonly characterized as property."[3] There is broad consensus among these opposing theories, then, that property confers on its owners a broad right to exclude. More specifically, owners have *in rem* exclusion rights, that is, rights of exclusion that are good against the world of non-owners, *ceteris paribus*. The preceding *ceteris paribus* clause papers over certain differences between the two dominant approaches to property, concerning perhaps especially what precisely the right to exclude actually excludes. But the two approaches agree that the right to exclude typically applies and also that where the right to exclude does apply, the right is stringent, placing demanding duties on others to respect it.

This is not coincidence. For the right is recognized by the law of torts as correlating to a strict duty to honor it and correspondingly strict liability for its violation. Indeed, the tort of trespass is a paradigmatic strict liability tort. Take a prosaic example. It may have been reasonable to build the fence where I did, for I placed it precisely where I was supposed to based on the professionally conducted survey on file with the county clerk, but the survey was mistaken, so my fence now sits on your land, and as a result, I have trespassed and am liable to you.[4] The fact that mine was a reasonable mistake has no bearing on the tortiousness of my conduct—it remains a trespass, even if innocent.[5] The placement of my fence violates your right to exclude any non-owner from your property, and that right stands against even reasonable intrusions. Every

---

"essential reference not only to the right to exclude simpliciter but also to the powers of title." James E. Penner, *Property Rights: A Re-Examination* (Oxford 2020), 27 n. 78. See also James E. Penner, "The 'Bundle of Rights' Picture of Property," 43 *UCLA Law Review* 711 (1996) and *The Idea of Property in Law* (Oxford 1997). I should add that little in the analysis that follows would change if the right to exclude were replaced at the center of property law by the subtly different right to exclusive agenda-setting authority as defended in Larissa Katz, "Exclusion and Exclusivity in Property Law," 58 *University of Toronto Law Journal* 275 (2008).

[3] *Dolan v. City of Tigard*, 512 U.S. 374 (1994), 384. See also *Jacque v. Steenberg Homes, Inc.*, 563 N.W.2d 154 (Wis. 1997) 159–60. For defense of the bundle-of-sticks approach, see e.g. Thomas C. Grey, "The Disintegration of Property," 22 *NOMOS: Property* 69 (1980), and Stephen C. Munzer, *A Theory of Property* (Cambridge 1990).

[4] For a variation on these facts, see *Burns Philp Food, Inc. v. Cavalea Cont'l Freight, Inc.*, 135 F.3d 526 (7th Cir. 1998). See also, *Pile v. Pedrick*, 31 A. 646 and 31 A. 647 (Pa. 1895), and *Golden Press, Inc. v. Rylands*, 235 P.2d 592 (Colo. 1951).

[5] Although reasonable mistakes and innocent trespasses will not be subject to punitive damages, while intentional trespasses may be.

common law jurisdiction is crystal clear about this, underscoring the fact that trespass is a strict liability tort.

It is this feature of property—the fact that the right to exclude is stringent, grounding the strict liability tort of trespass—that is taken by many to account for the outcome in *Vincent v. Lake Erie*.[6] In that famous case, the steamship Reynolds had docked to unload its cargo at a pier on Lake Superior when a storm arose. Though the ship had just finished unloading its cargo, such that its permission to dock was now extinguished, the Reynolds' captain ordered the ship's crew to keep the Reynolds fast to the pier to avoid facing the storm on open water, which would have risked the ship and its crew. In staying docked the ship was indeed saved, but the storm-driven wind and waves repeatedly threw it against the pier, which suffered damage as a result. The owner of the pier consequently sued the owner of the ship and a 3-2 majority of the Minnesota Supreme Court found for the plaintiff. The court held that while the Reynolds' captain's decision to stay tied to the plaintiff's pier was reasonable, the defendant nevertheless owed the plaintiff compensation for the resulting damage.

This case and its result has long preoccupied commentators insofar as reasonable conduct precludes liability in prominent domains of tort law. For example, that I took reasonable care in driving entails that, though I nevertheless accidentally crashed into and injured you, you have no viable tort claim against me. If the Reynolds' captain's decision to stay docked in *Vincent* was a reasonable one, why then was the Reynolds' owner nevertheless liable for the damage sustained by the pier? The literature that *Vincent* has spawned is vast and impossible to summarize. Francis Bohlen began analysis of the case when in 1926 he articulated the influential *sui generis* doctrine of "incomplete privilege" to make sense of the holding.[7] According to Bohlen, the Reynolds' staying fast to the pier was *privileged* insofar as it was reasonable, entailing that the owner would have been barred from preventing the ship from docking or casting it off after it had done so, but the privilege was *incomplete* to

---

[6] 124 N.W. 221 (Minn. 1910).

[7] Francis H. Bohlen, "Incomplete Privilege to Inflict Intentional Invasions of Property and Personality," 39 *Harvard Law Review* 307 (1926).

the extent that the ship's owner nevertheless owed the pier owner compensation for the damage sustained. While the concept of an incomplete privilege has proven to be an influential *characterization* of the puzzle of *Vincent*, however, it is not itself an *analysis* of it. Indeed, the notion of an incomplete privilege itself calls for analysis.

There is, though, a more theoretically compelling and parsimonious explanation, one offered and comprehensively developed by John Goldberg and Benjamin Zipursky.[8] They read *Vincent* as a straightforward trespass case. By intentionally staying docked after its cargo had been unloaded, the Reynolds exceeded the scope of its permission to be on the dock owner's property. It may have been reasonable for the ship to stay docked, in other words, but that fact is inapposite, for it intentionally touched the property of another without (contemporaneously operative) authorization. In remaining tied to the pier without the owner's authorization, in other words, the Reynolds was trespassing. By virtue of violating the pier owner's right to exclude, the Reynolds' owner was liable for the damage the ship caused while trespassing, even though its trespass was reasonable.

Now, summarized in this way, the holding in *Vincent* would seem to support not simply strict *liability* but a strict *primary duty* not to intrude on another's property, even if reasonable.[9] That is, if even the reasonable touching of another's property generates liability, perhaps that is because even the reasonable touching of another's property is prohibited. If true, this would emphatically vindicate the right to exclude that is at the heart of property. But it would also be doubly mistaken, both as a conceptual matter and as a matter of positive law. Consider these errors in turn.

The conceptual error consists in thinking a reasonable touching could be prohibited—it cannot. For a reasonable touching just is a justified one, justified conduct cannot be prohibited, so a reasonable touching of another's property cannot be prohibited.[10] This logic might

---

[8]   John C. P. Goldberg and Benjamin C. Zipursky, *Recognizing Wrongs* (Harvard 2020), 190.

[9]   For discussion of the relationship between strict duties and strict liability, see Stephen A. Smith, "Strict Duties and the Rule of Law," in Lisa M. Austin and Dennis Klimchuk (eds.), *Private Law and the Rule of Law* (Oxford 2014), 190–1.

[10]   See John Gardner, "The Mysterious Case of the Reasonable Person," in *Torts and Other Wrongs* (Oxford 2019), arguing that "reasonable" is synonymous with "justified." Note that while it has become commonplace to understand "reasonableness" through an economic lens,

appear mistaken. After all, the type of trespassory conduct that I first cited to illustrate the strictness of the tort—reasonably mistaken trespasses—can most certainly be prohibited. If a neighbor is about to build a fence on an owner's property on account of a reasonable mistake, the owner can get an injunction against the neighbor.[11] But cases of making a reasonable mistake in siting a fence or structure on another's property make sense as *reasonable* mistake cases because the mistake is made at t2, when the neighbor neither believes nor has reason to believe that they are in fact trespassing. If the owner approached the would-be trespasser at t1, before any trespass was committed, explaining that the land belonged to the owner, then any subsequent trespass would not be a reasonable mistake. Even simply acting to bar entry without explanation would likely vitiate the reasonableness of the would-be trespasser's mistake, for doing so would put them on notice that the property might not be theirs. Equipped with the relevant information, in other words, the would-be trespasser would no longer be an innocent one and their mistake would no longer be reasonable.[12] This conclusion cannot, however, be generalized. Notably, necessity cases do not have this same structure or these caveats. There is no mistake of fact in such cases that might be cleared up. Instead, the entry in a necessity case is reasonable full stop—it is justified—and thus it cannot be prohibited full stop.

This conceptual truth finds famous expression in black letter law. *Ploof v. Putnam*, itself cited approvingly by the *Vincent* majority, stands

---

thanks to Richard Posner's interpretation of Learned Hand's opinion in *Carroll Towing*, I make no such assumption, and nor does Gardner. See *U.S. v. Carroll Towing Co.*, 159 F.2d 169 (1947) and Richard A. Posner, "A Theory of Negligence," 1 *Journal of Legal Studies* 29 (1972). See also John Gardner, "What Is Tort Law For? The Place of Corrective Justice," in *Torts and Other Wrongs*, 43.

[11] A *quia timet* injunction is available when a defendant is about to commit a wrong but has not yet committed one. For discussion, see Stephen A. Smith, *Rights, Wrongs, and Injustices: The Structure of Remedial Law* (Oxford 2019), 147–9.

[12] I discuss the same point in a parallel context in John Oberdiek, *Imposing Risk: A Normative Framework* (Oxford 2017), 53–7. As a matter of positive law, even if this trespasser cannot for some reason be informed of their mistake before being barred from entering the owner's property, the owner could still rightfully exclude them. For their would-be entry, though based on a mistake that is reasonable, would nevertheless be based on a mistake. Entry would not be justified. It is notable, though, that the law at least under certain circumstances distinguishes the innocent from the non-innocent trespasser at the remedial stage: the innocent trespasser in a case like the one I am contemplating may only owe (permanent) damages, while the intentional trespasser is sure to be subject to an injunction, which will require (much more costly) removal of the offending structure. See *Golden Press v. Rylands, Inc.*, supra note 4.

for the proposition that one is permitted to enter the property of another, even without authorization, under circumstances of necessity.[13] The standing authority an owner typically has to prohibit entry onto their property gives way in cases of necessity because entry under those circumstances is justified. This is why Bohlen was correct to describe the rule in *Vincent* as a privilege at all. In *Ploof*, a landowner was held liable when his agent unmoored a small sailboat trying to dock at the owner's pier during a storm on Lake Champlain, casting the boat's occupants and cargo into the water. The mooring, the Vermont Supreme Court held, was permitted out of necessity. Necessity, in other words, justified what would otherwise have been prohibited, namely, entering another's property without the consent of the owner. Thus, as the Restatement puts it, according to the doctrine of private necessity, one is privileged intentionally to enter or remain on another's property when doing so is, or reasonably appears to be, necessary to prevent serious harm to oneself, one's property, or another.[14] Black letter law therefore recognizes the conceptual truth that the reasonable, justified entry onto or touching of another's property is not something that can be prohibited.

Still, what remains true, and what *Vincent* confirmed in the wake of *Ploof*, is that one who enters or touches the property of another without authorization is liable to the owner even if doing so is justified. It is this triad of propositions—the entry is a trespass, the trespass is justified, and the justified trespasser is liable to the owner—that I challenge.

III. The Boundaries of the Right to Exclude: *Ploof* and *Vincent* Revisited

The aforementioned combination of propositions provides an elegant solution to what is otherwise a puzzling aspect of *Vincent*. For that puzzle only seems to arise if one views the case through the lens of negligence. The tort of negligence revolves around unreasonable conduct: liability

---

[13] 71 A. 188 (Vt. 1908).
[14] Restatement of the Law (Fourth), Property, Vol. 2., Div. 1, Ch. 1. Trespass to Land, §1.20.

only attaches if the defendant acted unreasonably. Through this lens, there should be no liability in *Vincent* because the Reynolds' captain did not act unreasonably. And yet there is liability in *Vincent*. If *Vincent* is understood as a run-of-the-mill trespass case, however, there is no puzzle, for trespass grounds liability regardless of the reasonableness of the underlying conduct.

As John Goldberg and Benjamin Zipursky, the architects of this approach, articulate their position,

> Intentionally occupying or building on a swath of land is a trespass if in fact the land is possessed by another and the other has not permitted the occupation or building. The occupier's or builder's having behaved prudently or reasonably does nothing to defeat liability. Indeed, as *Vincent v. Lake Erie* famously demonstrates, even morally justified interferences with the property rights of another can be actionable in the law of torts.[15]

On their view, it would seem, what is puzzling about *Vincent* is why others have taken it to be puzzling.

Goldberg and Zipursky's characterization of *Vincent* as a trespass case is based upon the case's holding that the Reynolds' owner owed compensatory damages to the pier owner, and so founded, that characterization is difficult to dispute. But if one also takes judicial reasoning and language seriously in characterizing the law, something that Goldberg and Zipursky are committed to doing,[16] then it is less obvious that *Vincent* is a "plain-vanilla trespass case."[17] In this regard, it is notable that the *Vincent* majority itself rejected a trespass interpretation, a fact which Goldberg and Zipursky readily acknowledge.[18] Before reaching the normative question of whether the common law of trespass is

---

[15] John C. P. Goldberg and Benjamin C. Zipursky, *Recognizing Wrongs* (Harvard 2020), 190 (italics omitted). See also, John C. P. Goldberg and Benjamin C. Zipursky, *Torts: Oxford Introductions to U.S. Law* (Oxford 2010), 238–41.

[16] See Goldberg and Zipursky, *Recognizing Wrongs*, ibid., p. 47, arguing for "taking tort law at face value as lawyers."

[17] Goldberg and Zipursky, *Torts*, supra note 15, p. 240.

[18] As they put it, "[w]e think the *Vincent* court reached the right result, but needlessly complicated its analysis by denying there was a trespass." Goldberg and Zipursky, *Recognizing Wrongs*, supra note 15, p. 190 n. 11.

morally sound, then, it is worth taking *Vincent* as well as *Ploof* at face value to see just how unequivocally they can be restated as trespass cases.

The *Ploof* court, for its part, could not be much clearer in *denying* that the sailboat's mooring on the owner's pier was a trespass: "[t]here are many cases in the books which hold that necessity...will justify entries upon land and interferences with personal property that would otherwise have been trespasses."[19] If entries onto another's property borne of necessity "would otherwise have been trespasses," it means that entries onto another's property that are not made under circumstances of necessity *are* trespasses but that necessary entries are *not*. This is not an aberrant statement either. The Vermont Supreme Court repeatedly states this point in *Ploof*. The court observes, for example, that one traveling on a highway that suddenly and temporarily becomes obstructed "may pass upon the adjoining land without becoming a trespasser because of the necessity."[20] It further notes that "[a]n entry onto land to save goods which are in danger of being lost or destroyed by water or fire is not a trespass."[21] In these instances, while the entries are not authorized, they are nevertheless also not trespasses. *Ploof* itself emphatically underscores this, for the entry there was not merely unauthorized, it was outright resisted. And yet it was no trespass. *Vincent*, moreover, corroborates all of this. In its retelling of *Ploof*, the *Vincent* majority recounts that "where, under stress of weather, a vessel was without permission moored to a private dock at an island in Lake Champlain owned by the defendant, the plaintiff was not guilty of trespass...."[22] *Vincent* endorses this reading of *Ploof* and seeks simply to show that a finding of liability does not depend upon a finding of trespass.[23]

If one takes these opinions at face value, then, it would seem that they cannot be read as cases involving trespasses. For the opinions themselves deny that the necessary entries constituted trespasses. And they reach that conclusion on the force of the observation that necessity

---

[19] 71 A. 188 at 189.   [20] Ibid.
[21] Ibid.   [22] 124 N.W. 221 at 222.
[23] "If, in [*Ploof*], the vessel had been permitted to remain, and the dock had suffered an injury, we believe the shipowner would have been held liable for the injury done." Ibid.

justifies the touching of or entry upon another's property.[24] That the entries were justified is the reason why the entries were not, in fact, trespasses.

Yet the reason we are stuck with Bohlen's notion of an incomplete privilege is that the majority in *Vincent* found that although the Reynolds was justified in staying roped to the pier, it was liable for the damage it caused in doing so. It is this fact that Goldberg and Zipursky fix on in interpreting *Vincent* as a trespass case. On their view, the defendant's secondary obligation to pay damages implies the breach of a primary obligation, and specifically, the obligation not to touch the plaintiff's property without authorization. So, *Vincent* and *Ploof* really are trespass cases, according to this reading, notwithstanding the fact that the opinions themselves expressly deny this.

IV. Trespass to Land and the Primacy of Trespass against Persons

Still, the law's bottom line is clear. There is no room for debate that, in a private necessity case like *Vincent*, damages are owed as a matter of black letter law.[25] The Restatement is crystal clear about this. Taking the language and express reasoning in *Vincent* and *Ploof* at face value is nevertheless illuminating. These cases are forthright that conduct that would otherwise constitute a trespass is not in fact a trespass if that conduct is justified. It seems to me that those famous necessity cases get that right as a moral matter. An upshot of this, by my lights, is that our positive law gets private necessity wrong and stands in need of revision: by virtue of being justified, necessary entries onto another's property are

---

[24] See also *State v. Shack*, 277 A.2d 369 (NJ 1971) ("Hence it has long been true that necessity, private or public, may justify entry upon the lands of another").
[25] Note that public necessity cases depart from private necessity ones on this front. See e.g. *Bowditch v. City of Boston*, 101 U.S. 16, 18 (1879), and *City of Rapid City v. Boland*, 271 N.W.2d 60 (N.D. 1978). Note also that, as Ernest Weinrib points out in *The Idea of Private Law*, *Vincent* itself was decided by a bare majority of the Minnesota Supreme Court and "has been rejected by at least one other common law court." Ernest Weinrib, *The Idea of Private Law* (Harvard 1995), 197 n. 62. Specifically, in the Canadian case of *Munn v. M/V Sir John Crosbie* [1967] 1 Ex. C.R. 94, the majority reached the opposite conclusion as *Vincent*, citing the *Vincent* dissent in support of its holding.

not in fact trespasses, and therefore should *not be subject to liability,* at least as a matter of right.[26]

In this section, I begin making the case for that normative conclusion. I do so by locating the tort of trespass amongst other signal torts, and in relation to the tort of battery in particular. Contrasting the structure of trespass with that of battery helps to reveal why the positive law of trespass is misguided.

The tort of negligence today dominates both the practice of and theorizing about tort law, but the conceptual and normative font of tort law is in fact the tort of battery. Our concern with the careless treatment of people, around which the tort of negligence revolves, derives from our antecedent concern with intentionally wronging them, which is the basis of battery. Accidental wrongs are wrongs at all only because intentional wrongs are wrongs first. Another way to put the point is that what it is not wrong to do intentionally cannot become wrong when done unintentionally. The converse of this, however, is not true.[27] Intentional wrongdoing is therefore explanatorily prior to unintentional wrongdoing.

This same explanatory priority shows up *within* intentional torts as well. In such cases battery's priority is not, of course, secured by its intentional character, as it is with respect to negligence. For unlike negligence, these other torts share that same character. The priority is instead established by the fundamental importance of bodily autonomy, which the tort of battery protects. Consider assault. Battery consists in the intentional harmful or offensive touching of another without their consent, so assault, which consists in intentionally causing another to believe they are about to suffer a battery, is straightforwardly derivative. One can suffer an assault without suffering a battery, to be sure, but assault makes no sense as a wrong unless battery does. Intentionally causing someone to believe they are about to be touched in a harmful or

---

[26] See infra note 48 for an explanation of this qualification and its significance.

[27] As Judith Jarvis Thomson maintains, "other things being equal, it is permissible for A to do something his doing of which will impose a risk of harm H on B *if* it is permissible for A to cause B harm H. That, I think, seems plausible enough. If we could also say 'only if' with equal plausibility, then it would be plausible to think that risk-imposition generates no independent problem for moral theory.... But there unfortunately is what looks like good reason to think we cannot also say 'only if'." Judith Jarvis Thomson, "Imposing Risks," in *Rights, Restitution, and Risk* (Harvard 1986), 177.

THE TROUBLE WITH TRESPASS

offensive manner without consent is only wrong, in other words, because intentionally touching someone in a harmful or offensive manner without consent is wrong first. The same is true of false imprisonment, though the relevant derivation is perhaps not as obvious. It could not be wrong to confine people against their will if it were not wrong first to touch people in a harmful or offensive way against their will. This is not because false imprisonment makes essential reference to battery in the way that assault does—it does not—but because freedom of movement matters only if basic bodily integrity does. Being able to move one's body freely through space matters only because one's bodily autonomy matters, and that autonomy is, again, what the tort of battery safeguards. The wrong of confining another against their will, like the wrong of assault, is thus an extension of the wrong of harmfully or offensively touching without consent. False imprisonment only makes sense because battery does.

This one-way dependence holds with respect to the tort of trespass as well. Now, in the common law's original nomenclature, of course, every tort was a trespass. Every tort descended from the writs of trespass and trespass on the case, which revolved around direct wrongs to persons and property. This history, while no less contingent than any history, is nevertheless unsurprising. Given the conceptual pole position that I am claiming battery occupies, the history of tort law and the attendant nomenclature makes sense, for even if batteries are no longer denominated as trespasses, they are colloquial trespasses in the most basic sense. For they are violations of the autonomy of persons. The contemporary incarnation of the tort of trespass, though, is as a property tort. A trespasser is someone who intentionally touches or enters another's property without consent. And though we understand trespass differently and more narrowly than the early common law did, as focusing exclusively on property, the contemporary conception of trespass is related to the common law's original and more capacious conceptualization. That relationship is by now familiar. Much as negligence, assault, and false imprisonment all derive from battery, trespass is conceptually dependent upon battery. The contemporary tort of trespass is intelligible only because the contemporary tort of battery is intelligible.

This might be obscured by the history of the common law, in that trespass as originally conceived indiscriminately covered direct wrongs to persons *and* property. But as a conceptual as well as a normative matter, it is clear that the modern version of the tort of trespass answers to what we now denominate as battery. Why? People's *things matter* only because *people matter*.[28] What matters first and foremost are people; their things matter only because the people who own them do. This is not intended to be a Hegelian claim about the way that property and personhood are intertwined,[29] but a quite down-to-earth and even self-evident one. The things that are protected as property are important *to* their owners, it is true, but it is the importance *of* their owners that makes property important. One way to put this point is that the value of property cannot be understood without reference to ownership, a concept which depends upon there being an owner, whether individual or collective. Perhaps some things have intrinsic value apart from valuers, that is, apart from the existence of people who could value them—I take no stand on that question here—but no thing can be understood and valued as property absent an owner. The importance of property depends on the importance of people; if people did not matter, morally speaking, then neither would property. Trespass therefore depends upon battery.

The conceptual relationship between the torts of battery and trespass in particular is illuminating because it reveals shortcomings in our positive law's conceptualization of the latter. The tort of trespass as presently conceived within Anglo-American law is malformed, at once overdrawn and wooden. Its shortcomings are most obviously normative in my view, yet they are fundamentally conceptual in nature. The trouble with trespass is this. The tort of trespass owes its place in our constellation of torts to battery, the foundational tort, but the way that trespass is constructed suggests that it is battery, not trespass, that is derivative. This is because, in the most fundamental way, the tort of trespass protects property even more than the tort of battery protects persons. And that, it seems to me, cannot be right.

---

[28] The influential thing-based characterization of property that I am assuming is defended in Henry E. Smith, "Property as the Law of Things," 125 *Harvard Law Review* 1691 (2012).

[29] G. W. F. Hegel, *Elements of the Philosophy of Right*, Allen Wood (ed.), H. B. Nisbet (transl.) (Cambridge 1991), 1821. For discussion and defense of the Hegelian approach of property, see Margaret Jane Radin, "Property and Personhood," 34 *Stanford Law Review* 957 (1982).

This is apparent in the first instance in the very definitions of the *prima facie* cases of the two torts: one can commit a trespass even without causing any damage to the real property one touches, but one only commits a battery if one's intentional touching of another is harmful or offensive. The tort of trespass thus has fewer qualifications than the tort of battery—it is easier to wrong someone *qua* owner than it is to wrong someone *qua* person. That strikes me as backwards.

The second way in which trespass protects property even more than battery protects persons is brought into relief by *Vincent*, and it is this that I focus on in what follows. Though the touching was *justified* in that case, the touching was nevertheless the *basis of liability*. The law of battery, protecting persons rather than their property, however, admits of no such possibility. If one touches another with justification, one is not liable to them. This is evident in cases of self-defense. If I am attacking you, you may repel my attack with reasonable force, committing a *prima facie* battery against me. But because your self-defensive force is justified, you are not liable to me for the harm you inflict, assuming that it is proportionate. Justification negates liability. It does so because the justification fully rebuts the *prima facie* case of battery. That is, justification negates liability for battery because justification transforms what would have been a battery into a non-battery.[30] The same, however, is not true of trespass. Justification does not necessarily negate liability for trespass because, according to the law, justification does not transform the trespass into a non-trespass—the language of *Vincent* and *Ploof* notwithstanding. This, again, gets things backwards. As justification fully rebuts the *prima facie* case of battery, it should *a fortiori* fully rebut the *prima facie* case of trespass. Property should not enjoy greater protection in the law than persons, for things matter only because people matter. Our positive law should be revised to reflect that fact.

---

[30] As Heidi Hurd evocatively makes this point with respect to the justification of consent, "consent turns a trespass into a dinner party; a battery into a handshake; a theft into a gift; an invasion of privacy into an intimate moment; a commercial appropriation of name and likeness into a biography." Heidi M. Hurd, "The Moral Magic of Consent," 2 *Legal Theory* 121 (1996), 123. Note that Hurd mentions the transformative effect of consent on trespass; I argue that justification generally, and not simply the justification of consent, should have this transformative effect, converting what would otherwise be trespasses into non-trespasses.

V. Necessity, Self-Defense, and Justification

It might be objected at this point that I have drawn a false parallel between cases of necessity and self-defense, and that I cannot therefore appeal to the negating power that self-defense has with respect to the tort of battery to show that necessity should negate trespass. Self-defense, this line of reasoning holds, is qualitatively different from necessity. The *Vincent* majority itself seems to make this argument in maintaining, "[t]his is not a case where life or property was menaced by any object or thing belonging to the plaintiff, the destruction of which became necessary to prevent the threatened disaster."[31] The Minnesota Supreme Court seems to be distinguishing the facts of *Vincent*, where the plaintiff's property was passive and non-threatening, from a situation where the plaintiff's property actually threatens the defendant. The implication is that, where the plaintiff's property poses a threat, the defendant would be able to destroy that property out of self-defense and also escape liability for the destruction, just as in a standard self-defense case. Necessity, in contrast, does not operate in the same fashion according to the court.

The problem with this response is that it misidentifies what is normatively significant about necessity and self-defense. Each possesses whatever normative significance it has by virtue of being a species of justification. It is because self-defense is a justification that it negates the *prima facie* case of battery. Necessity should negate trespass for the same reason. In either case, the conduct is rightful because justified.

Or perhaps not. Goldberg (writing alone) challenges the analysis of necessity as a justification. On his view, necessity does not justify unauthorized entry onto another's property. In fact, he even denies that necessity excuses such entry. According to Goldberg, "[a] trespass committed out of private necessity is neither justified nor excused, which is why damages are owed for harm caused by such a trespass."[32] Tort law,

---

[31] 124 N.W. 221 at 222.

[32] John Goldberg, "Tort Law's Missing Excuses," in Andrew Dyson, James Goudkamp, and Frederick Wilmot-Smith (eds.), *Defences in Tort* (Hart 2015), 54. Goldberg is forthright in focusing on the status of necessity as a *legal* justification and excuse for trespass, not its status as a moral justification or excuse for trespass. In subjecting his position to scrutiny, I am trying to assess whether necessity's legal status can pass moral muster. That is not Goldberg's principal aim.

he maintains, "requires us to avoid trespassing on...others' property even out of necessity."[33] As Goldberg understands it, the tort of trespass prohibits unauthorized entry onto an owner's land no matter what. Thus, "a trespass done out of necessity is just that—a trespass."[34] Necessity still has a role to play in certain trespass cases, in his analysis, but not in *Vincent*. The role that necessity plays in trespass cases is instead revealed in *Ploof*, for *Ploof* but not *Vincent* involves conduct undertaken to defend property.

Goldberg notes that one may employ self-help to defend one's property from trespass, but there are limits to what one may do. Specifically, one may not act unreasonably in the defense of one's property. An owner is, for example, clearly permitted to lock their front door, and may be entitled to shove a trespasser out of their doorway, but an owner cannot (without more) use deadly force against a trespasser *qua* trespasser to protect their property.[35] This is the rub, according to Goldberg. For circumstances of necessity present owners whose property is being intruded upon with the highly-circumscribed choice of either not resisting the trespass and thus tolerating the wrong or ejecting the trespasser under life-threatening or otherwise too-dangerous conditions. Given this choice, Goldberg maintains, an owner must accede to the trespass. He makes this point by way of an analogy. While under normal circumstances you might be able to push someone else away to prevent them from spitting on you, you may not do so if the aggressive expectorator is standing on the edge of a cliff, because pushing them in that situation would be lethal, and killing another to avert a mere indignity is not reasonable.[36] Likewise in necessity cases. It is not that the entry is justified. It is no more justified than spitting. It is rather that there is no reasonable response that would prevent or terminate the entry. For any response that would prevent or terminate the entry would be disproportionately

---

[33] John Goldberg, "Inexcusable Wrongs," 204 *California Law Review* 167 (2015), 168.

[34] Goldberg, supra note 32, p. 62.

[35] See e.g. *Katko v. Briney*, 183 N.W.2d 657 (Iowa, 1971). The "without more" caveat and "*qua* trespasser" qualification is intended to cover cases that veer into self-defense in one's home, rather than pure defense-of-property cases.

[36] See Goldberg, supra note 32, pp. 62–3.

harmful, given the exigent circumstances, and so the only justified response to an unauthorized entry in such a case is to tolerate it.

Goldberg's stark and fundamental rejoinder, that trespass is trespass and necessity cannot justify it, is elegant in its simplicity. It allows Goldberg to stand on trespass's status as a strict liability tort and make the stronger claim, disputed above, that the tort also encodes an exceptionless primary duty to honor it. There are no justified trespasses on Goldberg's view, and so he is able to stick to the position that every trespass can be prohibited. *Ploof* only appears to stand for the proposition that necessary trespasses cannot be prohibited because the owner is not permitted to eject the trespasser. This fact is misleading, though, because the reason that the owner cannot eject the trespasser has nothing to do with the trespasser being justified; rather, it owes to the disproportionality and therefore unreasonableness of ejecting the trespasser when doing so would be unduly dangerous.

For all its spare elegance, however, Goldberg's position cannot be sustained as a moral matter. Before addressing its substantive shortcomings, note as a threshold matter that holding that an unauthorized entry onto another's property can never be justified—and that necessity in particular does not justify entering another's property—comes at the cost of rejecting (once again) the self-understanding of the relevant caselaw. The majorities in both *Ploof* and *Vincent*, after all, considered the underlying conduct at issue in those cases to be reasonable, which is to say justified. Those cases are, moreover, standardly cited as uncontroversial examples of justified entries.[37] Goldberg takes himself to be interpreting the law of torts, and considers the reasoning that courts engage in to be an important determinant of a sound interpretation. Now, in addition to rejecting the *Ploof* and *Vincent* courts' characterizations of the entries in those cases as non-trespassory, he has rejected their characterizations of those entries as justified. As an interpretation of the caselaw, then, his is increasingly strained.

---

[37] See also Joel Feinberg's famous hypothetical of the hiker who is caught in a storm and finds shelter by breaking into another's unoccupied cabin, which Feinberg asserts is "surely justified." Joel Feinberg, "Voluntary Euthanasia and the Inalienable Right to Life," 7 *Philosophy and Public Affairs* 93 (1978), 102.

It is the normative substance of his position, though, that is its biggest flaw. For Goldberg's position by implication treats the right to exclude as more important than the right to bodily autonomy. It puts things before people. Goldberg focuses on the limits of the right to defend one's property in analyzing *Ploof*, analogizing it to the limits of the right to self-defense. One cannot eject an unauthorized entrant on one's property in circumstances of necessity for the same reason that one cannot kill another to stop them from spitting on one: in both cases the response would be disproportionate. What is telling, though, is what happens short of these limits. For when disproportionality does not rule out responsive, preemptive self-help, it becomes quite clear that the right to exclude, protected by the tort of trespass, cannot be analogized to the right to bodily autonomy, protected by the tort of battery. For there are *countless* circumstances under which one may harm or even kill another justifiably without thereby incurring liability for battery, but there are on Goldberg's view *exactly no* circumstances under which one may enter another's property without their authorization. On his analysis, again, the entry in *Ploof* was unjustified, it is just that ejecting the entrants would also have been unjustified. In contrast, killing another in self-defense can be outright justified. One's property may never be justifiably intruded upon according to this logic, even though one may oneself be justifiably killed in myriad circumstances. The right to exclude is therefore more powerful than the right to bodily autonomy on this view. Or more pointedly, the right to property trumps the right to life. Surely that is mistaken. It is just another manifestation of the wrongheaded fact of positive law that the tort of trespass affords greater protection to owners than the tort of battery affords to people.

Goldberg's analysis of *Ploof* goes wrong, it seems to me, in offering the wrong kind of reason for why the entrants in the case cannot be removed. It is not that the owner was disabled from exercising his right to defend his property. It is rather that the entry itself was justified. As *Ploof* itself succinctly puts it, "necessity…will justify entries upon land."[38] Goldberg rejects viewing *Ploof* and *Vincent* through the lens of justification, maintaining that only in resisting that perspective can one

---

[38] 71 A. 188 at 189.

make sense of the fact that the law holds an entrant liable to the owner for any damage the owner sustains on account of the entry.[39] His argument, I think, misfires. Others, however, reach Goldberg's conclusion, that unauthorized entrants are liable as *Vincent* avers, without following him in jettisoning the framework of justification. Prominent among them are John Gardner and Gregory Keating, who maintain that one can preserve that liability while viewing the entries as justified. I close this section by focusing on Gardner's and Keating's distinct arguments. It is my conclusion that neither of their strategies succeed, the upshot of which is that there is no basis for holding those who are justified in entering another's property liable to those owners, at least as a matter of right.

Gardner's is a complex position that defies quick summary, but for present purposes the following statement will suffice:

> Torts are wrongs—breaches of obligation—and one owes damages for their commission even if one's wrong was justified, never mind excused. True, there are some torts, such as the tort of negligence, that are not committed if one acted with certain justifications. That one acted with reasonable (i.e. justified) care means that one did not commit this tort. These are special cases.... In general one owes reparative damages for torts as wrongs, never mind whether they are justified.[40]

He goes on to note that this is "the lesson" of *Vincent*, which he follows Goldberg and Zipursky in reading as a trespass case.[41]

Gardner's idea, in brief, is that an owner's interest in excluding others from their property grounds a normative reason, and that that normative reason remains in effect even if the circumstances justify not conforming to it. So, on Gardner's view, necessity justifies entering another's property, but that does not extinguish the reason-giving force of the owner's interest in exclusion. That still-standing, unfulfilled reason—the reason not to enter without authorization—still calls for conformity even though it

---

[39] Goldberg, supra note 32.
[40] John Gardner, "What Is Tort Law For? The Place of Corrective Justice," supra note 10, 70–1. Internal footnotes omitted.
[41] Ibid., 71 n. 68.

was outweighed under the circumstances. The only remaining way to conform to that reason, albeit imperfectly, on this approach is to hold the entrant liable to the owner for the entry.[42]

The problem with this tack should be clear by now. For one can say all of the same things about killing another person in self-defense. Anyone has an interest in being alive that grounds a normative reason not to be killed, but in justified self-defense cases, that normative reason not to be killed is defied. And yet there is no liability in such cases. Battery is not battery, in other words, if it is committed in justified self-defense. The host of reasons that count against killing people do not remain in effect, demanding conformity. They are not simply out-weighed but left standing, awaiting conformity in some imperfect way. Killing another with justification, instead, *negates* whatever reasons there are not to kill another person.[43] That is why one does not owe compensation to the (estate of the) person whom one kills in justified self-defense. In short, one is not liable because one has done no wrong.

The mechanics of the defense of private necessity should mirror this, but of course they do not. While necessary entries are permitted according to black letter law, there remains an underlying predicate—a wrong, in Gardner's view—that warrants liability. If this is so, the explanation for why Gardner does not treat battery the same way is fugitive. Either killing another in self-defense is a wrong notwithstanding its justification, in which case liability should follow, or killing another in justified self-defense is not a wrong, in which case liability should not follow. There is, in fact, no liability as a matter of positive law in cases of

[42] I defend a similar but importantly different position to Gardner's in John Oberdiek, "Specifying Rights Out of Necessity," 28 *Oxford Journal of Legal Studies* 127 (2008), 143–4. I argue there that while one has a *reason* to compensate, one does not have a *duty* to do so. I locate the source of the reason to compensate in value pluralism, which holds that values are irreducibly distinct such that the reasons they ground cannot always be conformed to. The basis of the reason to compensate in cases of necessity is "to make good on the unfortunate fact that some reason or reasons counting against what [the justified trespasser] did could not be accommodated in [the trespasser's] justifiable behaviour." This is only a reason and not a duty to compensate, though, because "one can only have a duty to compensate if the primary reason that one initially defied was a categorical reason, or a reason demanding compliance, and that is not what is being supposed here."

[43] Or at least it negates the otherwise decisive *categorical strength* of the reasons not to kill, even if it leaves a now-denuded, non-mandatory reason still standing. I leave this detail unresolved as my argument does not turn on its resolution.

justified self-defense, which in turn implies that killing another in justified self-defense is not after all a wrong. And it seems to me difficult to explain that fact without reference to the fact that the self-defense *is justified*. If justification is doing the relevant work, however, and Gardner admits that the defense of necessity is a justification, then entering another's property without authorization under exigent circumstances is not a wrong and should not be subject to liability.

To hold otherwise, once again, would be to privilege things over persons. Where Goldberg holds that the right to exclude (protected by the tort of trespass) is exceptionless, even though the right to bodily autonomy (protected by the tort of battery) is not, Gardner concedes that the right to exclude, like the right to bodily autonomy, admits of exceptions. This is what it means to say that the defense of private necessity is a justification. But Gardner nevertheless privileges things over persons insofar as he would countenance liability in cases of what he would call justified trespass, even though he would not in cases of justified killing. If things only matter because persons do, then the torts protecting things should not be more robust than the torts protecting persons, and yet Gardner endorses just that inversion.

One may still think that this conclusion gives short shrift to the possibility that Bohlen perceived, but did not explain, in identifying the category of an incomplete privilege. One might think that the steamship Reynolds was indeed justified in staying fast to the pier in *Vincent*, but only *on the condition* that it pay for any damage it inflicted on the dock. The notion of an incomplete privilege, on this view, can thus be understood as a conditional justification: the reason the Reynolds was justified in staying docked while remaining liable for the damage to the dock is that the Reynolds was only so justified because it was so liable.

This logic is familiar especially from the economic analysis of tort law. According to law-and-economics, tort law is necessary only because it is practically impossible to bargain in advance with everyone with whom one might interact to settle what rights and duties the parties have. As the parties to a tort suit are typically strangers, the transaction costs are simply too high. Thus, tort law is necessary, according to law-and-economics, only because contract law, whose bargains are necessarily efficient, cannot in fact address the problems that tort law confronts.

How does this motivate the idea of conditional justification? Economic rationality counsels filling out the content of tort law exactly the same way it counsels filling out the content of contracts that are rationally left underspecified on account of high transaction costs: determine what the parties would have bargained for.[44] Applying this logic to *Vincent*, the dock owner would presumably refuse to allow the Reynolds to dock without an assurance that the Reynolds would bear the risk of damage to the dock. And just as the dock owner would insist on conditioning the Reynolds' docking on the Reynolds paying its way, the Reynolds would accept that deal insofar as docking-but-paying is preferable to not-docking-and-sinking. Thus, the docking was justified, but only conditionally so.

This logic is not confined to economic analysis. Gregory Keating, for example, reaches a similar conclusion on the basis of his resolutely non-economic conception of tort law. On his view, necessity cases exemplify what he calls "conditional wrongs."[45] By Keating's lights, "[t]he wrong in *Vincent* lay not in the defendant's doing damage to the dock, but in the defendant's wrongful (or unreasonable) failure to step forward and volunteer in the aftermath of the storm to make good the damage to the dock."[46] Keating, then, also subscribes to the conditional justification theory of necessity cases: entries are justified under circumstances of necessity but only on the condition that the entrant compensates the owner for any damage done. That the concept of conditional justification can be reached via such different theoretical routes, moreover, would seem to provide powerful support for it. But the concept is deeply flawed. In fact, it is question-begging, and it is so regardless of the route

---

[44] For discussion, see Jules Coleman, "The Structure of Tort Law," 97 *Yale Law Journal* 1233 (1988), 1237–38.

[45] Gregory C. Keating, "Strict Liability Wrongs," in John Oberdiek (ed.) *Philosophical Foundations of the Law of Torts* (Oxford 2014), 301.

[46] Ibid., p. 302. See also Gregory C. Keating, "The Priority of Respect Over Repair," 18 *Legal Theory* 293 (2012), 323. It is worth noting that Goldberg and Zipursky cannot help themselves to this argument, insofar as their civil recourse account of tort law's remedial wing expressly denies that anyone incurs a duty upon wronging another. Instead, being wronged empowers plaintiffs to hold defendants liable; absent being called to account, defendants owe nothing to those whom they wrong. On their view, "the commission of a tort has a legal consequence. But it is not the creation of a legal duty owed by the tortfeasor to the victim. It is instead the creation of a legal power, and with it, a corresponding liability." Goldberg and Zipursky, *Recognizing Wrongs*, supra note 15, p. 163.

one takes to reach it. In *Vincent*, the question is whether the Reynolds owes compensation even though the ship was justified in staying docked during the storm. Replying that the Reynolds' docking is justified on the condition that it pay for any damage it causes presupposes that the dock owner had the standing not simply to demand that payment but to deny the docking in the event that no payment is forthcoming. But the existence of that standing is precisely what is at issue in this debate.

This is an abstract point that might seem obscure and therefore unpersuasive. The presupposition that the dock owner has the standing to demand payment for the use of their dock might seem warranted, and indeed obviously so. After all, one might think, the dock owner *owns the dock*, so of course the dock owner can condition the docking on a payment should the docking result in damage to the dock. The thought would be this. Under normal circumstances the parties would bargain over the terms and conditions of the docking, with the dock owner coming away with a contractual right to payment for the ship owner's entitlement to use the dock. But circumstances of necessity are far from normal. The exigent circumstances create high transaction costs that impede a contractual resolution, so hypothetical contract terms must be implied. And the terms that would be implied are precisely those that we see in *Vincent*: dock but pay.

To see why this move begs the question, consider again an analogy to battery and self-defense. Everyone has a right to bodily autonomy and integrity. It is this right that the tort of battery protects; one may not harm another precisely because people have this right. So, if one harms another under normal circumstances, one commits the tort of battery, and is liable accordingly. But if one harms another in justified self-defense, one does not commit the tort of battery and one is not liable to the individual one harms. It does not follow from this plain fact that the individual one harmed through justified self-defense does not, in fact, have a right to bodily autonomy and integrity. Of course they do. That is why, for example, even justified self-defense is subject to a proportionality limitation. But the possession of that right, protected by the tort of battery, does not prohibit justified interferences with the bodily autonomy that the right protects. And so there is no basis for liability in cases of justified self-defense. This is true even though the aggressor against whom self-defense may be exercised retains a right to bodily autonomy—even as their attack is being justifiably repelled. The fact that an aggressor possesses a right to bodily autonomy does not give them the standing to demand of their would-be victim either that they may not repel the attack or that, should they successfully do so through the use of force, they must pay for any injuries they inflict. To say that exercising self-defense in such cases is justified just means that the aggressor's right to bodily autonomy does not entitle them to bargain over the terms of its exercise. Conversely, to say that the aggressor is entitled to bargain over the terms of their putative victim's exercise of self-defense just means that exercising self-defense independently of bargaining is unjustified.

Just as an aggressor retains their right to bodily autonomy even as they are being justifiably repelled by force, an owner retains their right to property even as that property is being justifiably damaged. But it does not follow from this that the owner is entitled to bargain over the conditions of entry in circumstances of necessity, any more than it follows from an aggressor having a right to life that they are entitled to bargain over the conditions under which self-defense may be employed to repel their attack. The thought that entering another's property without authorization under circumstances of necessity is justified if but only if the entrant compensates the owner for any damage caused, then, begs the question. The notion of a conditional wrong, as well as the idea of an incomplete privilege that it is adduced to explain, is circular.[47]

VI. Conclusion

If what I have argued is correct, it follows that a long-standing position taken by the common law, that one who enters another's property out of necessity and hence with justification is liable to the owner, is difficult

---

[47] There is a conception of a conditional wrong that is not circular, but it is not Keating's (or Bohlen's) conception. For example, failing to compensate another for a wrong is a type of conditional wrong: it is a wrong because one has breached a secondary duty, and it is conditional because one only has a secondary duty if one breaches a primary duty. This is distinct from Keating's conception, for on his view, the duty to compensate is not secondary insofar as he does not believe that it is predicated on the breach of a primary duty.

to defend.[48] It seems to me that we should treat such a person no more harshly than we do the person who kills in justified self-defense—there should be no liability in either instance.[49] The law, I think, therefore stands in need of revision.

It might be tempting to resist so revisionary a conclusion on the grounds that it is possible to interpret the law in a way that leaves existing doctrine in place. That is, one might favor a methodology that prioritizes "fit" over "justification" in the interpretation of the law.[50] It is true that mine is, at bottom, a normative criticism of the tort of trespass as presently conceived. But it would be a mistake to characterize my approach as devaluing fit. I have, instead, widened the parameters of that criterion of interpretive success. I do this in two ways. First, I situate the tort of trespass among the other torts and seek a construction of it that reflects its place within that constellation. That trespass is conceptually subordinate to battery influences what I take the proper understanding of trespass to be.

---

[48] Difficult, but not impossible. As my riders "at least as a matter of right" throughout suggest, I think that there may be a more *instrumental* justification for liability in such cases, deriving from the importance of a settled property regime. This would be consonant with a conception of property that is thoroughly Humean in its conventionality. See David Hume, *A Treatise of Human Nature*, Book III, Henry D. Aiken (ed.) (Macmillan 1948 [1739]). (It may not be exclusively so: for discussion of the Kantian approach, which occupies a middle position between Hume's thoroughgoing conventionality and Locke's natural right account, see Martin J. Stone and Rafeeq Hasan, "What is Provisional Right?," 131 *The Philosophical Review* 51 (2022)). If such an account provides the justification for liability in so-called justified trespass cases like *Vincent*, however, then the account of the wrong of trespass itself also will be dramatically different from that typically presupposed by the law of torts. As Liam Murphy puts this point, "So the fact that general compliance with a certain rule-structured social practice produces value does not in itself establish the deontological force of the rules." Liam B. Murphy, "Purely Formal Wrongs," in Paul B. Miller and John Oberdiek (eds.), *Civil Wrongs and Justice in Private Law* (Oxford 2020), p. 33. It may also sever the bilateral plaintiff-defendant structure that is emblematic of private wrongs, such that the plaintiff may be entitled to redress, but not necessarily from the defendant. I leave further consideration of this possibility for another occasion.

[49] There is another option, not examined here, that would preserve the parity of killing in self-defense and entering another's property out of necessity, and that is to find that there is liability in *both* cases, rather than in *neither*. On this view, one would owe compensation to the owner whose property one entered justifiably, albeit without permission, but one would also owe compensation to the (estate of the) aggressor whom one justifiably killed. Property would thus be no better protected than persons, which is the fundamental shortcoming of the law. To accept this (differently) revisionist view, though, would require denying that justifications have the negating power that seems to be their hallmark, and which is any case usually acknowledged in law and morality. I thank David Brink for discussion of this possibility.

[50] See Ronald Dworkin, "Hard Cases," in *Taking Rights Seriously* (Harvard 1977).

Second, I also take seriously the language and express reasoning of the relevant caselaw, and do not take their holdings to be the only thing that must be made to fit. With respect to *Vincent*, of course, I admit that I cannot fit its holding into my characterization of the tort of trespass at all, for I deny that liability should have been found in that case. That makes my interpretation more strained than it might be. That omission is not, though, fatal. One might explain why in the following way. I side with the language and express reasoning of *Ploof* and *Vincent*, accept the holding in *Ploof*, but abandon the holding in *Vincent*. Goldberg, to cite a contrasting example, abandons the language and express reasoning of *Ploof* and *Vincent* but sides with the holdings in *Ploof* and *Vincent*. Courts of course focus on holdings. Theories of the law are more ambitious, for they attempt to explain, interpret, and justify. That project demands taking the language and logic of caselaw at least as seriously as its holdings.

Finally, though, it is the normative cogency of the position that the common law takes on the tort of trespass that I am challenging. Justification, and not just fit, matters. On this front, it seems to me, it is clear that the common law falls short. Trespass protects things, and things matter only because persons matter first. The tort of trespass therefore both conceptually and normatively answers to the tort of battery. It follows that trespass cannot protect things more than battery protects persons, and yet as the common law conceives of it, it does. That is the trouble with trespass.[51]

John Oberdiek, *The Trouble with Trespass* In: *Oxford Studies in Philosophy of Law, Volume 5*. Edited by: Leslie Green and Brian Leiter, Oxford University Press. © John Oberdiek 2024. DOI: 10.1093/9780198919650.003.0007

[51] My thanks to audiences at the USC Legal Theory Seminar, the Private Law and Practical Reason conference hosted by Notre Dame Law School, and the University of Pennsylvania Carey Law School, and in particular to Anita Allen, Mitch Berman, Bill Ewald, Kim Ferzan, John Finnis, Jean Galbraith, John Goldberg, Felipe Jiménez, Greg Keating, Sandy Mayson, Erin Miller, Paul Miller, Stephen Perry, Jennifer Rothman, Teemu Ruskola, Rachael Walsh, and Ben Zipursky. Thanks also to Caitlin Pennell for her excellent research assistance.